GLOBAL
FINANCIAL
APOCALYPSE
PROPHESIED

GLOBAL
FINANCIAL
APOCALYPSE
PROPHESIED

Preserving True Riches in an Age of
Deception and Trouble

WILFRED J. HAHN

DEFENDER
A DIVISION OF ANOMALOS PUBLISHING HOUSE
CRANE

Global Financial Apocalypse Prophesied

Defender
Crane, Missouri 65633
© 2009 by Wilfred J. Hahn

All rights reserved. Published 2009
Printed in the United States of America

ISBN 10: 0982323581
ISBN 13: 9780982323588

A CIP catalog record for this book is available from the Library of Congress.

Cover illustration and design by Michelle Hyunjin Kim.

Unless otherwise noted, all Scripture is taken from the New International Version.

DEDICATION

To my parents, Johannes and Selma.

And, also to my dear circle of family—wife, daughter, sons, spouses—and friends, who share the modern inconvenience of a biblical worldview.

A rich blessing, even the more so due to its rarity.

CONTENTS

LIST OF FIGURES

Figure #1

Incidence of Banking Crisis in All Countries, 1800 – 2007

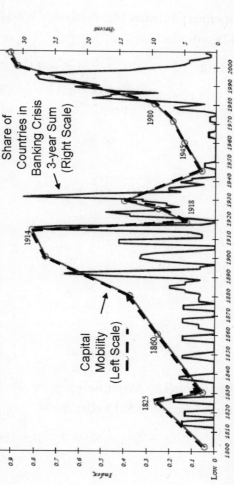

Source: Banking Crises: An Equal Opportunity Menace. Carmen M. Reinhart, University of Maryland, NBER and CEPR. Kenneth S. Rogoff, Harvard University and NBER. December 17, 2008, pg. 24.

Prophetic Global Crisis? The severity of the global financial crisis (GFC) of 2007 to 2009 has many convinced that it is of apocalyptic scale. For many reasons, the GFC certainly does not signify the start of the Tribulation, though it must be seen as part of the prophetic world-wide processes of globalization and globalism. Financial crises are not new as this chart shows. There have been many severe banking crises before and they all qualify as occuring during the days when "[…] people were eating, drinking, marrying and being given in marriage […] buying and selling, planting and building." (Luke 17:27-28).

PROLOGUE

An enormous global financial crisis has ravaged the world. It has been so shattering it has come to deserve its own acronym: the GFC. Viewed over the human timeline, there is no doubt it is a bellwether event, the significance of which must not be missed. It confirms a rapid road to the final global financial apocalypse that is clearly prophesied in the Bible, occurring as part of the Great Tribulation. The warnings are clear. Whether you are reading this book during the GFC, later during one or more of its deceptive recovery phases, or during a future global crisis, the perspectives provided will remain relevant and will help you weather such storms without being entrapped.

The global financial crisis signals urgent messages and questions at several levels.

First, these are personal. Have you placed your hope in the false idols of modern mankind? The realms of Mammon have been violently shaken upon their footings in recent times. As such, upon what firm foundation will you place your hopes now?

Moreover, are you aware that recent economic and financial troubles and various other commercial developments playing out across the world are part of a deliberate strategy specifically designed to annihilate the faith of Christians? Sadly, most believers today are falling prey to false gospels and these last-day troubles and traps by the thousands. Do you know why? Are you safe? How can you be sure?

Second, the GFC again is an admonishment to the entire world to turn from its primary worship and empty doctrines of prosperity. As its names implies, the GFC is a *global* crisis. The very fact that the recent financial crisis has impacted *the whole earth* confirms that the time is well advanced when God will finally punish and judge a "one world" that is united in its vain plotting against Him. That day may be here when "the nations rage and the peoples plot in vain" (Acts 4:25). How will the world respond to the clear disciplining and humiliating policy lessons of the GFC?

Many global observers have lately been bewailing and bemoaning what they perceive to be the destruction of "globalization." This was the great cornerstone to the worldwide humanist agenda to "plot against God." Commercial interconnectedness was to be the common interest pulling all mankind into one global society. This prosperous unification of mankind, often clothing itself under the altruistic goal of eradicating poverty and hunger from the world, would establish the foundation for universal peace. It would be a human project that renders irrelevant the sovereign rule of a transcendent God who claims to hold the salvation of mankind in His hand. Many of the pillars of globalization have now toppled, or at least have been shaken violently. Will the nations repent, or resurrect their fallen idols with even greater humanist buttresses and vain props of defiance? The answer to this question could make life much more challenging in the future, especially for Christians.

Quoting Martin Wolf, the respected economics editor of the

Financial Times who attempts to rationalize the many futile efforts of governments and transnational organizations to resurrect the pillars: "...it makes no sense to avoid action that would greatly lower the real economic costs of the crisis now, to eliminate a hypothetical and avoidable fiscal crisis later on. This would be like committing suicide in order to stop worrying about death."[1]

The world does know that long-term trends are definitely headed to a deadly end. But, it will not repent of its ways until the very last moment, if at all. Just how will it end? The Bible prophesies this outcome clearly, as we will review. The final global financial apocalypse is yet ahead...possibly very near.

Finally, the GFC holds special implications for America, and not just because "ground zero" for the GFC happened to radiate from this nation to the entire world.

America's ultimate destiny is indicated in the Bible. As will be discussed in this book, biblical prophecy does outline that America will decline in significance. After all, it is God alone who both raises and razes nations and appoints its rulers. He determines their time and domain. He judges them. "He brings princes to naught and reduces the rulers of this world to nothing. No sooner are they planted, no sooner are they sown, no sooner do they take root in the ground, than he blows on them and they wither, and a whirlwind sweeps them away like chaff" (Isaiah 20:23–24). The great empires and nations of the past all declined because of their dissipation, flaws, and sins.

PROGNOSIS FOR AMERICA

The prognosis for America as it stands currently is not bright. While such a morose view is now more readily accepted following the occurrence of the GFC, the question of exactly how the future will unfold cannot be answered with any precision. Events can proceed rapidly or slowly. A decline can be punctuated by one or more false dawns. In fact, you may be reading this book during one of these false dawns, when the theme of this book will seem outdated. Actually, that would be the most opportune time to heed the analysis presented here. These alluring but deceptive dawns are a necessary component of long-term decline and also afford the best opportunities for appropriate changes.

In any case, a trend of deterioration in America, as well as in some other nations, has long been recognized by common-sense, Bible-reading observers. To date, there are no hope-inspiring, long-term indicators—should nations not turn from their ways. Not only is this true in the economic and financial realms, but more significantly, in the areas of values and character.

America indeed has fallen into a grim financial pit. The impact of the GFC could not be more destructive for the U.S. were it specifically planned by its worst enemy. Not only has its financial system, once commandeered by the some of the world's largest financial titans, been reduced to technically bankrupt "zombie" companies, but its geopolitical influence has also begun to wane. Suddenly, the economic and financial policies of continental Europe are ascendant. Globally, members of a larger number of nations—including Russia, China, Brazil, and others—now sit as equals in various conferences. Most crucial of all, the core foundation of this nation, of any nation—the basic unit of family households—has been decimated by over-indebtedness and crashing wealth, the handmaidens of destructive life philosophies and religious debasement.

And now, a materialistically spoiled country of self-entitled, self-actualized consumers is left to dig itself out from under enormous debts and bankrupt systems. Will it knuckle down and rise to the occasion, as did some Asian countries during their time of crisis a decade ago? Or will it stoop to competitive larceny and anarchy?

Surely a nation such as America with so much Christian heritage will keep its composure and reconstruct its greatness in an orderly, self-sacrificing, national effort. While that is a hope-inspiring thought, it is not at all certain.

Is the financial situation of the United States terminal? The answer to that question depends upon the choices of this nation's citizenry. Will Americans repent and turn from their mass idolatries, Mammon-worship, and gods of greed and gain? Yes, it is true that God foreknows what this nation will ultimately choose, as well as the collective choices of a globalized world. But that does not mean America has no opportunity to turn from its ways.

To date, however, there is no sign of turning, despite the gut-wrenching, national reappraisals forced by the current economic hardships. After many years of fraudulent prosperity and unbridled greed, a culture of despondency, lost trust, desperation, and cynicism has given birth. The responses of policy makers to the collapse of financial institutions, housing values, and financial integrity have only confirmed a continuing state of deep corruption and deception.

No doubt many readers will resist this diagnosis. However, such a judgment is best deferred until we examine these developments under the light of biblical perspective. That is why this book's primary emphasis will be on laying out biblically grounded views of faith, materialism, Mammon, and idolatry rather than on in-depth economic analysis. There is no shortage of the latter; a wide range of opinion is available in many forums. Unfortunately, most mainstream economic views are misleading and misinformed. Why? Mainly because economics is a fraudulent science that refuses to recognize man as a free-willed creature who must answer to God. While surely offering needed stewardship advice, my main objective is to help readers see the deep deceptions and longer-running trends that are capturing Christians and leading to the final global financial apocalypse.

You will have noticed that I have chosen to capitalize the word "Mammon." This is deliberate, recognizing that the master the world has chosen to serve is in fact a spiritual hierarchy energized and led by the Deceiver. "You cannot serve both God and Money" (Matthew 6:24).

A CONTINUING GLOBAL SAGA

This book follows on the theme of an earlier work, *The Endtime Money Snare: How to Live Free* (Olive Press, 2002). The warnings of that book have mostly outlived their usefulness; many developments reviewed there have since come to pass.

I have long warned about the high probability of a massive financial and economic collapse through countless articles, papers, and reports I've written—both since and before—whether in professional, secular, or ministry circles. I saw it all as part of a longer-running process gripping the entire world that aligned with the foreknowledge expressed in Bible prophecy. The common unifying thread for the world of our time is global commerce and modern money, though it's surely only one facet of our diagnosis. Yet, these trends are the mediums of the increasingly invasive clutch of Mammon—an entity that has physical features yet is the main spiritual stronghold of a lost world.

The recent crisis, as is now well known, was compounded by a rampant real estate mania. America's real estate bubble was not the most extreme in the world, yet it was the most corrupt and vain. As early as 2004, it was possible to identify the dangerous trends underfoot in the real estate markets. It was obvious then that their continuation would lead to grief for the unwary. A May 2004 article entitled "A Warning That Hits Home"[2] clearly documented the emerging dangers. Even at that time, it could be discerned that there were spiritual dimensions and false idols in the looming real estate disaster. Quoting from the original article (since updated): "…some time ago home ownership began to be used as an instrument of ensnarement. Something that was good was taken to excess and directed to an evil end as materialism began to sweep the land."[3]

That financial instabilities were becoming ever more critical was repeatedly laid out. Weren't these warnings too early? No. The message was simply that the path taken, if not altered, would lead to disastrous consequences. The hope was that people would change their behavior and therefore avoid the consequences.

Please do not take these comments as a haughty "I told you so." In the first place, I take no pleasure in the actual occurrence of what I anticipated. It would have been better to be proven wrong, had it spared people some trouble. Frankly, no special education was required, because any discerning person would have feared the same outcomes. While it is true that no one can predict anything with precision, it is still possible to identify the season and the direction of the winds.

It is necessary to warn early; how else will people have sufficient time to respond and take precautions? It also is critically important to recognize the times in order to understand the cosmological, eschatological timelines that are unfolding. These perspectives and the desire to prepare readers for the difficult challenges ahead, again, motivated my writing of this book.

Now that the massive GFC has laid the world low, we must think about the dangers of the next stages of end-time commercial and financial developments. It is sure to be an even more treacherous and dangerously corrupt time. The end-time money snare is indeed progressing in leaps and bounds, having trapped legions of people through the deceits and corruptions that contributed to the GFC. There will be many more casualties, exactly as the Bible prophesies. But, the end-time money snare will likely proceed with different stages, different acts, and varied scenes. It is an agenda that is not intended to be visible to complacent, indulgent people—Christians or otherwise.

Of course, we cannot know exactly how future events will unfold. Though we will propose a number of possible scenarios, we still can't be sure which events will occur, and when. No one can. Those who do claim a skill of accurate prediction, especially if they are charging a fee for it, are deceiving you. Not only that, but they also reveal a lack of knowledge of the complexities involved in any scenario.

I have lived close to the hot flames of big money and greed, seeing money in motion, people in power, and avarice in action. My long-time experience in the global money world has at least taught me one thing—humility. Such past posts as a director of research for a major Wall Street firm, a globally ranked analyst and strategist, head of a multi-billion dollar global investment operation, and a host of other positions have allowed me a ringside seat to one of the most phenomenal and rapid end-time developments of human history: globalization.

Having experienced firsthand the treacheries of the Wall Street culture around the globe, I can be certain of at least two continuing developments—continuing deception and snares for the unwary. Thankfully, we can rely on the truth of the Bible to set our gaze in the right direction. Bible prophecy outlines the destiny of mankind and reveals its general course. Here, a much bigger timeline is outlined. The sweep of the Bible's statements are cosmological…they're certainly much bigger and more important than one event such as the GFC, significant as it may be in the eschatological timeline.

In this respect, it is important to understand that Bible prophecy is not the same as a forecast an economist might attempt. Prophecy is foreknowledge and sometimes also predestation, but it is not prediction. Prophecy reflects foreknowledge of the course of the world because God foreknows the choices of mankind, whether that of individuals, nations, or the entire earth. This may seem a subtle difference, but it is an important one.

God certainly knows what He will and must do. Yet, at the same time, mankind has been given choices with respect to its actions, worship, and affections. Yes, the revelations of the Holy Spirit will all come to pass. However, that does not mean our generation hasn't been given an opportunity to repent and change our ways. Therefore, in our treatment of Bible prophecy, we must leave open the possibility that certain prophesied events could very well play out much differently than we might think.

Yet, in spite of many warnings and disciplining, we know from the Bible that mankind, its nations, and societies will ultimately choose to worship Mammon and to pursue its own ways. It is by this light that we will review the significance of present-day trends and probe for the next stages following the GFC for which we must prepare.

The GFC crisis serves as a staging ground, perhaps one of many, for other end-time developments, as this book will further explain.

When a Change of View Is Necessary

Another reason prompting me to write this book is that much more information has become available since I wrote *The Endtime Money Snare*. New facts have emerged, and therefore some viewpoints need to be corrected or refined. John Maynard Keynes is reported to have said, "If the facts change, I change my mind. What do you do, sir?" As such, I must reconsider some previous opinions in the light of new information.

It's one of the realities of fallible mankind: No one is right all the time. No human being has full revelation—or could fully understand it all if it were given. Jesus Christ is the only Man who qualifies as having full revelation without error. Such brilliant people as John Calvin or Augustine, for example, may have benefited Christendom with important insights, yet they were not exempted from erring. Unfortunately, the downside of great repute was that their errors therefore also had a large legacy. Thankfully, my errors affect only a very small number of people.

Years ago, contemplating the looming probabilities of financial and economic instabilities, I could not know whether the next big global crisis would be the final one occurring in the Great Tribulation. We now know that it wasn't. We can know with certainty that the Tribulation period—the prophesied seven years of trouble—has not yet begun. The Antichrist has not come upon the world stage, nor has a peace treaty been arranged with Israel. Importantly, neither have the final ten kings who will collude with the Antichrist been identified.

Also, for those who hold to the belief of a pretribulational Rapture, this also can be taken as proof that the Tribulation has not yet begun. The Rapture has not happened; therefore, the seven-year Tribulation period cannot yet have begun. While I do believe that the Bible teaches a pretribulational Rapture, the views expressed in this book will be equally relevant to those who take different views on this doctrine.

Another perspective I have changed concerns America's role in the final global financial apocalypse. I once thought it likely that a financial collapse in America would be the contagious catalyst that would cripple the entire world in the final, end-time collapse. Here again, the balance of facts has changed. If anything, a continuing collapse of America and other key nations will drive the world into the arms of the prophesied coalition of ten kings. While America's troubles have rocked the entire world, causing major adjustments in trade and financial flows, other nations are now sufficiently independent and can, in time, successfully weather such storms.

Another crucial consideration I have jousted with uncomfortably has been the question of the Advent of the Lord. Scripture is clear on the point that we cannot know its time: "because you do not know the day or the hour" (Matthew 25:13). There is no contesting this fact. Rather, what has puzzled me has been the proper interpretation of the statement that "the coming of the Son of Man" (Matthew 24:37) would be at a time similar to that of Noah, when the world would be "eating and drinking" (Matthew 24:38), seemingly carrying on in happy complacency. This statement appears to imply that Christ's first return to receive the saints "in the air" (1 Thessalonians 4:17) cannot occur at a time of world crisis. If so, that implies that the Rapture could not occur at the present time of worldwide fear and angst. This point would also hold for a posttribulation interpretation for the Lord's first return. I now believe this to be an incorrect interpretation for a number of reasons.

As outlined in this book, the current financial tremors do not qualify as the extraordinary times of trouble at the time of Christ's return at the end of the Great Tribulation. Conditions then will be much worse. On the other hand, neither is the current GFC so traumatic that Christ could not return today. The current global crisis is not outside the experiential norms of the vast sweep of human history. What presently is viewed as a crisis in the minds of most people today is not bad enough to qualify as a time when conditions of "eating and drinking" are not occurring.

That people are experiencing the real troubles of being evicted from their homes in North America and thousands are starving or being maimed and killed in other parts of the world, sadly, must be considered a normal part of the baleful history of sinful mankind. Mankind still remains complacent, thinking that global solutions can be found to any problem.

LOOKING AHEAD, NOT BEHIND

The title of this book, as sensationalist as it might seem, has not been designed to scare readers into buying an advice service or yet another book. Sadly, it is an often-practiced and profitable tactic to sensationalize events that prey upon people's fears. A visit to the bookstore will confirm an avalanche of "gloom-and-doom" narrations and novels that have been rushed to the stores in recent times. Why? Scaremongering sells because there is widespread fear and confusion. People are looking for answers. Unfortunately, they will not likely find them in the books that follow every major crisis period. Why? They are all written after the fact…in this case, after the GFC. As such, these authors are much too late to offer any useful advice. Why did they not warn well ahead of time? Such cheap commercialism is not unknown, even among supposed Christian authors.

Given the obvious impact of the GFC, who needs experts to tell people what they already know has happened? In my view, it is irresponsible to hype up the bad news of plunging economic indicators, scaring people into taking actions and making decisions that are now much too late. Indeed, such things are occurring. To prey on the fear and anxiety these headlines generate is not doing anyone a service. In fact, unnecessary hysteria contributes to a tragic disservice.

Hyping up the sensationalist newspaper headlines is likely playing a part in an end-time trend that is contributing to a world with an ever-greater wealth skew and more entrapped, economically oppressed people. Why? Such perspectives are looking backward, not forward, and may be contributing to emotional, untimely, and inappropriate reactions. What this book proposes to do is to look *ahead*…to the next challenges that conspire to trap even more people in an end-time money snare. We should be looking toward the next challenges, not reacting to past events.

Much greater problems—much, much bigger problems—are ahead. But these scenarios will unfold in ways that will likely surprise most people. They will mostly be unsuspected, especially as gazes remain fixed to the rearview mirror. This must be the case, or such scenarios would not occur in the first place. Surprise and deception are necessary stratagems.

Summary Messages of This Book

The main message of this book is three-fold. Firstly, the final global apocalypse is indeed hurtling towards this world, not just because God has decreed it so, but in response to the choices of mankind. Any rational person—whether inclined to believe the Bible or not—can deduce that difficult times lie ahead, as we will show. The GFC, as frightful and difficult as it may be, is not the final apocalyptic event prophesied for the Tribulation period. Far from it. However, the GFC is very likely a characteristic end-time catalyst—perhaps even the final one—that hastens the world towards the final conditions that give rise to a ten-king global power coalition, the Antichrist, and the following Tribulation period.

The second message—a call to awareness—is that the future must be expected to unfold deceptively. Though the Apocalypse is certain, there will be false dawns—at least one—leading many people through successive cycles of false optimism, only to fall prey to further traps and disappointments.

Thirdly and most crucially, both Jews and Christians are the major intended casualties of the world's headlong flight into humanism and idolatrous materialism. The perilous time prophesied for Christians is now here. Do you see it? And, will you be safe? A virtual genocide of faith is occurring now…a veritable "Apocalypse Now" for the believer.

The great tragedy is that so few are prepared for these terrible times because they have been seduced by false gospels. One objective of this book is to show their interconnections with the GFC.

Who is not disoriented or blinded by prevailing secular values and a pagan society? In fact, steeped in this culture, we no longer recognize how deeply pagan our society has become. To emphasize: These are times of great deception and idolatry. Just how can we ensure that our faith remains pure and secure? This is the greatest challenge of the times. People indeed are having trouble with a very basic question: How now should we live?

A biblical view of our times, grounded upon truth, is the only one that promises peace and contentedness. Most importantly, such a long-term perspective can lead to bulging heavenly riches that will be eternally secure from Wall Street charlatans and the present earthly domain "where moth and rust destroy, and where thieves break in and steal" (Matthew 6:19). Hopefully, this book will help readers reaffirm essential eternal values and secure a realistic vantage point upon our times.

Figure #2

World Stock Market Value Crash
MSCI AC World Stock Market Index, Daily, US Dollars (October 1, 2007 – March 31, 2009)

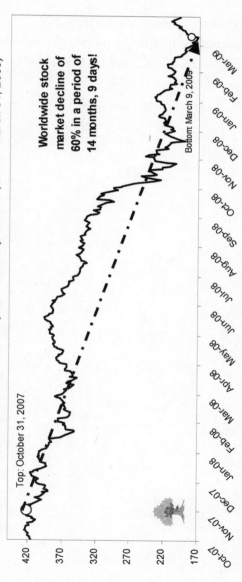

Top: October 31, 2007

Worldwide stock
market decline of
60% in a period of
14 months, 9 days!

Bottom: March 9, 2009

Source: MSCI/Barra, MSCI AC World Stock Market Index.   Format: Mulberry Press Inc.

All World Stock Markets Fall. Due to the advanced state of globalization, the brutal effects of the global financial crisis quickly radiated around the world. All stock markets of the world fell. In a period of a little more than 16 months, the entire quoted market value of all the world's equity markets declined 60%. This was unprecedented, considering its rapidity and global reach. As a consequence, the pension fund values for many Westerners were decimated. Is a lower low yet ahead? Or, will the world soon again enjoy soaring markets? Just how do these gyrations fit into the prophetic timeline?

1

FINANCIAL ARMAGEDDON
APPROACHING

In 2007, a worldwide, financial "heart attack" disrupted monetary systems and economic activity around the world. It soon cascaded into the most significant collapse in many decades, one of unprecedented global proportions. The crisis soon came to be infamously dubbed the "GFC" for "global financial crisis." Initial stages of collapse were even more vicious and virulent than occurred at the onset of the Great Depression of the 1930s. Just why should such a collapse occur now? What is its significance? Where will it lead for the world?

Tough economic and financial times certainly clamped down upon the entire world—most notably, the United States, Britain, and other high-income nations. Throughout the earlier stages of the GFC, securities markets were reeling, financial companies falling like flies, and almost everyone—from bankers to government policymakers—was panicked and fearful.

The catastrophic unraveling of the world's economic systems emboldened seers of all types as they smelled chaos and change—spiritually, geopolitically, socially, and economically. The rapidity of events fit their script. After all, consider the steepness of the initial plunges of various indicators, from global stock market prices to real estate values.

At one point, the entire global stock market had fallen 55 percent (as represented by the MSCI Barra, All Country World Index in U.S. dollars). Incredibly, the world's stock market wealth had more than halved, representing a decline of approximately $35 trillion in less than one year!

Of course, there had been rampant devastation everywhere, not just in the stock markets. U.S. housing values were sinking the fastest since the 1930s Great Depression, and everything from high-yield bond markets to art was deflating in value. With respect to global trade and a host of other economic statistics, record lows and precedents seemed to be occurring almost daily.

The speed of decline was so shocking and abrupt it seemingly fit into prophetic Scripture. The Baltic Dry Index, which tracks the cost of shipping freight on twenty-six major international trade routes, fell an unprecedented 95 percent from its peak of mid-2008. Global trade of goods shipments virtually came to a stop. This appeared to evince the scene depicted in Revelation 18: "Every sea captain, and all who travel by ship, the sailors, and all who earn their living from the sea, will stand far off exclaiming, Woe! Woe, O great city, where all who had ships on the sea became rich through her wealth! In one hour she has been brought to ruin!" (verses 17, 19).

It was not surprising, therefore, that various seers were sure that the Tribulation period was to start very soon. Some date setters even erroneously pinpointed its onset on December 21, 2008. In the same vein, these events evoked the terrifying emotions mentioned in Luke 21:26: "Men's hearts failing them for fear, and for looking after those things which are coming on the earth: for the powers of heaven shall be shaken." Everything looked grim and dark. At one point, according to a CNN opinion poll, nine out of ten people in the U.S. expected economic conditions to worsen.

The economic and financial dislocations resulting from the GFC had indeed shaken the confidence and complacency of everyone across the globe. There were and remain real fears that a global financial meltdown might ensue, one that would thrust civilization back into the Dark Ages. Could this happen? If not now, then perhaps in future years? In North America, such concerns were certainly understandable. The "perfect storm" of falling real estate values and financial asset prices, soaring and then crashing energy and commodity prices, the high debt-servicing costs of many households due to overindebtedness, and then a sharp economic downturn had the doomsayers in full bloom. Indeed, many indicators—viewed both domestically and globally—were worsening at a more severe pace than in recorded financial history.

More questions beckoned: Is another Great Depression in the offing? If so, just what will happen to America's economic position in the world? And, surely a question on the lips of many: Is the financial security of our very households at risk? We have posed many crucial questions, and not just because people may be vexed about their homes' values, investment portfolios, or jobs. Observers really have been worried about a final event…a financial holocaust. Any answer must deal with the near-term challenges as well as future outcomes that will extend from the GFC.

PONDERING THE SIGNIFICANCE OF THE TREMORS

Indeed, do the earth-shaking tremors of the GFC signify the start of the Great Tribulation and the soon-coming Armageddon, as some observers believe? Not only Christians, but virtually everyone is pondering such questions. News media reports about the various financial crashes and economic difficulties have been studded with words such as "Armageddon" and "the Apocalypse." Journalists have frequently described events as being of epic "biblical proportions."

The question of a "financial Armageddon" was openly and seriously addressed in the secular media. For once, a biblical topic was not being mocked. Big money and material comforts were on the line. Unfortunately, the answers often provided by Christian leaders proved misleading and harmful. Some even expressed glee that Armageddon was about to rain down. One would have thought that if a Christian really did think the wrath of God was about to fall down, such media exposure would have been seized to deliver an urgent call to repentance and salvation.

Even I was contacted for an interview by the secular National Public Radio in the U.S.[4] The reporters were ecstatic that they had found someone they thought could provide credible commentary on this urgent economic "end-of-world" topic. I was specifically targeted due to my "oddity" of being a former director of research for a major Wall Street firm who currently works and writes as a global chief investor officer—who is also familiar with Bible prophecy. I indeed was questioned: Did I in fact think Armageddon was underway? "No not yet," was my answer. While the GFC does have biblical significance, it certainly is not yet of biblical proportions. Moreover, the ultimate Apocalypse is surely coming nearer. We will yet provide the evidence for these conclusions.

The global financial crisis certainly does hold an important place on the cosmological timeline for humanity. That is a reasonable conclusion. It surely was not an accident, nor was it disconnected from human values and the state of morality.

After all, economies are driven by people. They may sometimes appear as aimless crowds who are illogical, greedy, and glandular, or as hard-working, sensible societies with a capacity for perseverance. Commerce and the movements of money are the result of people—humans beings—acting on their beliefs, expectations, wants, and needs. That necessarily involves choices and a faith system. This is an important point to reflect upon, as it plays a determining role in future events. Which of these will prevail or predominate now and in the future is the crucial question.

Contrary to common belief, financial markets and the state of commercial systems do not define the character and morality of a people. It is the other way around. The values and idolatries of society determine the state and nature of financial trends. Societies that evidence no belief in eternal consequences and are committed to the principles of humanism—the belief that the ultimate satisfaction of man is under his control and limited to his physical world—have the necessary relativism that greases the slope to massive financial and materialistic manias and the final busts. This progression is evident now, both in North America and other parts of the world.

As such, matters of human affections and religious beliefs are important determinants of financial and economic trends. This perspective will surely surprise many people who may have thought that financial markets are inanimate systems governed by such things as profits and interest rates. That is hardly the case. Money and markets are humans in action, whether for good or bad.

WHY SUCH IMPACT UPON AMERICA?

In the U.S., more than 1.5 million U.S. households were expected to default on their mortgages and possibly lose their homes in 2009. According to www.zillow.com, a real estate data service company, as many as 21.8 percent of all U.S. households at one point were upside down on their mortgages, meaning their houses were valued less than the mortgages outstanding. Worse was to come, in their opinion.[5] Such devastation of the wealth of American households seemed beyond belief.

The International Monetary Fund, surveying the damage of the GFC across the world, concluded that, besides Spain, America would bear the biggest brunt. According to this agency's estimates, the U.S. government deficit would be impacted by a cumulative $4.9 trillion, or an equivalent of 34 percent of the size of its economy. Globally, U.S. and other international financial institutions' losses as a result of U.S.-related securities were estimated to exceed another $4 trillion. It goes without saying that these are unprecedented losses.

But why was the GFC hitting America so hard financially and economically? The current troubles facing the U.S. were of epic scale and certainly much more severe than those occurring in other countries. Is it the natural outcome of bad economic policies and financial management—America effectively shooting itself in the foot? Or, is it possible that God was somehow playing a role, perhaps testing or disciplining the U.S.? If so, would these interventions also possibly be true for some sister nations like the United Kingdom and Canada? In the case of the U.S., had God finally remembered the sins of this once-"evangelistic," Philadelphian nation? We will briefly review the many views on this question in the next chapter.

AMERICA'S ROLE IN GLOBAL COLLAPSE

We can settle upon at least two conclusions of potential interest to observers of North America. For one, the U.S. and other countries facing similar difficulties—such as Britain, Spain, and Australia, to name the major ones in this group—could very well face a long phase of decline and financial hardship. It would not be surprising that they will come to the point of being eclipsed economically by other nations in the world. Even respected secular analysts and mainstream publications are of the opinion that this is occurring, should trends not change. Therefore, though we can be sure that the final collapse is not yet upon the world, this offers no assurance for America and other affected countries in the near term.

But what would happen to the world if the financial systems of the aforementioned bloc of nations actually were to collapse, as some observers fear? Isn't America so large and economically influential that such a development would spell certain doom for the entire world—in other words, be sure to trigger the prophesied global economic breakdown? Actually, whether or not the U.S. may possess a manifest destiny, financial troubles on this continent do not necessarily mean the entire world must be fated for immediate collapse. Some persuasive arguments support this view.

While the impact of the GFC falling upon the U.S. is indeed seen in terms of total humanity, isn't the U.S. so large economically that its troubles are sure to trigger worldwide collapses? It is most likely too pessimistic to conclude that the U.S.-induced credit crisis will sink the entire financial world. We also judge it to be the case that the U.S. is no longer large enough commercially to dictate the course of the entire world economy.

Here some history might be helpful. Some of the biggest banking busts in the past have cost on the order of 10 to 20 percent of economic output (gross domestic product), according to the studies of the International Monetary Fund. No doubt such crises were terrible and financially fatal for some individuals and companies, and the same holds true for the GFC. However, we can hazard a reasonable guess that the current crisis is ultimately survivable for the world's financial systems, at least for now. They will survive to see another day of crisis in the future. Many financial and monetary devices can be employed to resuscitate or manipulate the world economy. Indeed, major central banks around the world are throwing caution to the wind and beginning to "print" money. While such activities and others are likely to achieve a stabilization of economic conditions around the globe, they already set up the parameters for the next crisis...an even worse one.

As little as a decade ago or so, it would have been defensible to think that if America's economy collapsed, the entire world system would also face a terminal meltdown. Since then, it can be argued that the world power structure has changed significantly, not the least evidence of which has been the economic rise of Asia (including China, Japan, South Korea, and others), the rebounds of Russia and Brazil, and the increasingly financially powerful oil-exporting states.

We should be reminded here that whatever new prosperity may reappear, indeed perhaps in image only, will prove to be on very vulnerable footing. One day, to be sure, in the not-too-distant future, mankind's financial and trading systems will collapse. Just when will that collapse occur, if not now? We will explain that outlook in greater detail, as well as the required precautions, in Chapter 14, "Global Financial Apocalypse Prophesied."

PROPHETIC STEPPING STONE TO THE FUTURE

A key indicator of the world power shift now befalling America is China. Why this country? Because it has been the dominant proxy of change in the global economic/geopolitical sphere today. China, not the U.S., has been the key force of changing economic power in the recent past. It may come as a surprise that America is no longer the primary influence upon world economic growth.

America's troubles today in relation to China and the Asian manufacturing hub that it centers are as Europe compared to the United States in the late 1800s. Just as America was then the rising new competitive power in the world's export markets at that earlier time, so it is with China now. America eventually proved to be the key catalyst behind the financial collapses in Europe in the 1870s. Today, China is the price setter in many industries, now that it has become the world's second-largest trading nation.

That is not to say China won't face its own troubles in future years. However, at this time it is in a favorable position to continue increasing its financial influence and power.

China has become the U.S. government's largest foreign creditor, overtaking Japan in recent years. It owned $585 billion worth of U.S. Treasury bonds and agency bonds as of late 2008. Yet, China's gross domestic product (GDP) per capita ranks around the hundredth in the world. How is it that this relatively poor nation is financing the U.S.? While China sits upon nearly $2 trillion in accumulated foreign currency reserves, America is plunging ever farther into debt, its central bank, the Federal Reserve, buying up troubled assets and extending lending facilities to faulty banks.

We could cite many more statistics. Can there be much doubt that America's relative position in terms of its financial and economic clout in the world is waning? A report by the U.S. National Intelligence Council (NIC), *Global Trends 2025*, grudgingly admits as much: "The U.S. will remain the single most important actor in 2025, but will be less dominant." The report also states that the current trend of global wealth and economic power shifting from west to east is "without precedent in modern history" and will continue.

What should America do? Says Thomas Friedman, the populist *New York Times* columnist, in a November 16, 2008, article titled "Gonna Need A Bigger Boat: "…we need a president who has the skill, the vision and the courage to…inspire and enable us to do the one thing that we can and must do right now. Go shopping."

The solution to our hypercharged consumerism is more credit-driven shopping? It is an incredibly ill-advised answer, as it reveals the spirit of the original problems at fault. We must conclude that the old idols remain in the house. Despite the humiliating hardships of the GFC, policy makers do not show signs of changing course. "…they did not stop worshiping demons, and idols of gold, silver, bronze, stone and wood" (Revelation 9:20).

Blindness is as entrenched as ever. People do not know the purposes of the Lord. While the current crisis is now obvious to everyone, few still have any idea as to the next developments…the traps, both economic and political, and the rapidly nearing, multipolar reign of ten kings. The ten kings must come on the scene before the Antichrist is revealed. The prophet Daniel confirms this: "The ten horns are ten kings who will come from this kingdom. After them another king will arise, different from the earlier ones; he will subdue three kings" (Daniel 7:24).

In our analysis of Scripture and history, current events likely play a role in the stage-setting for the emergence of this ten-king, multipolar world order. This has critical implications for America's future. This ten-king world order must emerge before the Antichrist arrives on the scene. It is only for "one hour" that these kings will have the dubious honor of holding global power in the service of the Antichrist (Revelation 17:12). In Chapter 11, we will outline this earth-changing process in greater detail, as well as its implications for America. It holds great significance for the future of America.

MORE GLOBALIZATION AHEAD

To be sure, the GFC has caused an economic crisis that is most certainly the worst since the 1930s. But, it is not at all conclusive that the world's financial end is at hand, nor does the GFC spell certain doom for the majority of the world's population at this time.

If past trends are any guide, we should expect at least one more economic expansion period for the world, enveloping the entirety of all nations and ever more firmly entrenching mankind in the last-day money snare—the systemic Babylonian colossus of Bible prophecy. It could be argued that more than 60 percent of the world's population is only marginally participant in the world's emerging commercial structure. While there have been great strides to date in this respect, much more globalization could lie ahead. To what extent is impossible to predict.

Consider that if the entire world were to achieve only half the level of income or economic output as the high-income countries of the world today, the global economy would quintuple in size. One might imagine what such a boom would do to the environment and the prices of scarce energy supplies and other commodities. While unrealistic, the scenario nonetheless shows that another big world boom is still possible, though America and other high-income nations may continue to stagnate or decline.

While such an outlook may appear sanguine, it still represents a time of great economic and financial treachery. This cannot be said enough. We will lay out the likely characteristics of the period ahead in the next chapters. Importantly, in doing so, we will ground our analysis in a dispensationalist, pretribulational view.

Without a doubt, the world's financial system remains thoroughly compromised—a postmodern, relativistic, amoral net that is in the service of the Mammon spirit. It is specifically designed to deceive and entrap. Frankly, it is surprising how few Christians are wise to this reality. One dares not underestimate the deviousness that may be possible with respect to future trends.

KEY WORLD DEVELOPMENTS TO OBSERVE

Just what does the present global financial storm signify? As we have already begun to explain, Scripture provides clear guidance on this topic. We think the GFC signifies three developments.

To begin, nothing that has occurred has been an accident. Here, leaders and voters can be blamed. Any common-sense observer will confirm this view: The world is simply reaping what it has sowed.

A second and crucial significance of the GFC is that it intertwines and hastens this late, great race of global economic and financial integration. For this, accountability can be given to powers in high places (Ephesians 6:12), but also to flesh-and-blood complicitor-elites. Why? This current crisis will serve the familiar role of catalyst, drawing most nations together even closer and likely soon setting up the conditions for the last-day ten kings.

A third corollary development that must fall out of the prophetic fulfillment of ten kings is that the world must first enter an age of multipolarism. What is multipolarism? It is a world power arrangement balanced between many countries and not dominated by one or more powerful nations. Certainly, there can be no world power structure comprised of ten kings as the Bible prophesies if one superpower can ignore or undermine such a world order (see Daniel 2:41–42, Daniel 7, Revelation 12, 13, 17).

Is America now in the process of being downsized, making way for the ten-king, multipolar world to arrive? Bible prophecy confirms such an outcome. At some point, in some way, America must become a relatively smaller power. This process may require a long time. However, conditions are such that this shift on the world stage could happen rather suddenly.

Most definitely, the Bible clearly lays out the future, but it provides no specific dates for this dispensation. There can be no doubt that the world ultimately will face a complete financial and economic collapse. That day may be very near. However, for now, we can reasonably conclude that a global financial collapse of that type is not unfolding at present.

Though the GFC may certainly seem terrible, and economic conditions could get much worse, the great big, apocalyptic collapse is yet to occur. While this perspective will not likely provide the near-term reassurance most people are hoping to hear, the Bible does not fail to provide reasons for an attitude of contentedness, peace, and hope.

This is a most important perspective to understand and stand upon. If you are not firmly rooted in an eternal perspective of "true riches," you will be blown about like a reed in the wind during these very deceptive and troubled last days. In Chapter 16, we will return to the topic of riches and differentiate what the Bible calls "true riches" from other, more worldly, concepts of wealth.

THOUGHTS TO PONDER

Viewed from the frenzied vantage point of the global financial crisis, indeed, calamity has fallen upon the world—and most terrifyingly upon America. Trillions of dollars of financial value have been lost; the value of our mutual fund holdings has collapsed; pension funds have been eviscerated of their ability to fund our future income support; millions have lost their jobs; and countless numbers have been evicted from their homes.

Such widely broadcast developments easily lead to a mass hysteria from which it is difficult to separate oneself. Worries and anxieties quickly threaten to overwhelm our souls. It is a sign of the times. No one disputes that commercial challenges have fallen upon the world. However, we can at least ensure an appropriate state of mind by acknowledging the meaning behind Christ's question: "Who of you by worrying can add a single hour to his life?" (Luke 12:25).

Let's realize that spiritual and eternal views—in other words, perspectives on the real issues that matter for the long term—so easily risk being overlooked during anguished times. As such, the agitated popular view at present is dangerously out of focus, particularly in North America.

Any extraterrestrial visiting this planet and seeing the enormous gyrations in financial markets in recent times would greatly wonder about a civilization that is so fickle about the value of its wealth. Of course, reading the diagnosis that the Bible presents, we know better. This world—which Christians surely live within, but whose values we do not endorse—is vulnerable to mankind's idolatries and vain confidence. In fact, it is hubris taken to the extreme—mankind's confidence in its surveys of confidence—that has brought the planet to this brink.

Great global events such as are occurring now must be seen as part of mankind's progression to an end…actually, to one of several ends still ahead, as the Bible tells us. But it is not yet the start of the Great Apocalypse, though it is surely very close. You may be surprised to learn just what Bible prophecy has to say of future events in this respect. We will look at the reasons for these perspectives in Chapter 14, "Global Financial Apocalypse Prophesied."

Some countries stand to emerge much weakened, and others will be in a more powerful position. For now, the key development to see is that the world will have moved to a more centralized, globally coordinated state. What we are witnessing today is simply part of the pattern of that long-continuing process.

But what about the role of Christians? Many today take delight in the belief that they will not suffer in any troubles of the Tribulation period...particularly financial losses. Why? Because their hearts and affections are entirely ensnared in materialism and greed right now. Doing so, they show themselves to be "earth dwellers."[6] In response, we are reminded of these three points:

- **Above all, the Lord's return is imminent.** Whatever the theories or speculations, we could be with Him at any time and our sojourn upon earth completed. We would have no more chance to set things right, to shed our idolatries and worldliness. The bema seat of judgment lies ahead.

- **Certainty about the specific time of future events in this present dispensation has not been given to man.** We have not been given the ability to accurately predict the near-term future. Thankfully this so. It would be a much more chaotic world than it already is if humankind were given the capacity to know the near-term future...in other words, perfect future visibility. It couldn't work, given mankind's fatal penchant for money, security, and self-reliance. Imagine! If we did know the exact timing of future events, everyone would act on this information at the same time, thus changing the future. It would be a maniacal and even more volatile world. As the Bible indicates, the love of money is a primeval force: "For the love of money is a root of all kinds of evil" (1 Timothy 6:10).

We can know the general season and such things as the destination point of the path upon which the world is traveling, but we are not given the hour or the day. This means that even though we may theorize that another global economic cycle may be underway at some point, and that the final, "big financial meltdown" needs wait until the Tribulation, these give no assurances of anything near term.

With respect to the world's headlong rush into the "last-days super-religion"—the merging of God and Mammon—we can be sure of its occurrence. The world is on a path to destruction...morally, economically, and spiritually. We have the more sure word of prophecy on this point. On this road, we can expect serious, scary financial tremors, as well as wars, pestilences, earthquakes, etc., through which many people (greedy, naïve, or otherwise) will suffer or profit greatly.

- **Deception and corruption remain the mode of the world's developing systems.** The successive economic booms of the world...the temptations of the rising end-time apparition of great wealth or the "deceitfulness of wealth" (Matthew 13:22)...the greater material comforts or the "worries of this life"...the "anxieties of life" (Luke 21:34)...the ever-ensnaring end-time money trap...they all play upon the affections of Christians. Who then can sustain such an assault and still stand ready at all times for His coming?

The GFC must be seen as a sign of the times, a symptom of extremely materialistic and corrupt era that can be expected to continue if the Lord does not first return. So that our faith doesn't become frayed and despondent, we must not think that our righteous living during this larcenous and desperate financial time will "receive anything from the Lord." How many Christians today have this perspective, thinking that their prosperity will be protected because of their faith?

Actually, among the many disastrous consequences of the conditions leading to the GFC are many Christians who have lost faith in a God who was only to bless America with a surfeit of material goods and monetary wealth. Crucially, as this book will show, this deceptive, corrupt teaching lies at the very foundation of the troubles that America and other nations are experiencing. Readers will be surprised to learn that the GFC has a Christian footprint.

To ensure that we can withstand the challenges of the current time upon our faith, and keep from falling for the "prosperity dealmaking" with God, it is essential to take heed of James' admonition: "If any of you lacks wisdom, he should ask God, who gives generously to all without finding fault, and it will be given to him. But when he asks, he must believe and not doubt, because he who doubts is like a wave of the sea, blown and tossed by the wind. That man should not think he will receive anything from the Lord; he is a double-minded man, unstable in all he does" (James 1:5–8).

GLOBAL
FINANCIAL
CRISIS IN
PERSPECTIVE

Figure #3

World Financial Securities & Position Value Boom

Trend compared to world average annual income and arable land per person, 1982=100, 1982 to 2008

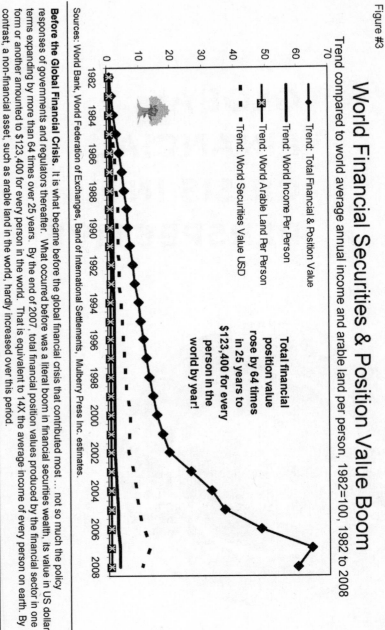

Legend:
- Trend: Total Financial & Position Value
- Trend: World Income Per Person
- Trend: World Arable Land Per Person
- Trend: World Securities Value USD

Total financial position value rose by 64 times in 25 years to $123,400 for every person in the world by year!

Sources: World Bank, World Federation of Exchanges, Band of International Settlements, Mulberry Press Inc. estimates.

Before the Global Financial Crisis. It is what became before the global financial crisis that contributed most .... not so much the policy responses of governments and regulators thereafter. What occurred before was a literal boom in financial securities wealth, its value in US dollar terms expanding by more than 64 times over 25 years. By the end of 2007, total financial position values produced by the financial sector in one form or another amounted to $123,400 for every person in the world. That is equivalent to 14X the average income of every person on earth. By contrast, a non-financial asset, such as arable land in the world, hardly increased over this period.

2

FINANCIAL PROPHECIES
AND AMERICAN OMENS

No, the world is not likely witnessing the final global financial apocalypse. Recent financial events ricocheting around the world are surely part of the process that will eventually culminate in that prophesied time when the world will suffer many troubles. But for now, if anything, current financial downturns represent another, though significant, station stop on the road to a thoroughly globalized world and a launch point for the next worldwide economic boom should the Lord tarry. According to our pretribulational, premillennial framework, the Great Apocalypse is still ahead.

Bible readers who understand things of the end (eschatology) know that an economic and financial control structure takes form (Revelation 13:17); a boom in false wealth takes place (James 5:3); and an elite group of wealthy complicitors emerges (Daniel 11:39)—even as a greater part of humanity becomes entrapped slaves. All these processes, though not yet complete, are clearly seen today. Much worse manifestations occur in the Tribulation itself. While we cannot know the exact time when any crisis will occur, we at least know that the great apocalyptic events all play out on a global scale inside the future seven-year Tribulation period.

Consider that the global trend of financialization is the bedrock—the very seedbed—of the end-time power structure that underpins the last-day ecumenism and rule of the final False Prophet and Antichrist, respectively. The trends of globalization, globalism, financialization, corporatization, etc.—all of which are related—provide the sinew and connectedness of a last-day world that has staked its hopes and faith upon the common commercialism of mankind.

SYSTEMS CANNOT PASS AWAY
BEFORE THEIR TIME

All of the above comments draw the deduction that none of these outcomes can happen if the world's financial system collapses before its time. It is a perspective that also applied to the Y2K ("year two thousand") hysteria that swept the world in the late 1990s. At that time, many Christian pulpits and Christians ministries were taken in by the hysteria, with a number of pastors and leaders advising people to buy generators and extra water supplies.

It proved to be prophetic hype gone awry. To recall, the Y2K mania ended up being more of a psychological crisis than an unsolvable technical problem. Some intrepid observers early on defused concerns about Y2K with the simple observation that computer technologies were essential to global interconnectedness and therefore were absolutely necessary to bring about a number of conditions clearly prophesied in Scripture. Particularly, Dave Hunt presented this perspective in his book, *Y2K: A Reasoned Response to Mass Hysteria.*[7]

It was a logical conclusion that the world would not succumb to a Y2K-type holocaust before the prophesied Antichrist could complete his world-ensnaring program of rule. Yet, while this biblically-derived position was correct in the case of the Y2K issue, there indeed was a technical problem that needed repairs. In this sense, some hysteria certainly would have ensured that these repairs would be made well in advance.

To illustrate the role of fear being a motivating driver in this situation, I recall the time in the 1990s when I was managing a large global investment operation and needed to plan for the Y2K issue in various parts of the world. Frankly, it was actually comforting to witness the high levels of concern at the time. Why? It ensured motivation and resolve to work out what was really a simple technological problem. If there had been no hysteria, perhaps the Y2K technical problem would not have been solved as quickly.

The same consideration now applies to the world's developing financial system and the current crisis. Fear now hastens the actions and interventions of policymakers around the world. In the case of the United States, many new and unprecedented measures have been taken to counter the financial troubles. Many of these new programs are unfortunate and will likely prove ineffective. As a result, governmental controls will become more intrusive.

This also stands true on a global scale. The pace of globalism can be expected to be hastened. In later chapters, we will review some of these developments in greater detail. However, here we simply want to distinguish between what we can know in advance according to Bible prophecy and the likely actions that can be expected to play out today in alignment with that ultimate destiny.

The Antichrist needs an integrated, functioning, global, financial system to carry out his agenda. Otherwise, how would it be possible for the False Prophet to implement the controlled conditions of "buying and selling" (Revelation 13:7)? Therefore, we can conclude from these prophecies that the final, world-spanning financial crisis cannot occur until well into the Tribulation period. Before that time, smaller financial crises will occur—including the GFC—but these will all be survivable and will play a facilitating role in prodding further global commercial and monetary convergence. In that context, the present GFC, as shattering as it may be for a time, should be considered smaller in scope. But none of these comments should be taken as a reason for complacency. A continuing process is underway that, through boom and bust, invariably moves the world to greater interconnectedness while entrapping people in ever greater numbers.

AMERICA'S ROLE IN THE GFC

As it happened, the direct impact of the credit system breakdowns of the GFC in the beginning was largely confined to the Western nations. America was at the very epicenter of the crisis. This came as no surprise, given the excessive indebtedness and other economic and financial ailments that had gradually beset America. America's current troubles had "not been sleeping" (2 Peter 2:3). Its woes were certainly the product of past choices, those of corrupt leaders as well as households and individuals.

A progressive slide toward materialism and various kinds of idolatry, greed, and lawlessness has been documented for many decades. In fact, this beginning slide was detected by both Christian and non-Christian writers 150 years ago and more. In recent years, there have been clear warning indicators that any common-sense observers could have discerned for themselves. So why should there be surprise that finally the "chickens have come home to roost"? The Bible clearly says, "Do not be deceived: God cannot be mocked. A man reaps what he sows" (Galatians 6:7).

AMERICA'S SLIDE ENABLED BY FALSE PROPHETS

Throughout this long slide in America, a long line of false prophets and soothsayers has popularized the ideas that there are no consequences for poor stewardship and revelry, that "you can have your cake and eat it, too," and that there is no such thing as sin—let alone its consequences. These messages offered pleasing license to complacently rush down the broad road to the financial difficulties America and the world are experiencing today. Very few wanted to know the ultimate consequence of overindebtedness, asset bubbles, and credit manias, the ever-more-extreme chasms between the incomes and wealth of the rich and the middle class.

America, the richest nation in the world, became the world's biggest debtor, at times borrowing as much as 75 percent of the entire world's excess savings. Its financial systems became progressively more corroded as pension systems, both public and private, became underfunded. Households no longer saved; instead, they relied upon ever-rising housing prices. Further, credit institutions became clogged with massive amounts of low quality and speculative debt assets.

Virtually every economic sector became engaged in the alchemy of creating figments of wealth. All of these developments were evident. Yet, no shortage of Wall Street economists and public policy makers dreamed up inane theories intended to substantiate the durability of these reckless developments. There was also a host of false prophets who gave the entire prosperity mania their religious blessing and supplied it with a spiritual pedigree. We will deal with this most abominable "Christian" phenomenon, the most corrosive and destructive of all, in Chapter 9.

As for the role of influential leaders in America's financial circles, a quote originating from an observation by John Maynard Keynes of a similar period in America, the late 1920s, is most apt. That period also experienced a surge of financial lawlessness and rampant greed, though not nearly attaining the heights of sophistry witnessed in recent decades. Keynes said: "Even in such a time of madness as the late twenties, a great many men in Wall Street remained quite sane. But they also remained very quiet. The sense of responsibility in the financial community for the community as a whole is not small. It is nearly nil."[8]

Significance of a Slumping U.S. to the World

While there surely are real troubles for many households in North America, we must take a global view and not forget that there is a world financial system today much bigger than just America. Then just how significant are the recent economic troubles of America in relation to the whole world? Of course, the answer depends upon whose perspective we adopt. Americans may exaggerate this linkage due to the real-life impact and immediacy of current financial troubles.

To illustrate this point, we use the example of Indonesia here (and again in a related perspective presented in Chapter 3). Consider that country, which has the fourth-largest population in the world—227 million people—as compared to the U.S. population of 307 million. According to 2008 estimates of the International Monetary Fund (IMF), Indonesia has a gross domestic product (GDP) of $488 billion in equivalent U.S. dollar terms. The U.S. economy, measured at $14,195 billion, by comparison, is gigantic—namely, it is twenty-nine times larger.

Consider that during the Asian crisis of 1997–1998, an Indonesian citizen would have been tempted to draw the same apocalyptic inference for the rest of the world as an American might in the troubled times of 2008 and 2009. Indonesia then seemed to be in a literal meltdown. Many of its citizens suffered; some even starved. Yet, while that country's economy contracted by more than 20 percent between 1997 and 1998, the stock market collapsing steeply, to conclude that the sky was falling upon the whole world would have been incorrect. The same perspective now applies to America, though the comparative metrics of the illustration are exaggerated.

Just how would God compare these two crises? Was Indonesia's crisis lesser because this country only represented 0.8 percent of the world economy versus 23.5 percent for the U.S. share? Was its plight insignificant because this country represented such a small share of total world wealth and was considered a geopolitical pipsqueak? Or, does God look upon the number of individuals? As already observed, the populations of these two countries are roughly in the same league.

The Bible clearly reveals that the Lord cares for each soul individually, and that everyone is important, whether rich or poor. "Are not two sparrows sold for a penny? Yet not one of them will fall to the ground apart from the will of your Father. And even the very hairs of your head are all numbered. So don't be afraid; you are worth more than many sparrows" (Matthew 10:29–31). If that is so, surely God places more importance on people and their numbers rather than on the contrived power measurements of mankind, whether economic or otherwise. Therefore, from this vantage point, troubles unfolding in the United States would be a small crisis in comparative global terms, as God would see it. After all, the United States accounts for only 4.5 percent of the world's population.

When the Bible says the world will be generally unaware of the coming days of the Son of Man, "eating and drinking, marrying and giving in marriage" (Matthew 24:38), this does not necessarily mean that every tribe, nation, and state will be experiencing the same levels of complacency, economic buoyancy, or recession. A serious economic crisis in America in and of itself therefore is not sufficient reason for the Lord to wish to delay His return.

DIVINE OMENS IN THE AFFAIRS OF AMERICA

While secular observers see humanist solutions to current problems, others are sure they see epochal significance in recent tremulous trends. To the more apocalyptically minded visionaries, the entire earth is now hanging on the cusp of a very important threshold. If so, just what lies beyond? What purpose is served by the present world financial crisis? Here any semblance of consensus ends, even within Christianity, as we will review shortly.

Some put significance into the fact that the Mayan calendar has an end point of December 21, 2012. While Bible-reading Christians assuredly know that the Lord's coming is very near, they also know that no specific dates or signal events are pinpointed on any calendar for the church.

Now that the GFC has erupted its retributions upon America, and there is not yet much contrition to be observed for past follies, moralists have been quick to see God's hand at work. Many who are inclined to take a religious perspective now interpret the consequent disasters as a direct and divine disciplining of America by God. The more extreme in this camp even believe God has selected America's troubles as a catalyst for the final global collapse for the entire world. How are they certain this is the case? Apparently, inauspicious omens have been observed, testifying that God has verifiably intervened to unleash financial bedlam as vengeance for this nation's supposed greed and materialistic idolatries.

Famously, the fact that the Dow Jones Industrials stock market index fell exactly 777 points on September 29, 2008, is selected as one such omen. More than one Christian commentator has openly stated the divine significance of this occurrence. The number seven in the Bible is often used to signify completeness of God's plans. A triple seven, namely the number 777, therefore holds much greater significance as an omen, some believe. Is such an interpretation valid?

Other similar omens have been conjured. Consider that the massive stock market declines of October 2008 were greater than those of the infamous October 1987. The time span between these two collapses was exactly twenty-one years. The number twenty-one is the product of three times seven. Are these sevens also a coincidence? Or, what about the curious timing of the demise of the financial firm of Lehman Brothers in early September 2007, widely considered to have been the catalyst triggering the disastrous worldwide market deluge over the following two months? The capital deficiency of this company was announced to regulators precisely seven years after the 9/11/01 attacks to the day. Here again, a number seven pops up. Could the repeated occurrence of the number be just a coincidence, or does it indeed signify a divine role in the GFC? It would be impossible to prove this, although there would be no harm in taking admonition from such numerical alignments.

NOTHING ESPECIALLY OMINOUS

One must wonder why God would use such subtle omens, if at all. To begin with, these interpretations are highly subjective, open to a wide range of supposed meanings. The definitions of the omens themselves are conveniently selected. Consider that there is a long list of financial indicators from which to select one's ominous number indicator of choice. There are also many different stock market indices. Why is only one taken to be a special omen, and not others? We must conclude that these random indicators are not omens at all, and cannot be validated.

In any case, the number seven would be only of divine significance to Bible-studying Christians. More often in the secular world, a triple seven is seen as a lucky number. Some slot machines in casino halls pay off winnings when the gambler hits the 777. One can reasonably wonder why the number six doesn't come up more frequently in these supposedly divine signals of the displeasure of God instead. Six, after all, is the number of man and his own ways; a triple-six—666—is the number of the final, demonically inspired idolatries of mankind.

Would it be of any significance then that the intraday and final low of the U.S. stock market crash of 2008–2009 was exactly 666? (March 6, 2009, Standard & Poor's 500 Composite stock market index.) It surely was a significant decline as far as stock market crashes are concerned, representing a cathartic decline of some 60 percent in real terms (here another six) from its earlier peak in 2007.

Certainly, serious lessons are to be learned from the GFC. Other than this general message, it cannot be concluded that extraordinary, divine warnings are seeded into any number occurring on any particular day. However, some stock traders did think it significant that the stock market then surged from its low by 13 percent to the end of March 13, a week later. The coincidence of several thirteens in this instance was not taken as being ominous, to be sure. After all, markets were rising in this case.

Our reluctance to see any omens in these numbers in no way denies the importance of numbers mentioned in Bible prophecy. We are best to find meaning in these numbers, rather than the random statistics produced by modern financial markets. We will discuss the interesting interconnection of the number 666 in Chapter 8.

BIBLE PROVIDES BETTER OMENS

God long ago made mankind aware of His thoughts and purposes, most importantly sending His Son, Jesus Christ, as a witness. "For since the creation of the world God's invisible qualities—His eternal power and divine nature—have been clearly seen, being understood from what has been made, so that men are without excuse" (Romans 1:20). As such, it is not necessary for us to look for omens of our own definition, no matter how spectacularly coincidental, in order to discern the Lord's actions and interventions. While Christians "have the word of the prophets made more certain" (2 Peter 1:19), the rest of the world also remains without excuse to know and acknowledge God.

This indictment is even more valid today. Why? The first verified appearance of the prophesied Christ has already occurred. If He "…had not come and spoken to them, they would not be guilty of sin. Now, however, they have no excuse for their sin" (John 15:22). Moreover, God "has given proof of this to all men by raising him from the dead" (Acts 17:31). Given that we have Bible prophecy to guide us as "a light shining in a dark place" (2 Peter 1:19), we do not need to look for hidden or cryptic omens to discern the future. If anything is hidden to the common eye in our culture, it is the deep idolatry and pagan ways of our society.

AMERICA AND DIFFERENT PROPHETIC INTERPRETATIONAL SYSTEMS

There are other Christian perspectives on America's possible divine or prophetic roles in the world that do not depend on numerical omens. For example, consider the Dominion Theology theorists, also called Reconstructionists, who, among other beliefs, hold that Christians will reform the entire world before Christ returns. It is a group that is gaining in influence and feeling rather triumphant over the specter of the GFC. Various proponents of this view have long predicted that a global financial and economic collapse will occur, causing the demise of secular culture and governance. The occurrence of the GFC to them now qualifies as evidence that such predictions are finally coming true for the world.

The problem here is not so much that Reconstructionist predictions will not eventually prove true in the case of financial collapse. It is that the Reconstructionists generally take an amillennial or postmillennial stance and therefore are waiting for the collapse to occur so that Christian rule can seize supremacy over world systems that have proven morally bankrupt. They then expect to transform the world into a state of peaceful readiness for Christ's eventual return. Not surprisingly, these theorists are known to display glee at every hint of financial crisis. Are they right that the final, definitive global collapse is now underway?

Also, the lately re-proliferating offshoots of British Israelism, also called Armstrongism after the late Herbert Armstrong, are also feeling strengthened. Many of the organizations in this varied movement are prolific in disseminating their views. Among these are the Philadelphia Church of God and the Living Church of God. Generally, they take the view that America and other Celtic-related nations are really offshoots of the supposedly long-lost tribes of the house of Israel. These Armstrong groups take differing stances on the Rapture, historicism—the belief that some historical events during the Church Age are literal prophetic fulfillment of Bible prophecy—and various Jewish ordinances.

Yet, taken together, their interpretation of Bible prophecy generally produces the conclusion that all the supposed modern-day country members that stem from the original ten tribes of the house of Israel will face a severe disciplining and weakening prior to the Tribulation and the return of Christ. This group identifies the United States as being the modern manifestation of the Manasseh branch of Joseph. As Joseph was given the double portion by Jacob, his two sons, Manasseh and Ephraim, each became one of the twelve tribes of the Israelites. According to this system of prophetic interpretation, Ephraim today is represented by Britain and other European countries correspond to the remaining tribes. In the Armstrong view, recent financial troubles are part of the last-days judgment upon the ten tribes of Israel, and the demise of America is prophesied. Are they right?

AMERICA TO FACE THE SAME PROPHECIES AS ISRAEL?

That America is often seen in Scripture has a long tradition. This began with the early Puritan immigrants, who saw themselves as Israel going to a new land and even subduing Canaanites in the form of North American Indians. America regarded itself as a modern-day parallel to ancient Israel, both in terms of experience and destiny. Walter Russell Mead, a member of the Council on Foreign Relations,[9] writing in *Foreign Affairs*, comments:

> The United States' sense of its own identity and mission in the world has been shaped by readings of Hebrew history and thought.... From the time of the Puritans to the present day, preachers, thinkers, and politicians in the United States—secular as well as religious, liberal as well as conservative—have seen the Americans as a chosen people, bound together less by ties of blood than by a set of beliefs and a destiny. Americans have believed that God (or history)...[has] brought them into

a new land and made them great and rich and that their continued prosperity depends on the fulfilling their obligations
toward God or the principles that have blessed them so far.
Ignore these principles—turn toward the golden calf—and
the scourge will come. Both religious and nonreligious Americans have looked to the Hebrew Scriptures for an example
of a people set apart by their mission and called to a world-
changing destiny.[10]

This perspective Mead describes is still quite strong today. Troubles and disasters—from the September 11, 2001, terrorist attacks and
the effects of Hurricane Katrina upon New Orleans in 2005 to recent
economic troubles—are popularly seen as direct divine interventions
of warning or disciplining. Moreover, America's fate is seen as either
dominating or determining the fate of the world. While many may
be inclined to take the perspective Mead describes, it doesn't provide
any specific insight to the question of premillennial global collapse or
proof that the GFC has prophetic implications for America alone. Yet,
all of the above views intermingle with the baited question of whether
indeed a global collapse has a specific prophetic role for America.

RECOVERY ATTEMPTS BEFORE FINAL JUDGMENT

Summarizing our views, the great global collapse and its various sub-
sidiary judgments prophesied in the Bible are not unfolding at present.
The Bible has the final say as to when this collapse occurs, and that is
in the future, as we will show in detail. That said, it remains true that at
this time globalism and the vulnerabilities of the world's systems continue to build toward that ultimate outcome, and in that way could be
viewed as prophetic fulfillment. But the final collapse is not yet.

Not only can this view be proven from Scripture, it can also be logically deduced as we have shown. After all, a functioning global financial and trading system is essential to bring the world to the apex of the Antichrist's reign inside the Tribulation period. As prophetic events of the Great Tribulation are yet to occur, a widespread, terminal, global collapse now would be before its time. As such, we can know that a crippling and terminal global financial collapse is not going to happen at present.

The world's systems are certainly and indelibly proceeding to an end point. In that sense, many of the trends we are witnessing today—globalism and globalization, for example—could be viewed as prophetic preparation, in that they play a role in the continuing process toward the ultimate and literal events the Bible prophesies. We can validly expect that overall world financial systems will not "melt down" before their time. They may suffer tremors, hair-raising crises, temporary panics, and so on, but not an incapacitating, terminal meltdown. Why? It stands to reason that they must remain operational for at least the early stages of the Tribulation period.

That said, collapses of lesser types have occurred and can occur any time. In fact, this has been the normal course of history. Some nations have risen in power; others have fallen or been overturned. There have been recessions, even world-shaking depressions (as in the 1930s), and countless currency crises and individual country disasters.

Yet, the world's systems, though battered, were patched together only to advance to a more heightened state of globalization. It does not counter Scripture or violate the immediacy of Christ's return to conclude that this pattern will continue. Even should the U.S., traditionally seen to be the economic locomotive of the world, experience near-calamitous conditions, an analytical argument can still be made that this view would still apply to the world.

Final judgments are ahead. Every other entity in the Bible,

whether city or nation, that has pridefully held itself out as self-suf-
ficient and smug has been judged. We are given many examples in
the Bible of the consequences of pride, arrogance, and man's reliance
upon his own tools and systems. Not only does God specifically punish such attitudes; it seems that the consequences of mankind's hubris
and over-optimism are even part of the natural laws of economics. In
this sense, the financial troubles being experienced by the U.S. and
other nations are part of this general paradigm.

Christ said, "In this world you will have trouble" (John 16:33).
Right from the time of Adam, hardships were pronounced for man.
"Cursed is the ground because of you; through painful toil you will
eat of it all the days of your life. It will produce thorns and thistles
for you, and you will eat the plants of the field. By the sweat of your
brow..." (Genesis 3:17–18). In that sense—the natural consequences
of past actions, in other words—current credit crises and economic
troubles have come.

In time, we can be sure that the entire world, the nations, and all
individuals will be judged. The greater part of these peoples will face
the wrath of the Day of the Lord. And, in this regard, as the apostle
Peter understood, "Their condemnation has long been hanging over
them, and their destruction has not been sleeping" (2 Peter 2:3).

It is the same way with the Babylonian systems described in Revelation 17–18. "God has remembered her crimes" (Revelation 18:5).
All the excesses, unrepented-of injustices, and inappropriate affections of the past will eventually catch up with both individuals and
nations. These consequences will have been hanging over them for
some time...they have not been sleeping, for God indeed remembers
unrepented crimes.

In conclusion, we can be sure that it will not be until the second
half of the Tribulation—"the terrible day of the Lord" (Joel 2:31)—
when global systems begin to totally break down and all the final col-

lapses and wealth overturns that we have contemplated in this chapter will begin to occur. Until that time, systemic or geopolitical troubles of a lesser type—though surely disastrous and frightening for those involved, as they are today—will continue to unfold. These types of crises continue to drive the world into higher states of globalism and globalization. The GFC should be seen as a transition period to that future time when centralized economic power can be given to one man, the Antichrist.

THOUGHTS TO PONDER

What of the tough times being experienced by Christians during various difficult times now and in the future? God in His goodness may very well choose to use such times to discipline His people, individually or corporately, weaning them off of the dependencies of earthly wealth and humanistic self-reliance before Jesus Christ returns. We should be grateful if this would happen.

The Day of the Lord is certainly near, this being either the short or long day—i.e., the final half or the entire seven-year period, respectively. But we wonder why so many alternative perspectives—from different Bible prophecy interpretational systems to calendar watchers to the Islamic and the occultic—all seem to be feeling validated by recent world financial trends. Only one event is not taken seriously at this time: the expectation of the sudden return of Jesus Christ "when ye think not" (Matthew 24:44, King James Version).

We are therefore encouraged to "Keep your lives free from the love of money and be content with what you have, because God has said, 'Never will I leave you; never will I forsake you'" (Hebrews 13:5). We can provide no assurance that individuals or specific countries such as the United States might face even tougher times ahead. Yet, such a conclusion is entirely in alignment with Scripture, for we are counseled to place our entire hope in our Lord. That does not mean we are to abdicate common sense or any responsibilities of stewardship, but we are simply not to fear other things more than God. "...do not fear what they fear, and do not dread it. The LORD Almighty is the one you are to regard as holy, he is the one you are to fear, he is the one you are to dread, and he will be a sanctuary..." (Isaiah 8:12–14).

Figure #4

Housing Bubble: U.S. Labor Versus Housing Prices

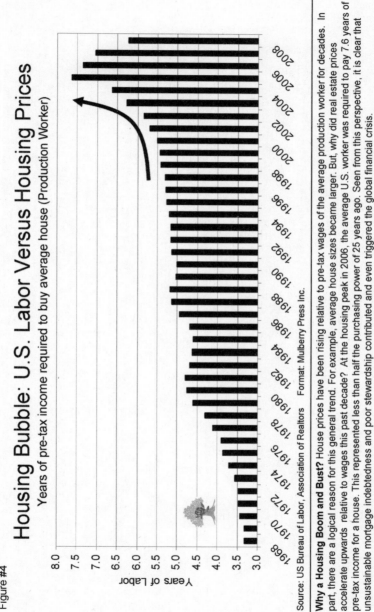

Years of pre-tax income required to buy average house (Production Worker)

Source: US Bureau of Labor, Association of Realtors   Format: Mulberry Press Inc.

Why a Housing Boom and Bust? House prices have been rising relative to pre-tax wages of the average production worker for decades. In part, there are a logical reason for this general trend. For example, average house sizes became larger. But, why did real estate prices accelerate upwards relative to wages this past decade? At the housing peak in 2006, the average U.S. worker was required to pay 7.6 years of pre-tax income for a house. This represented less than half the purchasing power of 25 years ago. Seen from this perspective, it is clear that unsustainable mortgage indebtedness and poor stewardship contributed and even triggered the global financial crisis.

3

CONFUSING, DISTRUSTFUL TIMES: A GROUNDED PERSPECTIVE

We have posed some broad opening perspectives with respect to the scope of the GFC. Moreover, we have shown the penchant of many observers, Christian and otherwise, to search for its significance for the world's future. Could the GFC have a prophetic role? Has the final descent into the Tribulation period begun? Will America recover from its troubles to reaffirm its influential role in the world? We want to urgently return to these questions and begin to present the sobering and eye-opening answers the Bible provides.

However, there is one other foundation we must address first. Not only is there much confusion and ignorance about basic biblical prophetic perspectives, there is much misunderstanding as to the real workings of present-day economies and financial markets. Before we probe the spiritual significance of world financial trends evident today, let's first attempt to correct common misconceptions and counter any possible confusion that may exist. It will also provide us a firmer foundation to provide answers about how Christians can be better stewards of their possession in the challenging scenarios likely

ahead. To do so, we will next review seven basic perspectives that will
aid in this preparation.

TRAVELING WITH THE CROWD

We start with a very basic lesson about crowd psychology and the
challenges it can pose to the actions of both individuals and nations.
To begin, if you are relying upon newspapers and mass media to
inform your worldview—let alone your opinions and decisions—you
will be vulnerable to being carried away by the crowd and becoming
confused by the noise. Critically, you could become the prey of those
who take advantage of people's emotional swings. Crowds are usually
wrong and misdirected.

To avoid the critical error of running with crowds, here are some
general rules to consider. First, always look past the sensationalist
headlines…well past them. Why? Remember that all reported news
concerns the past. By definition, news only refers to trends and events
that have already happened. While that may seem an obvious statement, it highlights an important point: People are more influenced
by what has happened in the recent past than by what is a reasonable
expectation for the future. Therefore, most people—including, for
that matter, professional economists—extrapolate past trends into the
long-term future. This rarely yields a correct perspective.

As Malcolm Muggeridge once famously said, the "media is the
message." We are reminded that the media is the world's collective
mouthpiece of humanistic perspectives. It likes to perpetuate the idea
that only what is in the focal eye of the populist media is the essence
of the current moment of human existence. Not so. No matter how
the world may choose to view the significance of the times, our perspectives are to be framed by a biblical worldview, recognizing that

the "ecclesia" are those who are called out from the world, remaining impervious to its fashions and fears. Jesus prayed that we be taken "...out of the world [and protected] from the evil one" (John 17:15). Again, He said: "I have chosen you out of the world" (John 15:19). The world's opinions therefore are not generally relevant to the Christian life. One needs to screen the message of the media. The popular focus of the times is apt to deliberately mislead because it is the perspective of a lost world.

Last, in this connection, we want to be alerted to the pull of mass psychology and the idiocies produced by the crowd. The popular media has great influence over the shared views and perceptions of a populace. The distribution systems of modern media have become so pervasive and broad they wield enormous influence over the opinions and mood of societies...even over the entirety of mankind. Today, fewer than ten firms—all of them global giants—dominate world media, whether radio, television broadcasting, cable, print, or the Internet. They include world-spanning companies such as Sony, News Corporation, Time Warner, Viacom, Disney, Bertelsmann, and others. By some estimates, fewer than fifty companies control the world's media.

Rupert Murdoch, arguably the world's most powerful media mogul who built News Corporation, famously predicted that the world would have only three large media companies in three years.[11] While his forecast was somewhat aggressive in terms of the predicted concentration of media companies, it is nevertheless true that global values are becoming increasingly monolithic. When the majority of people share the same fears, beliefs, or greed, it can be challenging to maintain an independent course as an otherworldly individual. Moreover, it is the nature of cliques and larger crowds—therefore, also the world—to hold irrational beliefs and to be wrong and misguided. Even those who are widely thought to be wise are proven to be fools, says the Bible (Romans 1:22). "For the wisdom of this world is fool-ishness in God's sight. As it is written: 'He catches the wise in their craftiness'" (1 Corinthians 3:9).

What all these realities implore is that we remain critical and inde-pendent of the populist philosophies of the media and our clique. We need to think for ourselves as to the significance, dangers, and oppor-tunities of the financial and economic bedlam of recent times or any other time. Rather than looking backward, we should be looking for-ward. It is not unbiblical to do so. To Isaiah, the Lord said: "Forget the former things; do not dwell on the past. See, I am doing a new thing! Now it springs up; do you not perceive it? I am making a way in the desert and streams in the wasteland" (Isaiah 43:19). The apostle Paul said, "Forgetting what is behind, and straining toward what is ahead, I press on toward the goal to win the prize for which God has called me heavenward in Christ Jesus" (Philippians 3:13). Let's not allow the past to dictate our future, whether in perspective or deed. Moreover, we must not fall prey to the manias and irrationalities of crowds.

Besides backward-looking biases, one other troublesome facet of today's crowd behavior is very revealing. The deep pessimism reveals a highly distorted value system. While other cultures would consider plagues, pestilences, and famine the worst that could be feared, our high-income societies consider one thing worse: The destruction of wealth. Our ultimate definition of disaster is a materialistic one, fix-ated as it is on the ups and downs of "cyberbit" financial asset values, home prices, cyclical patterns in employment and commerce, and other such things. An apocalypse in these regions of the world is more defined by a lack of things than life-threatening conditions.

Finally, just where should we find our information about the future, at least to the extent that this is available? The popular media? If so, you'll need to wait until the future is reported after the fact.

Discerning, Bible-reading people can do much better than that, as we will learn in the next perspectives.

Rising Above Lies and Selective Statistics

While the popular focus of crowds can be dangerous to our perspective, so could our interpretation of information and statistics. Most everyone is familiar with the quote from Benjamin Disraeli (the first and only prime minister of England of Jewish heritage): "There are three kinds of lies: lies, damned lies, and statistics." He said this back in the mid-1800s. Today, statistics are many times more treacherous than at that earlier age.

We can only attempt brief review of this important topic here. Suffice it to say that statistics have become a very sophisticated and deliberate form of deception in the public sphere. Under the guise of seeming precision, statistics can deliberately lead to misinformation. Partly, that is also attributable to how people mentally process statistics. Misinterpretation is particularly rampant in the case of economic data. Very few people—including so-called professionals—are able to interpret economic statistics reliably.

During my time as a research director of a major Wall Street investment banking firm, one of my big concerns was always the misuse and ignorant interpretation of statistics. All analysts know how to produce reams of statistics, but very few can validly interpret them to draw out the true, underlying, causal meanings.

You may be surprised to learn that statistics do not have a claim upon truth—far from it. Nor can statistics be used to predict the future, as many people seem to believe. With respect to economic data—almost all of it portrayed in the form of statistics—there is also the practical matter of first understanding the definition of the data. To briefly illustrate, consider the significance of the following statement:

> March 6, 2009 (Bloomberg)—The U.S. unemployment rate jumped in February to 8.1 percent, the highest level in more than a quarter century, a surge likely to send more Americans into bankruptcy and force further cutbacks in consumer spending. Employers eliminated 651,000 jobs, the third straight month that losses surpassed 600,000—the first time that's happened since the data began in 1939, Labor Department figures showed today in Washington.

Reading this, you may conclude that employment conditions today are the worst they've been since 1939. Actually, the reader has not been given enough information to draw a firm conclusion of any kind. You would first need to know the definition of "unemployment." This is a statistical definition that has changed many times over the years. Next, you would need to place this statistic in historical context. In reality, U.S. unemployment conditions at times in the past have been much worse than quoted above (for example in 1982, when unemployment under the definition of that time hit 9.7 percent). Of course, the population of the U.S. and the size of its workforce—another concept subject to somewhat arbitrary measurement and definition—are some three times larger today than in 1939.

In any case, the news services that choose to portray this information in such a sensationalist form have an agenda. They sell news, and pessimistic headlines surely sell newspapers. At other times, reporting euphoria suits the general interest. Statistics are interpreted and presented in a very biased fashion. This can contribute to the emotional swings of crowds.

This simple illustration, of course, is not intended to deny that economic downtrends are significant and that joblessness is rising. The point here is simply to raise awareness that statistics can be a powerful tool of misinformation, both intentional and accidental. You need not be so deceived. Strive to tease out the truth from statistics—the closest semblance to reality possible—rather than uncritically accept a biased portrayal. Also consider how economic data, which is always backward-looking and often subject to "spin," may influence the popular mood and psychology of crowds around you.

WHAT GOES AROUND COMES AROUND

If you are a discerning person, you likely were not overly surprised by the news reported by media scribes during the global financial crisis. For several reasons, you would have already known that mankind's economic and financial systems have cyclical patterns and vulnerabilities. First, you realized that financial economies are driven by fallible, fleshly humans who are not always rational and logical.

Second, you knew that from time immemorial, the ebb and flow of commerce has coursed through ups and downs, steps backward and steps forward. Sometimes, such trend changes are caused by external shocks such as droughts or other natural calamities, perhaps plagues or disease. At other times, more likely to occur in our modern era, cyclical monetary and economic systems are the more frequent cause. That economies should experience recessions followed by expansionary periods is not much different than the regular cycles found in natural ecosystems.

That said, every now and then—and much, much more frequently than the merchants of perpetual prosperity would like us believe—big economic and financial busts do occur. These types of downturns are also quite normal. Yet, most people are always shocked and surprised when these downturns come. They may have become swept up in the popular idolatries of the times; chased after false gods of prosperity and fleshly affections; believed the populist predictions of demagogues, politicians, and economists alike; forgotten that the god of this age is a great deceiver; or simply listened to an ill-informed stockbroker.

Countless domestic economic recessions have occurred throughout the world over the last century. There also have been many crises that have included banking and currency collapses, not to mention deep recessions. A research paper issued by the International Monetary Fund (IMF)[12] counts over forty-two such instances around the world between 1970 and 2007 alone, instances in which all three types of crises occurred simultaneously. Amazingly, 124 currency crises have occurred over this period. Much less frequent but normal are the big downturns—the really big collapses involving economic depression, banking system implosions, and sometimes causing global financial contagions.

LARGE BUSTS NOT UNUSUAL

A report that provides helpful insights studied twenty-one such "mega" occurrences back over a little more than a century.[13, 14] The more recent examples occurred in Japan (1991), in South Korea during the Asian crisis a decade ago, and in Sweden (1991). What can be concluded from such studies? For one, big crises do happen fairly regularly, and the one impacting the U.S. and other nations around the world as part of the GFC was not much different in character to date. The follies of "economic man" that crest from time to time have occurred for millennia. Says the writer of Ecclesiastes, "What has been will be again, what has been done will be done again; there is nothing new under the sun" (Ecclesiastes 1:9).

That said, while there may be similar patterns, significant differences are in the details. Also, we must consider the cosmological timeline of mankind. The state of humanity and its systems today are much later and fuller in the eschatological chronology. Yet, we could safely conclude that the GFC as experienced in North America and the world would still qualify as occurring during the days when "...people were eating, drinking, marrying and being given in marriage...buying and selling, planting and building" (Luke 17:27–28). The GFC, as disruptive and destructive as it has been, still does not qualify as an event that is outside normal human history. For those who believe in the Rapture and that it is not likely to occur during tribulational times, this observation counters the argument that the Lord cannot return at this time.

The GFC, as apocalyptic as it may seem to North Americans, still qualifies as a regular part of human existence. George Friedman, the intrepid geopolitical expert of Stratfor, puts it this way: "There will be wars, there will be poverty, there will be triumphs and defeats. There will be tragedy and good luck. People will go to work, make money, have children, fall in love and...hate. That is one thing that is not cyclical. It is the permanent human condition."[15] Though it may seem so to some people, the Great Tribulation has not begun. We can be sure that the economic and financial collapses will be much greater at that time, as it will then be a result of the wrath of God Himself. We will take a more detailed look at this future outcome, the global financial apocalypse, in Chapter 14.

The Late, Great GFC Compared to History

Just how does the recent financial crisis compare to others that have been researched? Compared to the average historical experience of the twenty-one major financial crises (referred to earlier, and also including the 1930s Great Depression in the U.S.), the GFC in America to date is not yet much worse than average. Of course, we can only speak to the statistics available at the time of writing. A number of different scenarios can unfold from this point.

However, let's compare the development of the GFC to date against history. For example, consider that the average stock market decline during those twenty-one periods was a drop of 55 percent in real terms (meaning adjusted for inflation). By comparison, U.S. equity markets had already fallen over 60 percent in real terms during the recent experience (based on the Standard & Poor's 500 stock market index, peak to trough). Whereas real prices of housing declined an average of 36 percent over the twenty-one sample periods, this is already near being exceeded in the U.S. (perhaps cumulating to a total real decline of as much as 45 to 50 percent or so by the end of 2009).

The only major impact upon the U.S. of the current downturn that has not yet matched or exceeded the sample average is the decline of the economy itself. Here the average experience was a peak-to-trough decline in the economy of 9 percent in real terms, requiring approximately 1.9 years.

The point of this brief comparison is not to make any prediction, but rather to show that the recent crisis has not proven itself extraordinarily unusual when viewed against the big busts of history. The global financial crisis therefore does not qualify as an apocalyptic event.

It may very well be true that the worst is already behind for the current stage of the troubles. We also recognize that our brief comparisons have only referred to the average "crisis experience," and not the worst, in our sample set. Therefore, further deterioration is possible. While one should never say "never," at the same time, we shouldn't overlook the fact that mankind's monetary systems are fiat contraptions expressly designed for manipulation. In times past, when all else has failed, policy makers have always resorted to policies leading to inflation...sometimes, to massive runaway price spirals. Given recent actions of major central banks, an inflationary outcome of some type is already underway, though not broadly recognized.

We will review some of the possible scenarios ahead. These range from a meteoric worldwide inflationary boom to a long-term economic depression. Whatever scenario will manifest itself, few will correctly anticipate the next phase of troubles.

CRISES: MORE TOLERABLE WHEN THEY HAPPEN TO SOMEONE ELSE

We now know that the economic and financial crises of the scope now being experienced in the United States, while rarer, are nonetheless within the normal range of human experience. What is significant, of course, is that such a major crisis should strike America at this time. In many ways, it has been deserved, as have most other such busts. However, for the sake of balanced perspective, we again point out the experience of Indonesia during the Asian crisis of 1997–1998. Why? Because this nation is the closest in population to the U.S. and it suffered a terrible economic depression only a decade prior to the GFC.

North Americans today want to believe that their economic

downturn is unjust, undeserved, and especially bad; that there is some special significance because it is happening to an advanced country thought to be Christian; and that the crisis is so significant that it must be of divine origin. Actually, when compared to the Indonesian experience, North Americans protest too much.

According to estimates by Goldman Sachs, the cleanup of the U.S. banking system may cost the equivalent of as much as 40 percent of GDP. In Indonesia, stabilizing its failed banks at that earlier time cost approximately 50 percent of GDP. Indonesia's stock market fell more than 93 percent in U.S. dollar terms and its economy contracted more than 20 percent over the 1997–98 period. Though 230 million people live in Indonesia, this scale of human suffering at the time (hunger and riots resulted) did not signal the beginning of the Apocalypse, nor did it generate much concern in North America. The troubles of other people are rarely considered as severe as when we experience them for ourselves.

Sadly, the world remains in a continuous state of various crises, including such heinous things as genocide, famine, and wars. By comparison, is it so remarkable that a financial crisis should also fall upon developed countries such as Canada and the United States from time to time, especially if it is deserved? To date, troubles have only been limited to financial and economic dimensions. There has been no widespread famine or pestilence. In any case, even if a country were considered to be Christian, would that imply that trials would never come upon its land? The Bible says, "He causes his sun to rise on the evil and the good, and sends rain on the righteous and the unrighteous" (Matthew 5:45). Calamities do happen to Christians. In fact, some types of troubles are the direct consequences of unfortunate decisions and ill-advised behavior. Christians are not given impunity from the physical consequences of bad choices.

As the apostle Paul warned the early church, using the experiences of the ancient Israelites:

> For I do not want you to be ignorant of the fact, brothers, that our forefathers were all under the cloud and that they all passed through the sea. They were all baptized into Moses in the cloud and in the sea. They all ate the same spiritual food and drank the same spiritual drink; for they drank from the spiritual rock that accompanied them, and that rock was Christ. Nevertheless, God was not pleased with most of them; their bodies were scattered over the desert. Now these things occurred as examples to keep us from setting our hearts on evil things as they did. (1 Corinthians 10:1–6)

Just because Christians may be led by the Holy Spirit and walk under the miracle of salvation, they are not preserved from the earthly consequences of sin and error. Therefore, Paul admonishes us to avoid the following mistakes:

> Do not be idolaters, as some of them were; as it is written: "The people sat down to eat and drink and got up to indulge in pagan revelry." We should not commit sexual immorality, as some of them did—and in one day twenty-three thousand of them died. We should not test the Lord, as some of them did—and were killed by snakes. And do not grumble, as some of them did—and were killed by the destroying angel. These things happened to them as examples and were written down as warnings for us, on whom the fulfillment of the ages has come. So, if you think you are standing firm, be careful that you don't fall! (1 Corinthians 10:7–12)

BEWARE OF ECONOMISTS BEARING FORECASTS

To this point in our analysis, we have made many references to economic concepts and we have quoted economic data. We have even risked a few general macroeconomic predictions. We need to recant. In case you didn't know, the field of economics is not a science—far from it. At best, it is a field of study that may offer some practical tools and concepts. But more generally, the use of economics for predictive purposes and public policy must be seen as a secular religion.

The truth is that the prescriptions of macroeconomics are no more effective than voodoo. It is a faculty of study assigned to the humanities. Therefore, to the extent that policy makers have put their faith into macroeconomics, we all have been deceived by false prophets and a fraudulent belief system. The late, great GFC reveals this to be the case. Why? The vast majority of the prophets and high priests of modern macroeconomics did not predict the economic wreckage of the current crises (practically none of them!). What has been witnessed, therefore, is a systemic failure of the economics profession.

A small number of scholars has emerged, scholars who are bravely exposing this empty tower of macroeconomics. In one report critical of the macroeconomics profession, the authors pull no punches. They point out that:

> "...systemic crisis" appears like an otherworldly event that is absent from economic models.... The economics profession has failed in communicating the limitations, weaknesses and even dangers of its preferred models to the public...makes clear the need for the establishment of an ethical code.... In hour of greatest need, societies around the world are left to grope in the dark without a theory.... The tradition [of crisis phenomena] has been neglected and even suppressed. [16]

Apart from these brave academics and a few others, the scientific fraud and failure of macroeconomics qualifies as one of the most unspoken facts in history. Yet, at the continuing gatherings of international economists recently, no one admits to this dismal record. The obvious failure remains an open, unspoken secret. They continue on with their voodoo, further offering up policy prescriptions to governments intended to rescue countries from the current crisis. The blind lead the blind.

Of course, once the GFC befell the world, the divinations of most economists revealed a future so dire that massive money interventions by central banks were considered essential. In other words, they effectively argued that massive deceit and theft are necessary to counteract the past follies of policy makers, regulators, and various business executives. We observe that one evil begets another. These emergency prescriptions will be no more effective in solving the oppressive economic problems of the world today than a "bloodletting" is likely to heal a patient suffering from dementia.

The whole field of directing government economic policies or predicting the future through macroeconomic theory is really no more valid than following pagan omens and the false visions of prophets of old. Beware! It has yet to be proven that an economist is a more successful investor or forecaster than anyone else: "Physician heal yourself" (Luke 4:23).

DELIVERED FROM THE TRIBULATION?

Many commentators have noted the significant wealth losses experienced by Christians. For example, quoting a typical comment: "Americans have lost some $3 trillion in wealth, as the markets have plummeted some 30 percent." Ignoring that this statistic is out of date, just what is the point? Apparently there was gnashing of teeth. Christian businesspeople, not to mention families and households, were gripped with great fear and looking for a special word from the Lord. Tough business conditions are surely not pleasurable, whether for business manager, owner, or employee. Apparently, Christian businesspeople somehow feel they could deserve vindication or absolution from the effects of the GFC.

Some balance is needed here, as we are dealing with an elitist Christian perspective. Why is it expected that God should deliver Christians from the GFC? While preservation from the global financial apocalypse that is yet to come (this being representative here of the Tribulation period) can be expected, this would really only apply to Christians whose hearts are free of the materialistic idolatries to begin with. Most Christians today betray a very worldly and amoral view when it comes to matters of comfort and prosperity. Of course, all humans are predisposed to enjoy similar fleshly pleasures. God did give us the capacity of pleasure for our blessing. Yet, in doing so, we realize that a pleasure cannot be consumed or enjoyed without at least some consideration of values and morals. This also applies to the pleasures of wealth and financial gains.

MONEY: THE COMMON DENOMINATOR OF TRUTH?

Can you think of a situation in which a huge financial gain might be immoral? No doubt, quite a number of such personal scenarios could be imagined. Let's next consider the same question on a more macro plain, applying it generally to life around us. For instance, if world real estate values are soaring, is that a good thing or a bad thing?

While it may feel pleasurable at the time, we (after the onset of the real estate crisis) can surely recognize that such a development might not have a pleasant consequence. While people may celebrate a sensation of becoming wealthier when the house they own rises in price, they somehow overlook that they really did not become wealthier at all. If an automobile were to become more expensive, we wouldn't think we had become wealthier, but rather poorer. Rising costs relative to our incomes actually reduce one's standard of living. Overlooked in the case of rising residential housing prices is that those who have yet to buy a home—the younger generation, for example—have become relatively impoverished.

In any case, just who has determined that financial upturns are no more allowed by the Lord than downturns? Why is it that Christians are less inclined to seek the Lord's direction when times appear to be easy and prosperous from a worldly perspective—when inflated millions and trillions are pumping up monetary wealth and society's arbitrary and imperfect indicators of well-being are all rising (i.e., stock markets and economic growth)? It reveals a duplicitous and false standard.

Financial and economic indicators are not to be uncritically adopted by Christians as the measure of what good and right. That the Dow Jones Industrial stock market index should rise is no sure indication of a positive development or the validation of a benevolent situation. It may the exact opposite, perhaps part of an illusory wealth bubble that ensnares many people. That being the case, just where were these Christian commentators when these corrupt financial conditions began to occur in the first place? There were few warnings.

More likely, that earlier time of false prosperity, when real estate values and stock markets were rising, was wrongly taken as a validation of God's overall blessings. After all, much of these apparently halcyon times were underpinned by illicit and corrupt developments. Couldn't these conditions popularly perceived as "blessed" also not have occurred because God relented and gave people up to the results of their own perversions and idolatries? (See Romans 1:24.)

Surely, during recent times, terribly corrupt and idolatrous conditions swept the U.S. and most of the world. These conditions can be expected to worsen over time, as epic monetary manipulations now undermine any hope of peaceful stewardship and ethical reward. That financial indicators themselves are deceptive and spiritually unreliable is a crucial realization too few Christians have pondered.

As troubling and deceitful as the times may be, we must still strive to make the best moral decisions we can. We are not absolved from the task of godly stewardship of our possessions and planning for our retirement. However, it remains very difficult to extricate ourselves from the influences of pagan perspectives that are so deeply embedded in our societies. We will return to the topic of personal stewardship, laying helpful guidelines in Appendix 1.

Here is an important question that you must answer for yourself. Jesus said, "No man can serve two masters: for either he will hate the one, and love the other; or else he will hold to the one, and despise the other. Ye cannot serve God and mammon" (Matthew 6:24, KJV). If these opposites are mutually exclusive, then is it really possible to wholly serve God while employing the score-keeping values of Mammon? If you are called to obey the Lord and it costs you do so in earthly monetary terms, what values will guide your decision? Would you allow your faith to cost a job promotion...perhaps a lucrative profit opportunity? Your answer will reveal whom you really serve: "For where your treasure is, there your heart will be also" (Matthew 6:21).

FICTITIOUS FUNNY MONEY

One cannot discuss wealth without differentiating its modern popular conception from true, earthly wealth. To the point of total blindness, the wealth most everyone identifies in our age of global capital is mostly a mirage. The trillions that North American households supposedly lost in recent times—just where did it come from in the first place? Was it legitimate wealth to begin with? Or was it just an illusory, manipulated contrivance? Seen in the aggregate, the answer is the latter. Indeed, some people did achieve enormous gains in relative wealth during the preceding financial bubble, but the vast majority did not. If anything, the world's distribution of wealth is becoming ever more skewed. In America, this wealth skew is becoming even more extreme. If trends do not change, its wealth distribution is headed for the high level of income inequity observed in some Latin American countries. According to the surveys of the World Bank, the U.S. distribution of wealth is the most distorted of all high-income countries.

Just what relation is there between financial market values and wealth? Very little. We live in times of fiat money. This means that money issued by governments and central banks has no fixed call upon true wealth—namely, the fruits of mankind's labor or the earth's physical resources. Money can be manufactured independent of real savings and wealth. Though most major central banks around the world try not to overly abuse this power of money creation, there are times when policy makers believe there is little other option. Indeed, such were the times during the GFC.

Consider that the central banks of England, the U.S., Japan, and Switzerland did choose to resort to "printing money" in response to the GFC. These are among the major central banks in the world. What is meant by the phrase "printing money" is that these central banks are now effectively creating money out of thin air—by fiat decree, by the stroke of a pen. Such actions dilute the value of money that is already in existence, not to mention the savings deposits of hard-working people. It is grand theft, deception, wizardry of a type and scale as never seen before. In practical terms, the purchasing power of your savings and current income will not stretch as far in the future.

APPARITIONS OF WEALTH

In recent decades, there has been another rather nefarious development in respect to financial market wealth. Consider that policy makers long ago recognized that the surest way to make people feel happy and prosperous is to have the perceived wealth of their homes and financial assets rise. Even most Christians have fallen for this hollow ruse. This new demagoguery became brazen in the early 1990s, openly endorsed in intellectual circles. A quote reflecting this thinking states that: "…now many societies, and indeed the entire world, have learned how to create wealth directly. The new approach requires that a state find ways to increase the market value of its productive assets." Such an economic policy that "aims to achieve growth by wealth creation therefore does not attempt to increase the production of goods and services, except as a secondary objective."[17]

The point to recognize is that the apparition of rising wealth—by hook or crook—is to be focused on, not the real aspects of human labor, financial conditions, or anything else. Wealth—even if only a flickering, volatile imitation—has become the focus of adulation.

The core of this rotten ideology is found in high places. The lure of financial wealth—more, exactly, the perception of wealth—has become a deliberate policy tool. Wealth goes before all and is above all. Make most people think that they are becoming wealthier and that more wealth gains are probable, and national prosperity and economic growth will be sure to follow. This "hoodwink" ensnarement played a great part in the current economic troubles now being faced by North America and other nations. Frankly, many people were carried away by their lusts.

What's the bottom line...the profitable conclusion? Don't be fooled or ensnared by manipulated money. Do not allow affections to settle upon such hollow promises of temporal prosperity and therefore lose sight of eternal riches. The Bible couldn't provide a clearer warning:

> People who want to get rich fall into temptation and a trap and into many foolish and harmful desires that plunge men into ruin and destruction. For the love of money is a root of all kinds of evil. Some people, eager for money, have wandered from the faith and pierced themselves with many griefs. But you, man of God, flee from all this, and pursue righteousness, godliness, faith, love, endurance and gentleness. (1 Timothy 6:9–11)

THE BINARY NATURE OF WEALTH

To this point, we have not yet discussed the definition of "real wealth" and "eternal riches." We already reviewed two other concepts of wealth—illusory wealth as differentiated from true earthly wealth (the fruits of labor and the created physical firmaments). However, before doing so, we must first highlight one additional transitory aspect of earthly wealth. While newspapers may focus on losses, bankruptcies, and indebtedness, they usually ignore the other side of the equation. As every asset is owned by someone, every transaction must have a buyer and a seller; every borrower, a creditor. As Isaiah put it: "…for seller as for buyer, for borrower as for lender, for debtor as for creditor" (Isaiah 24:2). The visions of Zechariah shown in Chapter 5 of the book of the same name further testify to the effects of the binary nature of the world's commercial systems.

We seem to be dwelling on a redundant point. Yet, its implications are not generally realized. While many trillions of dollars of wealth may be disappearing into the ether for some people, for the most part, someone else is gaining in relative wealth. It is true that capital can be destroyed and that the world in a capitalistic sense will be poorer in such cases. Generally, however, wealth is more likely to be transferred to someone else or is converted to a different form during times of economic crisis or financial inflation.

To be sure, these processes have been underway these past few years as for centuries before. To illustrate, consider who might have benefited from the issuance of subprime mortgages. Some finance firm then sold these mortgages to the issuers of asset-backed paper. Someone built or sold the homes that went up in price to ridiculous extremes relative to household income levels. While AIG, the American insurance company, may have lost a reputed $170 billion in underwriting credit default insurance, the counterparty who bought the insurance in the first place was being paid off. The point to realize here is that while the popular media may be deflecting attention because of its biases, another perspective must not be overlooked.

Times of financial crisis, conditions of ongoing corruption, and ever-easier opportunity to defraud or outwit the masses continue to lead to ever-widening wealth skews, as already pointed out. The corollary to that condition for society is ever-increasing economic oppression, a trend of growing anxiety over the cares of this world for a greater majority of people. We will outline the tragic significance of this development for the world and Christians in Chapter 14.

Thankfully, there is one type of wealth over which one need not agonize or worry. Christ revealed its identity: "Provide purses for yourselves that will not wear out, a treasure in heaven that will not be exhausted" (Luke 12:33).

WHOM TO BLAME

Great crises, whether financial, economic, or otherwise, always involve victims and sacrificial lambs. During such times, it is convenient and politically expedient to assign blame. It soothes the national conscience. Therefore, upon whom do we pin the tail this time? Who might be the vulnerable sacrificial lambs?

Less than a decade before the GFC, such people as Martha Stewart, Bernhard Ebbers of WorldCom infamy, Enron Chief Executive Officer Kenneth Lay, Tyco International chief Dennis Kozlowski, and others were marched in front of the news cameras on their way to court or jail. It came to be called the "perp walk." Some identified themselves as Christians. These scapegoats were no worse than many other businesspeople. They just happened to be caught in the public eye. If anything, they reflected the accepted culture of the times—a cheating culture.

Who might be officially blamed this time? Could it be the high-profile elites, the great conspiracy groups such as the Illuminati, the international bankers, perhaps? No, we do not ascribe to such theories in isolation of the biblical view. People of all kinds were involved, from pauper to prince.

It is confounding how many intelligent Christians lose their focus in the area of conspiracy theories. Doing so, they trap themselves as purveyors of the social gospel. Yes, there are conspiracies in the world and there are a lot of rich, corrupt people. Of course, not all rich people are corrupt, though the Bible sometimes assumes this to be the case. For example, see James 2:6 and 5:1.

Scripture clearly equates conspiracy schemes with the antichrist spirit. The apostle John said, "This is the spirit of the antichrist, which you have heard is coming and even now is already in the world" (1 John 4:3). Everyone is vulnerable to playing a role, whether small or large. There can be any number of antichrists in this sense; the Bible indicates that there will be many. "Dear children, this is the last hour; and as you have heard that the antichrist is coming, even now many antichrists have come. This is how we know it is the last hour" (1 John 2:18). Simply complying with the world's values and its humanist agenda makes one a conspirator… a mini antichrist. The spirit of the Antichrist really aligns all individuals, groups, and nations who betray a spirit of rebellion against God, whether elites or not.

But this should not make any complicit people our enemies or the target of our condemnation. We are reminded that "we wrestle not against flesh and blood, but against principalities, against powers, against the rulers of the darkness of this world, against spiritual wickedness in high places" (Ephesians 6:12). This is not a single spirit, but a hierarchy of demons led by the "kosmokrator," the chief angel, Satan. It is against this conspiracy that we wrestle—not against deceived, mortal human beings.

Our time is therefore better spent praying for conspirators and antichrists, whoever they may be, and pursuing a biblical faith life. Elitists, globalists, or whatever other "one-world-order" villains there might be are no different or worse than the vast humanity that has been either misled or blinded by this world's "prince of the air." All other conspiracy theories are really unnecessary distractions to Christians.

It is the basic nature of humans to love money, to share in "the cravings of sinful man, the lust of his eyes and the boasting of what he has and does" (1 John 2:16). Every person, whether elite or common, must accept responsibility for his or her actions and idolatries. The difference, if any, is that the sins of some people can affect the entire world; for others, their sins only affect their immediate families or themselves.

ROLE OF THE CHURCH

It is not the great commission of the church to convict and hunt down sinners. If one should want to make it a life ambition to scalp so-called global conspirators, to hang Wall Street manipulators, or perhaps to incarcerate sex trade workers, one is free to do so. But we must not claim that this is a Christian mission. God has set rulers and governments in place to establish earthly justice and to carry out such initiatives.

The church first is to preach the gospel that man is a sinner and headed for damnation, and that only by acknowledging Christ as Lord, Son of God, and Savior will he be saved. Then, once imbued with the living Holy Spirit, the convictions of sin will emanate from the heart. The scalpings, condemnations, and hangings will not lead to repentance that offers eternal life. The Bible repeatedly says that the Spirit is the sword (Ephesians 6:17 and Hebrews 11:34), and so is the Word (Revelation 2:16 and 19:15). If we are to engage in any offensive actions, it must be with this sword, not with our social, activist programs.

THOUGHTS TO PONDER

History and the Bible warn us about another people who, time and again, have been appointed the scapegoats. It is a history of great tragedy and injustice.

Many times in the history of the world, the Jews have been the convenient whipping stock for financial collapses. Tragically, it has happened many times. For various reasons—mainly because God decreed that they would be separate and dispersed until their millennial restoration—these special people, called to be God's servants, have excelled wherever they've been given an opportunity. Indeed, Wall Street today is home to a disproportionate number of Jews. Many have high-profile positions. For example, the two recent central bank governors in the U.S., Allan Greenspan and Ben Bernanke (the very two who presided over the current monetary malfeasance of grand scale), are Jews. Larry Summers, Robert Rubin, and Timothy Geithner—in fact, half of the Treasury secretaries since 1995, this period widely acknowledged as the big bubble years of financial alchemy—have been Jews. We need not go on.

The American Jew has experienced a Golden Age since the 1950s. America has prospered because of the liberties and acceptance it has bestowed upon this people…the "apple" of God's eye (Zechariah 2:8). But the lessons of history now urge a special caution. Every Golden Age for the Jew to date, whether experienced in Spain, Russia, Poland, Germany, or other countries, has come to a close. As Christians, we must pray that this does not happen again and that the demonic spirit of anti-Semitism doesn't cause America, indeed even ourselves, to have any complicity in such evil. It is an urgent task for evangelical Christianity. In Chapter 10, we will tackle this very difficult and sensitive topic—Jews, Gentiles, and money.

Figure #5

Delusions of Wealth: US Household Impoverishment
Home Equity Ratio and Home Value/Disposable Income (1952 to 2008, Quarterly)

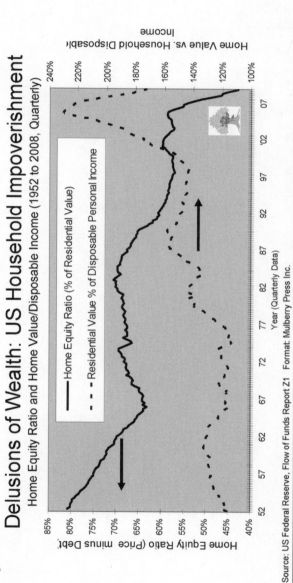

Home Value vs. Household Disposable Income

Home Equity Ratio (% of Residential Value)

- - - Residential Value % of Disposable Personal Income

Year (Quarterly Data)

Home Equity Ratio (Price minus Debt)

52 57 62 67 72 77 82 87 92 97 '02 '07

85% 80% 75% 70% 65% 60% 55% 50% 45% 40%

240% 220% 200% 180% 160% 140% 120% 100%

Source: US Federal Reserve, Flow of Funds Report Z1   Format: Mulberry Press Inc.

A Remarkable Real Estate Crash. In recent years, accelerating in 2003, U.S. residential real estate climbed in value as prices soared. By mid-2006, the value of all U.S. residential real estate reached $21.7 trillion. It would be logical to conclude that the average American household was becoming wealthier as the value of their homes rose. Remarkably, this did not happen. On average, most householders refinanced their homes and spent their gains. In 2009, Americans now have the lowest home equity in history … probably less than 40%.

4

IDOLS THAT TOPPLE AND TOTTER: A MODERN REDISCOVERY

In earlier chapters, we briefly touched on some prophetic perspectives, both those of the Bible as well as the apocalyptic views of other visionaries and theorists. Now that we attempted to clarify current trends and challenges individuals may face in stewarding their possessions and retirement investments, we are ready to return to the task of researching the biblical view on our current times of materialism and crisis. We first must tackle a distasteful subject—idolatry. What is it, and what forms does it take?

Surely, this topic could not be relevant to the many nations today with historical Christian heritage—and certainly not America. After all, doesn't the large majority of America's populace believe in the existence of God? Is it not true that the largest, most vocal group of evangelical Christians resides in North America? Surely then our societies have no large complicity in the types of worldwide conditions that a sovereign God declares He will judge with wrath in the near future? To answer this question, we must first seek a biblical perspective and establish a proper measuring line for this determination.

Just what is the essence of idolatry? We can begin by first looking to the experience of the Israelites for an ancient perspective. From the beginning, the Israelites were admonished not to worship idols. During their wanderings through various nations after coming out of Egypt, Moses warned: "You saw among them their detestable images and idols of wood and of stone, of silver and gold. Make sure there is no man or woman, clan or tribe among you today whose heart turns away from the LORD our God..." (Deuteronomy 29:17–28). Furthermore, "Do not make idols or set up an image or a sacred stone for yourselves, and do not place a carved stone in your land to bow down before it. I am the LORD your God" (Leviticus 26:1).

Prophet after prophet, priest, and king warned about the dangers and futility of following the nations' idols made of wood, stone, gold, and other materials—idols that cannot see or hear. Even the pagans were reprimanded and punished for praising idols. For example, Belshazzar, the last Babylonian ruler, was judged and found wanting for celebrating his idols of "gold and silver, of bronze, iron, wood and stone" (Daniel 5:4, 23). Yet, the Israelites persisted, saying: "We want to be like the nations, like the peoples of the world, who serve wood and stone" (Ezekiel 20:32).

That was a long time ago. Reading these accounts today, it all sounds so primitive, so irrelevant to our time. Modern, civilized people do not worship idols made of wood and stone.

Or so we think. We read this in the book of Revelation: "The rest of mankind that were not killed by these plagues still did not repent of the work of their hands; they did not stop worshiping demons, and idols of gold, silver, bronze, stone and wood—idols that cannot see or hear or walk" (Revelation 9:20). This reveals a fact that is shocking to the sensibilities of modern man. We see a pagan civilization worshiping material idols in the future. Yes, in the future—from at least our day and right into the Tribulation period. Actually, pagan idolatry today is as rampant as perhaps never before. Do we recognize it for what it is?

TOTTERING IDOLS REQUIRE PROPPING UP

What is an idol? Consulting a dictionary, we read descriptions such as this: "a representation or symbol of an object of worship...a false conception,"[18] and so on. The Bible, however, provides an easy, useful definition: An idol is any object of human reliance that is vulnerable to toppling. For example: "A man too poor to present such an offering selects wood that will not rot. He looks for a skilled craftsman to set up an idol that will not topple" (Isaiah 40:20). This is a most humorous depiction. After all, why worship something that we ourselves must prevent from toppling with our own hands?

Again, Isaiah tells us: "The craftsman encourages the goldsmith, and he who smooths with the hammer spurs on him who strikes the anvil. He says of the welding, 'It is good.' He nails down the idol so it will not topple" (Isaiah 41:7). Jeremiah, too, made the same observation: "...they cut a tree out of the forest, and a craftsman shapes it with his chisel. They adorn it with silver and gold; they fasten it with hammer and nails so it will not totter" (Jeremiah 10:3–4). God must surely laugh at mankind's attempts to build and set up his own gods. He probably chuckles that mankind does not see the futility of idols if they must be nailed down and defended. Gideon's father, Joash, when coming to his senses after Gideon smashed his idols, said: "If Baal really is a god, he can defend himself when someone breaks down his altar" (Judges 6:31). Anything mankind allows to become an idol will be sure to disappoint and come up empty.

This is one of the key lessons of the recent storm of economic and financial tremors that has radiated across the world. Idols topple and totter. Many things held to be venerable emblems of mankind's achievements and hopes have wavered during the GFC. Comically, they must therefore be propped up by man.

Consider that some of the world's biggest and most swaggering companies, once revered as unstoppable global juggernauts, have needed propping up.

The largest U.S. bank failure occurred—Washington Mutual Inc., with $307 billion in assets. The largest insurance company needed to be rescued—American International Group. The world's one-time largest car company, General Motors, was technically bankrupt, requiring bailout financing from governments. The biggest investment banks (Merrill Lynch, Morgan Stanley) all needed government help. One of the largest and most trusted investment funds ended up utterly worthless, due to the Ponzi scheme swindle of Bernie Madoff. Fifty billion dollars disappeared into thin air. (All of these entities were headquartered in the United States.) They could no longer stand on their own.

Not to be overlooked, of course, are the phenomenal crashes of various financial markets themselves. As already observed, at one point in 2008–2009, the entire world stock market had fallen by more than 50 percent (measured in U.S. dollars) from the previous year. Surely, the widespread belief that modern-day financial markets—the supposed source of prosperity and wealth of mankind—would continue to rise to ever-higher extremes qualifies them as idols.

PHILOSOPHIES AND VIEWPOINTS
ALSO TOTTERING

Certain popular beliefs regarded as doctrinal truths to the humanist mind have also been tottering. Consider that the year 2009 was, even early in the year, on track to record the largest decline in global trade since World War II. Trade has been the central pillar of globalization and the long-promoted condition that will knit mankind into a common mutual dependency. As already mentioned, it is believed by humanists that once mankind's prosperity is tightly interdependent globally, the required incentive for world peace will have been established. But now, many fret that the means to achieving this ideal is under threat. Indeed, globalization may take a step backward during the present worldwide economic downturn.

However, in the end it is likely that most nations will recognize that it is much too late to disengage from world intercourse. As it is, given the experience of the Great Depression of the 1930s, policy makers are today extremely wary of protectionist trade policies. There are no longer any easy exits from the road to globalism given the advanced state of global financial interconnectedness and trade. In 2007, developing countries—numbering more than ninety nations—derived more than 50 percent of their economic activity (GDP) from exports.[19] That was double the trade intensity of 1995, only twelve years prior.

The Bible allows us to know that the nations will eventually huddle together to prop up their three favorite idols of the end times—the "unknown god," the "foreign god," and the "god of fortresses" (Daniel 11:38–39)—that were unveiled in my earlier book, *The Endtime Money Snare*.

Other long-held notions are also under threat. The case for "free-market-based" economics is threatened. Just what is meant by the term "free market"? It is the simple, liberal idea that people, if left to act freely in their own concepts of morality and self-interest—without much government or regulatory intervention in markets—will together achieve progress and greater prosperity for the world. This is the sure path to a world without poverty, it is thought. To no surprise, policy makers have again discovered that too many people have been acting too freely in pursuing their own selfish interests. Uncontrolled greed eventually devours its own house, weakening its very timbers and stones. That is an aspect of the curse to which Zechariah's vision of the great flying scroll points (Zechariah 5), the result of a global commercial system built upon the cornerstones of "stealing" and "lying." This curse "will remain in his house and destroy it, both its timbers and its stones'" (Zechariah 5:4). The full meaning of Zechariah's prophecies is the subject of Chapter 7.

We are not being overly harsh in our views. Why? Consider these three widely held economic maxims: "1. Man seeks to gratify his desires with the least amount of exertion. 2. Man's desires are unlimited. 3. Man hoards consciously and systematically." [20] These are not our own definitions. These maxims of "self-interest" are in fact enthroned and institutionalized as advanced, sophisticated theories today. It all represents a grisly, competitive world in which mankind celebrates the satisfaction of self. It is the worldly parallel to the terrible times that Paul sees invading the church in the last days: "People will be lovers of themselves, lovers of money, boastful, proud, abusive, disobedient to their parents, ungrateful, unholy, without love, unforgiving, slanderous, without self-control, brutal, not lovers of the good, treacherous, rash, conceited, lovers of pleasure rather than lovers of God…" (2 Timothy 3:2–4).

PROPPING UP THE GOLDEN FINANCIAL IDOL

We live in a day when mankind has reached the highest zenith of self-determination ever in history. Today, man is in the position to seek global solutions. God, who chose to reveal Himself through His Son, Jesus Christ, is not allowed into the public square of debate for the answers to mankind's problems. The boards and committees of cities, states, countries, and transnational organizations do not think to consult Him or observe His statutes. They choose to make their own way. They think: "He will not see us" (Ezekiel 8:12), and, "What does God know?… Thick clouds veil him, so he does not see us as he goes about in the vaulted heavens'" (Job 22:13–14).

Nowhere is this attitude more brazen than in the field of economics. We can best understand its revolutionary, "end-time" impact upon mankind's rebellion if we see it for what it is: a religion, a global religion. It is one of those disciplines that is not a science, but rather closer to sorcery in its recent globalist applications. That is not to say certain economic principles do not have their uses. Yet, most economic macro-policy theories—ideas that are applied by governments to manage economies and societies—remain just that, theories. None can be marshaled to create a certain outcome in the future.

Yet today, the entire world awaits the wizardry of the economic guru, the modern-day seat of the False Prophet. For example, the new economic advisors of the U.S. Obama administration: Timothy Geithner, Paul Volcker, Robert Rubin, Larry Summers, and Laura Tyson—all very smart people—have been called in to steady the tottering economic edifice. It is expected that their recommendations of various policies of economic tinkering will overcome America's deep troubles. They are likely to be no better than the advisors of Nebuchadnezzar's day. That indictment is not meant to be disrespectful, but reflects the hollowness of economic macro-theory today.

Yet, economic policy advisors are sought to solve challenges on a global scale. They devise ways to get the world back on the road to peace and prosperity. Most of these efforts are underpinned by the notion that future prosperity can be manufactured at will…conjured out of midair…and that past sins and excesses have no consequences. No. God says He "cannot be mocked" (Galatians 6:7). He says that whatever you sow, you will reap. It is a spiritual law as well as one that applies to the physical world. To the extent that the world's policy makers and economists ignore this admonition, they are "pillow prophets." Against their high imaginations, God says: "I form the light and create darkness, I bring prosperity and create disaster; I, the LORD, do all these things" (Isaiah 45:7).

Change Expected in the Millennium

In the present dispensation, the prince of the air continues to rule the earth. Though God is on His throne and Jesus Christ remains seated at His right side, Satan still is allowed great influence in the world of man. While God clearly has the uppermost power, declaring that it is He who sets up and deposes rulers (meaning also under His allowance), Satan is still able to entice key people with "the kingdoms of the world and their splendor" (Matthew 4:8).

Nebuchadnezzar, the most illustrious of all the Gentile potentates the Bible informs us about, pictured as the head of gold, finally bowed down to the God of the Bible. After being deposed from his throne and punished for seven years, he came to his senses, acknowledging, "Now I, Nebuchadnezzar, praise and exalt and glorify the King of heaven, because everything He does is right and all his ways are just. And those who walk in pride he is able to humble" (Daniel 4:37). His experience serves as a foreshadowing of the future, seven-year Tribulation. At the end of it, mankind will finally acknowledge that "everything He does is right and all his ways are just" (Daniel 4:37).

In the Millennium age, a new economic system will prevail, one that will be based on completely different doctrines. Yet, they are doctrines of old, long counseled by the Scriptures. They are based on the one surefire strategy that will never fail. One three-word verse unlocks this key: "Love never fails" (1 Corinthians 13:8). Both royal laws are extensions of this doctrine: one directed toward God and the other to our neighbors without favoritism (James 2:9). When the Lord returns and restores all things (Acts 3:21, Matthew 17:11), surely the world under His rule will be based on these royal laws, not on today's worldly economic maxims that focus on self. Regrettably, various teachers who identify themselves as Christian today endorse this veneration of self.

THOUGHTS TO PONDER

Do we recognize the idols of wood and stone today? They may be robed in the supposedly sophisticated concepts of our time; therefore, they are much more deceptive. At the same time, these idols are as arrogant and deadly as ever.

You can either choose to serve God or Mammon—the spiritual entity incentivized by money and the harbor of all idolatry. This is a Bible verse we have all often heard (Matthew 6:24). But do we really understand what it implies for the world in which we live? It speaks of a polarity that gives rise to a great struggle and the ultimate curse. We can choose to serve the One, yet the other is always seeking our affections. Our eyes wander between them all too easily. No matter our best intentions and devotion, idolatry is always only a hairbreadth away…perhaps a brief flicker of wandering affection. Yet, in repentance, we are saved from our sins.

Referring again to the polarity between God and Mammon, the disciples were gravely puzzled by this apparently irreconcilable chasm. Jesus said: "'I tell you the truth, it is hard for a rich man to enter the kingdom of heaven. Again I tell you, it is easier for a camel to go through the eye of a needle than for a rich man to enter the kingdom of God.' When the disciples heard this, they were greatly astonished and asked, 'Who then can be saved?' Jesus looked at them and said, 'With man this is impossible, but with God all things are possible'" (Matthew 19:23-26). We therefore trust in the God of the impossible, accepting His salvation through His Son, Jesus Christ.

Eventually mankind will come to the point when idols of gold and silver will be thrown into the streets. "In that day men will throw away to the rodents and bats their idols of silver and idols of gold, which they made to worship. They will flee to caverns in the rocks and to the overhanging crags from dread of the Lord…" (Isaiah 2:20–21). This prophecy aligns with the event John saw, as described in Revelation 6:15: "Then the kings of the earth, the princes, the generals, the rich, the mighty, and every slave and every free man hid in caves and among the rocks of the mountains."

By showing that the world is indeed full of idols and idolatry, we conclude that modern pagans must exist. The next chapter addresses their surprising identity.

PROPHETIC
PERSPECTIVES
ON TODAY

Figure #6

Western Offshoots Declining: Economies, 1500 AD to 1998

Economic Size by Major Regions & Powers, GDP, Billions 1990 International Dollars

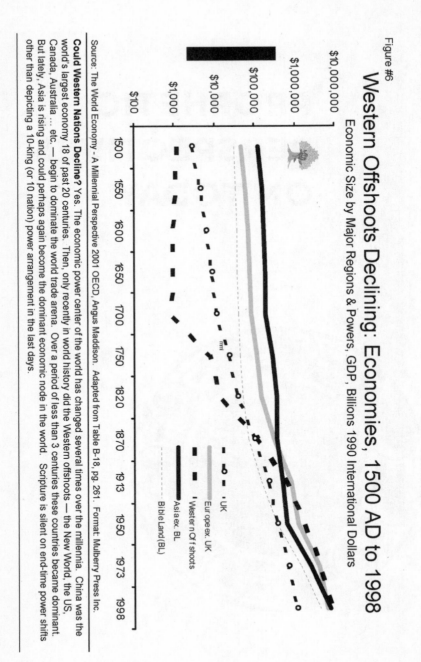

Source: The World Economy - A Millennial Perspective 2001 OECD, Angus Maddison. Adapted from Table B-18, pg. 261. Format: Mulberry Press Inc.

Could Western Nations Decline? Yes. The economic power center of the world has changed several times over the millennia. China was the world's largest economy 18 of past 20 centuries. Then, only recently in world history did the Western offshoots — the New World, the US, Canada, Australia .... etc. — begin to dominate the world trade arena. Over a period of less than 3 centuries these countries became dominant. But lately, Asia is rising and could perhaps again become the dominant economic node in the world. Scripture is silent on end-time power shifts other than depicting a 10-king (or 10 nation) power arrangement in the last days.

5

THOROUGHLY SOPHISTICATED, MODERN PAGAN

Indeed, our modern-day cultures do worship gods of wood and stone. If anything, idolatry is more advanced and sophisticated than ever before. The idolatry depicted in the Bible was usually associated with pagans. With so much idolatry in the world, just where are the pagans found today? Surely modern man has evolved to a much more rational and enlightened state than the ancient pagan. We would be hard-pressed to think of our society as deeply pagan. Isn't a pagan some wild native in a loincloth, perhaps running around in the jungles worshipping the sun god? Actually, there are in the world today pagans much more basal and arrogant than might be found in the jungle. It is another blunt question for which we best turn to Bible for our perspective.

EVOLUTION OF THE SOPHISTICATED PAGAN

Paleontologists speak of Neanderthal Man, Australopithecus, and many other prehuman forms that were purportedly forbearers to we modern-day Homo sapiens. The evolutionary processes that these represent supposedly happened over many millions of years ago. Of course, removed from literal biblical interpretation, we know that this whole field of study remains highly imaginative and speculative. There is now already a long legacy of the Bible having trumped the skepticism of science on many issues, whether historical, physical, or otherwise. All the Bible has proven true. Because all that has already been fulfilled or discovered has proven 100-percent accurate biblically, it takes only a small leap of faith to acknowledge that the rest of the truths in the Bible science still argues with will also require a revision in the latter. That truism applies to science, therefore also to the theory of evolution. With respect to physical evolution, the Bible doesn't mention any different species of humans, sub-humans, or any developmental biological stages of mankind. As it happens, there simply isn't any proof for the theory of evolution. It remains a religion. Nor is there any difference between ancient humanity and people today. Man's basic characteristics, both physical and temperamental, have not changed one iota.

With respect to humans, the Bible only makes one major distinction among mankind that is racial—that between Jew and Gentile. Yet, even more importantly, the Bible makes another distinction among humans—that between the pagan and the righteous. Here we see the real evidence for evolution, although a spiritual version: paganism. The pagan is alive and well today. However, he has become quite sophisticated in his fables, as we will discover. Virtually all anthropologists agree that today the earth's sphere is populated by the so-called modern man. In contrast, Bible prophecy speaks of the modern pagan man of the end times. Today, we find him as the fittest creature inhabiting and dominating the earth's new economic sphere. Do you recognize him for who he is?

FINDING ANCIENT PAGAN MAN

To discover the modern pagan man, let's first examine the character and behaviors of the ancient pagan. The Bible offers a detailed description. However, to get a balanced and accurate picture, we need to do a brief word study. There is no specific word in the Bible for pagan. In fact, we will not even be able to find the word "pagan" in some Bible translations (for example, the King James Version, International Standard Version, American Standard Version, and others). Why? Because it is a word meaning that originated only later in New Testament times.

Today, we commonly take the word "pagan" to describe a heathen person who worships other gods or idols, and who is outside the Christian or Jewish faith. In biblical times, a heathen was virtually synonymous with idea of a Gentile, though there were believers in God who were not Hebrew. Before Christ died for the sins of all and extended salvation to the Gentiles, the Gentiles and heathens were essentially the same. At the beginning of the New Testament era, most Jews still considered their newfound salvation through the Messiah as a progressive fulfillment of the existing Jewish faith. The religious world had not yet definably split into Jews and so-called Christians. It took a little while before it was broadly recognized that there were Christian Gentiles who were neither heathen nor Jewish. Therefore, at the start of the Church Age, only one Greek word was still used to describe both Gentile and heathen—"ethnos." This word appears 167 times in the New Testament. The point of this is that in our study of the "evolutionary" pagan, we will only look to those verses of the New Testament where the word "ethnos" is clearly in the context of the newer sense of the word—a heathen.

A study of the Bible reveals many common characteristics of the "pagan." We will review five of these, all of which are directly linked to the evolution of our materialistic modern pagan man.

1. Self Interest.

"If you love those who love you, what reward will you get? Are not even the tax collectors doing that? And if you greet only your brothers, what are you doing more than others? Do not even pagans do that?" (Matthew 5:44–47). In these verses, Jesus makes the point that the "pagan" people operate purely out of self-interest. Their actions are motivated by their own wants and pleasures, the personal pursuit of happiness and comforts. They only love those who love them and revile those who likewise repudiate them.

Today, some two thousand years later, this pagan characteristic of self-interest has greatly evolved, and is now held up as the very force leading the world to betterment, continued progress, and prosperity. In fact, supposedly advanced economic theories hold this impulse of "self-interest" in high esteem, representing a rapid transition that has taken place in less than a few hundred years. It is a foundational tenet of market-based capitalism, the term used for today's type of commerce (which, by the way, has little to do with capitalism in its original sense). The main result is that the entire world has become deeply commercialized. Increasingly today, commerce is the prime reason for existence and the very definition of life.

What does the Bible say about the "self-interests" of modern pagan man? It provides a clear message for societies that choose to define existence in purely pagan terms—in other words, societies that have given themselves over to the rule of economics and Mammon. The examples of Tyre and Babylon are poignant examples. Neo-Babylon was all about business. According to studies, Babylonia was essentially a commercial civilization. Virtually all of the documents that have survived from this culture are business documents. Another prime example is the history of Tyre, the extreme commercialization of which the Bible itself provides clear documentation.

The city of Jericho may be another, and even earlier, example. Probably the most ancient habitation in the world and one of the most prosperous, it was selected by God to be the first city to be conquered by the Hebrews as they entered Canaan. In fact, this city was the only one miraculously destroyed, and the only Canaan conquest that was annihilated—women, children, livestock, and all. God wanted it completely expunged. Why? Could it have been because of its idolatrous commercialism? God didn't want any of Jericho's culture to rub off on Israel. Joshua even prophesied that whoever would resurrect the city of Jericho would suffer the loss of his first and second born (Joshua 7:26). Exactly as prophesied, this occurred six hundred years later during the reign of Omri, when Hiel of Bethel did so (1 Kings 16:34).

2. Worry about Material Things

Pagans are totally consumed with material things, according to Scripture. "So do not worry, saying 'What shall we drink?' or 'What shall we wear?' For the pagans run after all these things, and your heavenly Father knows that you need them" (Matthew 6:31–32; see also Luke 12:29–30). By this definition, then, it would be pagan to only preoccupy oneself in the pursuit of possessions and lifestyle. Scripture refers here to only two items—food and clothing. In the society of that day, both things defined lifestyle as well as the necessities of life. This verse is therefore not only referring to mere subsistence. Clothing and food both have a necessary function. To attribute any other value to them is idolatrous and pagan.

Of course, in the modern age, lifestyle is defined by many more things than just food and clothes. To be sure, there are premium brands in clothing— top designer names, the latest accoutrements. The same is also still true for some foods. The finest wines are sought; the food brands that are the most effectively advertised are the ones people strive to buy. Mostly today, lifestyles are defined by other baubles such as expensive Swiss watches, luxury cars, the latest gadgets, palatial homes, and much else. To have all these things is the epitome of the successful life, the trappings of elite existence. That's the implicit goal and value of a society of pagans. "Running after these things" is part of a highly sophisticated culture of branding, consumer surveys, advertising, and psychological research. In this sense, there has been much change over the centuries and millennia. Here again, we see evolution underway to the modern pagan man. Viewing the massively endemic commercialization of America and other nations, it is hard to imagine that much more evolution could yet lie ahead.

3. Concern about Tomorrow

Societies that don't put their faith in God, by definition, must worry about the uncertainties of tomorrow. The Bible says it should be otherwise: "But seek first his kingdom and his righteousness, and all these things will be given to you as well. Therefore do not worry about tomorrow, for tomorrow will worry about itself. Each day has enough trouble of its own" (Matthew 6:33–34). This verse is connected to the two verses before it (Matthew 6:31–32) that speak of pagan practices. In that context, we understand that worrying about tomorrow is a "pagan" preoccupation of the "ethnos." These worries about the uncertainties of tomorrow have driven a monumental amount of economic and financial evolution over past decades and centuries, and have clearly added to the intensity of the commercialization of human life.

The introduction of insurance is just one such example. No doubt, the vast array of insurance products available provides useful services. Also, in recent decades there has been a boom in sophisticated financial instruments that, in turn, have underpinned an unprecedented rise in global financial wealth. Many of these instruments are based on mathematical concepts that seek to overcome the uncertainties of tomorrow. Few people are either expert or aware of these trends in the wild jungles of advanced economic and financial innovation. Meanwhile, back on Main Street, life is clearly different as a result of these many services that cater to the "uncertainties of tomorrow." Today, no one would think of not having life, home, or auto insurance. Most would agree that it is unwise not to have an IRA or a pension to protect against the uncertainties of retirement. Just taking the few services mentioned leads to at least five different purchases on a monthly installment plan. To the extent that a chronic worry about the future has led to increasing commercialization and idolatry is clearly pagan. This intensification of "worries over tomorrow" is therefore an identifier of modern pagan man.

4. Self-Indulgence and Debauchery

The Bible clearly refers to people who live lives of dissipation and indulgence as being pagan in character. Paul identified the Hebrews as having acted like pagans when they had parties and revelry while Moses was up on the mountain (see Exodus 32). "Do not be idolaters, as some of them were; as it is written: 'The people sat down to eat and drink and got up to indulge in pagan revelry'" (1 Corinthians 10:7). The apostle Peter takes the same view. "For you have spent enough time in the past doing what pagans choose to do—living in debauchery, lust, drunkenness, orgies, carousing and detestable idolatry. They think it strange that you do not plunge with them into the same flood of dissipation, and they heap abuse on you" (1 Peter 4:3–4).

Revelry, debauchery, bacchanalian feasts, and wild sensuality were seen as being part of the worship exercises of the pagans. The Amplified Bible also mentions frivolousness and hilarity. These aspects of paganism are highly promoted today. Why? It's good for business… good for economic growth. Morality is not the relevant question. Revelry and frivolousness add to economic growth, whatever forms it may take. Businesses that are on the leading edge in this regard often are the most successful. Television programs and movies that cater to this trend are an example. Many more could be listed. It's part of a sophisticated economic culture. Increasingly, these pagan "lifestyle" activities now may include mindless entertainment, drugs, pornography, and much, much more. The modern pagan man guiltlessly consumes and indulges.

5. Ultra Competitiveness

The Bible pictures pagans as being competitive. They are seen vying for the fulfillment of their personal wants. As already reviewed, they "run after" the things that they want (Matthew 6:31). Jesus indirectly points to another competitive behavior of the pagans: "…whoever wants to become great among you must be your servant, and whoever wants to be first must be your slave—just as the Son of Man did not come to be served, but to serve, and to give his life as a ransom for many" (Matthew 20:26–28). Apparently, He said this while in Jericho—the city rebuilt from the ruins of ancient Jericho. In contrast, "The kings of the Gentiles lord it over them; and those who exercise authority over them call themselves Benefactors" (Luke 22:25). By inference, pagan society is marked by "one-upmanship," the desire to be the "top-dog" as society would define, and to rule over others. Achieving these goals requires competitive behavior.

Of course, we recognize that commercial competition is one of

the most venerated principles on earth today to ensure efficient economic growth and prosperity. Nothing is wrong in trying to strive for
improvement if the motivations are healthy and balanced. However,
the type of competitive behavior identified here is the jungle rule,
"survival of the fittest." It is a type of competition devoid of charity
or love for others. This form of competitiveness is deeply embedded
in pagan society—our society. Even something as simple as buying a
security on a stock exchange for the sake of gain embodies the notion
that one person's success can only come at the price of another person's
predicted misfortune. Be that as it may, that's the accepted way of
modern pagan man.

Having reviewed just five of the pagan characteristics of ancient
mankind, we indeed see proof of evolution. Yes, all the basic characteristics of mankind remain the same. Yet, we do see that there has
evolved a modern, sophisticated pagan. Anyone who truly under-
stands the workings of the great global commercialization that now
reigns must face the extent of the paganization of today's world. Brief
as our description has been, the world of modern pagan man sets a
stark contrast to the primitive heathen of ancient times. Our modern
society—yes, even nations with a strong Christian witness—is deeply
pagan. Admittedly, many are blinded to this reality. It is both the
result and cause of the pervasive and corrupt commercialism and crass
materialism that has swept the world. The Bible's prophecies foresaw
that eventuality.

The most grievous aspect of these end-time developments is the
impact upon the morality of Christians and the changing teaching of
churches that hold themselves out to be Christian. We therefore now
want to turn our attention to these dangerous dynamics. To do so, it
is first imperative that the Christian be made aware of just the how the
science of the supposed evolutionary human has been turned to prey
upon the end-time pagan and unaware Christians.

PREYING ON THE MODERN PAGAN

Every person who has given his or her life over to the lordship of Jesus Christ will be familiar with the dilemma Paul describes in Romans 7. Why is it that the very thing that we do not want to do, we often end up doing? Most of us can identify with the well-worn saying, "The spirit is willing, but the flesh is weak."

Paul wrote, "As it is, it is no longer I myself who do it, but it is sin living in me. I know that nothing good lives in me, that is, in my sinful nature. For I have the desire to do what is good, but I cannot carry it out. For what I do is not the good I want to do; no, the evil I do not want to do—this I keep on doing. Now if I do what I do not want to do, it is no longer I who do it, but it is sin living in me that does it" (Romans 7:17–20).

We see that mankind is hardwired to sin. This trait—the sinful nature mentioned more than twenty times in the New Testament—is coded right into our genetic makeup. That pretty much explains why the world today remains corrupted by the flesh and is thoroughly pagan. The apostle Peter identified this condition as "corruption in the world caused by evil desires" (2 Peter 1:4).

To no surprise, this battle with the flesh has become all the more acute and difficult in these latter days. Whereas once society may have considered it a virtue to overcome the innate human vices, today it has become respected, high science to exploit these same sinful weaknesses. Just as precision missiles today can thread their way through to a small target, the human's fleshly senses are being assaulted as never before.

How so? In recent years, scientists and psychologists have developed a major new field of study generally referred to under the names of neuroscience and cognitive psychology. While having a number of focused specialties, the underlying premise of this research is the same. It tries to discover the basic "coding" of the natural or instinctive man. In other words, these analysts seek to understand the basal nature that operates outside the area of thought and consciousness. Why? To be better able to develop techniques that directly appeal to people's base instincts. Even more sinister—though few will publicly admit to this—is the goal to better manipulate people's decisions by bypassing their minds.

How is this being done? To explain, let's review a few developments in this field.

The Sciences of Marketing

What is the biggest problem facing marketers today? Apparently, it is the rational brain. Says Clotaire Rapaille, author of *The Culture Code*: "In a three-way battle between the cortical, our higher, thinking brain; the limbic, the home of emotion; and the reptilian areas, the reptilian always wins."[21] This reptilian part of the brain, as he identifies it, is the home of the instinct and is only accessible through the subconscious. Therein is the challenge for marketers, change agents, and scientists alike: how to appease the reptilian part of the brain through the subconscious mind. To do so, however, it is necessary to circumvent the thinking brain that might otherwise refuse to comply with the marketer's wishes.

Researchers in this field claim that the instinctive and physical systems of the human organism are coded to respond in preset ways. The flesh, left to its animalistic, nonthinking mode, will always opt for gratification, reproduction, and survival no matter the cost—moral or otherwise. Therefore, any proposal to these basal instincts is sure to be more successful.

Money matters are another key area that attracts much behavioral analysis. As might be guessed, the vast preponderance of this financial research is not inspired to help make the average investor more successful, but rather for the financial industry to exploit human behavioral weaknesses. It too has made a high science out of studying the "biases of the flesh." According to one author familiar with these techniques, "[Wall Street firms] actually prefer a market filled with irrational investors. That way they can manipulate you easily without you ever really knowing it.... and [they have] refined 'mind control' to a high art."[22]

This field of study has a scientific-sounding name: "neurofinance." There are great hopes for this research. "The brain scientists are the wave of the future in the financial world," says one noted expert, Daniel Kahneman, a 2002 Nobel laureate for his pioneering work in neurofinance.[23] Why should finance be such a promising area of study? Apparently, researchers have discovered that the human brain lusts after money just like it may crave sex. Professor Brian Knutson of Stanford University made this "startling" finding by sending volunteer students through an MRI machine. [24] (One wonders what this scientist would discover if he were to put a Bible through an MRI machine.)

Another way marketers or change agents can circumvent mature, rational human responses is by targeting children. Children have a large influence over their parents, controlling a large portion of buying decisions. According to the estimates of James McNeal, an expert on the techniques of marketing to children, children under the age of fourteen influence as much as 47 percent of household spending in the U.S.[25] There is a logical reason this is happening. Many companies have discovered it is much more lucrative to market to the children of a household than to a parent.

Why "suffer the little children" (Matthew 19:14, KJV)? Marketing experts know that children are much more impressionable than adults. Many of these children will not have reached the age at which they know right from wrong (Isaiah 7:15–16). Children are by nature uncontrolled hedonists, and impulsive. The assault upon the instincts of vulnerable children ingrains fleshly gratification at a very early age, further preparing the way for a world of hedonists whose stomachs and cares of this world will compete for any interest in the gospel truth. Not heeded at all are the Bible's warnings that apply especially in the case of corrupting children: "But if anyone causes one of these little ones who believe in me to sin, it would be better for him to have a large millstone hung around his neck and to be drowned in the depths of the sea" (Matthew 18:6).

A Buyer's World of New Religious Values

Just what is the significance of this scientific focus upon instinctive, unthinking behaviors? It certainly aligns with conditions of the last days described in the Bible. While most of the research in cognitive sciences may have direct application to the world of consumer marketing, its influence actually goes far wider and deeper. It is shaping a world where basic human instincts and indulgences are idolized. Crucially, it paves the way for a new, worldwide religion—the type that allows religion and commercial Babylon the Great to merge, to fuse into that fuzzy amalgam outlined in Revelation 17–18.

The apostle Paul's account of a time of rampant individualism, indulgence, and lack of control fits with the general direction observed today. People will be "lovers of themselves," "without self control," and "lovers of pleasure" (2 Timothy 3:1–4).

This connection may not seem apparent to people who live in the prosperous Western world. However, a perspective of Lord Saatchi (executive director of M & C Saatchi, a major advertising firm) will provide a bridge to this understanding. He bemoans the modern development of the "digital native." He identifies these as members of the younger generation today who process information much differently due to their upbringing connected to earphones and a diet of video. Their attention spans are short and their recall ability has declined significantly, he argues. The answer? His counsel to companies seeking to be more effective marketers to this generation is to find one word—just one word—that associates a value with this modern, "fleshly" person. Using heavy religious allegory, Mr. Saatchi says, "In the beginning was 'the word'…discover it and you have the route to salvation and eternal life," meaning commercial success.[26]

Crucial to see is that Mr. Saatchi is connecting "values"—not value, as in a good price, but as in a philosophy or meaning—with a commercial transaction. Since values are the domain of religion, then each brand or product associated with a "value" then becomes a mini religion. For example, Nike, the maker of sporting goods, has as its slogan, "Just do it." This is a statement of philosophy, not a product attribute. It promotes an identity with a certain lifestyle.

It is critical to see that spiritual and psychological destruction go hand in hand with an overladen merchandise culture. Says another marketing expert, "The difficulty now is that every consumer need we have has already been satisfied by at least twenty products. That is why in the most successful businesses, innovations must be driven by marketing rather than product design.[27]

What is being said here? Consumer brands are now a figment of strong "psychological propositions"…in other words, "values." And, if values rather than function are the appeal to sell merchandise, then we are already fast on the way to the apocalyptic, Babylonish culture shown in Revelation 17–18. In fact, it could be argued that most societies already fit this description.

Unleashing the Beast in the Church

The indulgent, instinctive, and fleshly consumer is the essential under-pinning of the end-time ruling colossus comprised of commercialism and religion. To this end, consumers are unreasoning beasts rather than "people led by the spirit" (Romans 8:14 and Galatians 5:18). However, to this point we have only discussed the ways of the world and its increasing sophistication at manipulating and exploiting the sinful nature. As we have shown, these techniques are well honed and now are merging into religion.

Unfortunately, this is not the full height of the corruption. The same techniques are being employed in the world of religion. Here we observe that instincts and fleshly desires are also being expressly catered to...yes, even in evangelical Christian circles.

Religion today, like most products, is sold. Surveys are conducted as to what is wanted. Religious "products and goods" are then designed in terms of consumer benefits and the appeasement of "fleshly "val-ues." Of course, this is not a new challenge for the church. Back in New Testament times, such approaches were already evident, though not yet sanctioned by advanced science.

The difference today is that such techniques are the product of precise method and science. Significantly, too, this is prophecy being fulfilled. Jude records the apostles as saying, "'In the last times there will be scoffers who will follow their own ungodly desires.' These are the men who divide you, who follow mere natural instincts and do not have the Spirit" (Jude 18–19).

It is the corrupt human instinct of these religious leaders in the first place that misleads many. "They are like brute beasts, creatures of instinct..." (2 Peter 2:12). "...things they do understand by instinct, like unreasoning animals—these are the very things that destroy them" (Jude 10).

THOUGHTS TO PONDER

The descriptions of the "ethnos"—these meaning "pagans"—in the last days already align with what we see unfolding in the world today. Surely, an anthropologist examining the records of the time described in Revelation 17–18 would scientifically validate that era as the time of the proud, modern pagan man. It is clearly a civilization marked by extreme consumption, endless wants, materialistic idolatry, and a fixation on wealth. The evolution of this "pagan" is truly advanced.

This description matches the human species of our time.

How many of us might find similarities with the modern pagan way of life? It is an important and timely question. Only the surviving, unbelieving "ethnos" and the surviving Jews are the ones who in the end—after the Great Tribulation—finally do come and worship before God. "For all 'ethnos' shall come and worship before thee; for thy judgments are made manifest" (Revelation 15:4, KJV). After all, "Every knee shall bow," (Isaiah 45:23).

Where should be found the true and reliable "neurological" leading during times such as now? Clearly, we are not to be led by instinct and the fleshly nature. And, forbid that anyone might prey upon such basal pagan instincts in order to promote and popularize false gospels. Paul pleaded, "Make room for us in your hearts. We have wronged no one, we have corrupted no one, we have exploited no one" (2 Corinthians 7:2). Yet, people ruled by their instincts readily ran after the false teachers who appealed to their fleshly senses.

But how to escape the dilemma Paul describes, especially in a time of a surfeit of temptation to the fleshly nature as we live in today? Paul says we should live by the Spirit (Romans 8:12–14), and to "clothe [ourselves] with the Lord Jesus Christ, and…not think about how to gratify the desires of the sinful nature" (Romans 13:14).

While the world shouts its cacophony of temptations and hurls its "flaming arrows" (Ephesians 6:16), more than ever we truly need to be shut in with Christ. He is the only one who can satisfy:

"The LORD is faithful to all his promises and loving toward all he has made. The LORD upholds all those who fall and lifts up all who are bowed down. The eyes of all look to you, and you give them their food at the proper time. You open your hand and satisfy the desires of every living thing" (Psalm 145:13–16).

One day, all the "ethnos" will sing a new song: "You are worthy to take the scroll and to open its seals, because you were slain, and with your blood you purchased men for God from every tribe and language and people and nation. You have made them to be a kingdom and priests to serve our God, and they will reign on the earth" (Revelation 5:9–10).

Figure #7

Representative World Trading Trends

Goods and Services Trade (Exports Plus Imports/ World GDP) and World Stock Market Turnover/GDP

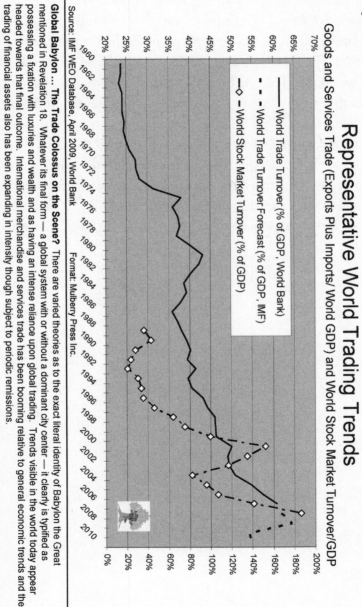

—— World Trade Turnover (% of GDP, World Bank)
- - - World Trade Turnover Forecast (% of GDP , IMF)
– ◇ – World Stock Market Turnover (% of GDP)

Source: IMF WEO Database, April 2009, World Bank

Format: Mulberry Press Inc.

Global Babylon ... The Trade Colossus on the Scene? There are varied theories as to the exact literal identity of Babylon the Great mentioned in Revelation 18. Whatever its final form — a global system with or without a dominant city center — it clearly is typified as possessing a fixation with luxuries and wealth and as having an intense reliance upon global trading. Trends visible in the world today appear headed towards that final outcome. International merchandise and services trade has been booming relative to general economic trends and the trading of financial assets also has been expanding in intensity though subject to periodic remissions.

6

THE BABYLON OCCLUSION:
HERE AND NOW

As the previous chapters have revealed, we can easily be blinded to idolatries. Our familiarity and contentedness with many of society's values can be the cause. This condition leads to other potential blind spots. In this chapter, I want to attempt to remove an optical occlusion in relation to the topic of Babylon—namely, "Babylon the Great" mentioned in Revelation 17 and 18. In doing so, we step on thin ice.

The topic of Babylon in prophetic Scripture is one of the most actively debated in Christian circles. The most contested portion, of course, has to do with questions of future fulfillment. Here we see a myriad of interpretations ranging from the increasingly popular position that modern-day America is end-time Babylon to strict literal interpretations that emphasize a physical rebuilding of Babylon, situated in present-day Iraq, as the final totality of fulfillment. Respected prophecy students hold different views. There are also dozens of interpretations in between that can be quite bizarre.

The word "Babylon" appears 294 times in the Bible (KJV). Numerous prophetic statements are made about this entity in its various forms, many of them already fulfilled. A number of these prophecies are mirrored in the treatments of Tyre in Scripture, another city Bible prophecy speaks of (at least twenty-three times). The topic of Babylon is obviously very important. Therefore, it is unfortunate that so much confusion exists in relation to its future fulfillments. Just what is the Babylon of future fulfillment?

BABYLON SEEN IN AMERICA

As mentioned, a view growing in popularity is that America is final, end-time Babylon. Certainly, this is not the case. It is not difficult to disprove this view. America has surely been a major contributor to the development of the characteristics of a modern-day Babylonian system. But that does not make the U.S. or New York City literal, end-time Babylon. At the same time, it may be understandable why this interpretation is gaining prominence.

Therefore, before focusing on the Babylon Occlusion itself, let's first deal with the question we have posed concerning America. We next list a few key reasons America is not Babylon the Great.

1. America is a young country. Statements about Babylon the Great in the description found in Revelation 18 obviously rule out America as Babylon the Great. Consider these two: "Rejoice saints, and apostles, and prophets. God has judged her for the way she treated you" (verse 20) and "In her was found the blood of prophets and of the saints, and of all who have been killed on the earth" (verse 24). In no way is America responsible for "all who have been killed on earth," nor is she alone or otherwise responsible for how apostles and prophets have been treated. America hasn't been around that long, nor has it existed throughout the ages. What has existed all that time is the "spirit" behind Babylon, the same spirit that propels the present-day world system of finance and commerce as it did in the day of Tyre, ancient Babylon, and other worldly regimes.

2. Which country requires rebuilding? A number of respected prophecy scholars believe the ancient city of Babylon will be rebuilt. We will not examine this position here. However, if this interpretation is correct, it certainly precludes America being Babylon the Great. After all, does America need to be rebuilt? This is outside the bounds of reason. If so, America also must be the same Babylon that was destroyed some two and one-half millennia ago.

3. Better candidates exist. If America is thought to be Babylon the Great of Revelation 18, then why wasn't the great British Empire a better candidate for this position in the days of her prime? Britain had a much bigger realm—"upon which the sun never set," it was said—than does the U.S. today. Historians generally agree that Britain has left a much bigger stamp upon the world than America has to date. Moreover, Britain even had a bigger influence upon world trade and finance in relative terms at its height of power. The great Gilded Age of the late nineteenth century witnessed a globalization that some economists argue was even greater than today's era. If so, why would the very capstone of last-day economic idolatry that is called Babylon the Great be a smaller manifestation of this literal prophecy than has ever occurred before in human history?

4. The U.S. is not a prophetic marker. A more recent argument pinning the Babylon tail upon the U.S. is this one: As America is occupying Iraq, it is reasoned that since all former world kingdoms mentioned by the prophet Daniel ruled the area of Babylon, the U.S. reveals itself to be the final, seventh kingdom mentioned by John the Revelator. This argument falls flat on a number of points. The most obvious reason this argument is incorrect is that, in character, most all Bible prophecy is centric to the Jews, Israel, and Jerusalem. Babylon and its ancient kingdom never were a part of the land of Israel. According to prophecy, Babylon will remain a region outside the future and expanded millennial area of Israel. As such, Iraq or Babylon is not a marker of the prophetic timeline outlined either in the book of Daniel or Revelation. If this theory were correct, again: Why isn't Britain—or even the Ottoman Empire—considered one of the world kings mentioned by Daniel? Iraq was under British rule after its invasion in 1917 and up to 1941, this following the breakdown of the Ottoman Empire. After World War I, Iraq was under British mandate and control for more than thirty years. Using this reasoning, both the Ottoman and British empires should have been part of Daniel's prophetic timeline, which they are certainly not.

5. America currently accounts for a large portion of world trade, yet it remains a fraction of the total. The U.S. is not even the world's largest exporter; Germany holds this position. The Babylon the Great that the Bible depicts is an entity that accounts for the majority, if not all, of the trade flows that take place under the rule of the world's kings, captains, and trade. Similarly, the final events of end-time Babylon involving its destruction impacts the entire world, and not just one country in any one hemisphere. Yes, America may have a significant economic influence upon the world, but it is not the hub of the world's trading systems as Babylon the Great will be. There is much data to prove this assertion. Consider that of the ten busiest container ports in the world today, none is found in America. Seven are located in Asia, two in Europe, and one in the Middle East.

Though our detour has been brief, we can safely conclude that America is not Babylon the Great. Yet, that conclusion leaves little room for comfort. It can be still true that America and other Western nations are deeply infiltrated and compromised by the ancient spirit of Babylon. Like no other nation before it, America is the best-fitting foreshadowing of future Babylon to date. Just as the Roman Catholic Church of today may be the closest type of Mystery Babylon the Great—the apostate, religious entity of Revelation 17—that the world has produced to this point, the final, literal fulfillment still likely lies ahead in the Great Tribulation. That may leave time for the further evolution of these entities, though perhaps not much.

We will return to the question of America's prophetic role in Chapter 11.

SEVERAL BABYLONS

One thing is certain: If the word "Babylon" in the Bible is construed as only referring to the original progenitor of this word in the Bible—in other words, the original city of ancient Babylon—the Bible will be proven inconsistent and contradictory. It will not make sense, and must stand accused of holding error and confusion rather than the error and confusion being in the mind of the interpreter.

Any scholar who has studied the question of Babylon's future identity must admit that this is the case. Try as one might, ascribing a single entity or concept to the name of Babylon in the Bible is like forcing a square peg into a round hole. Though this writer certainly does not profess to have the full and correct answer to this question, we can all at least agree to this general conclusion. Indeed, none of the attempts at deciphering all references to Babylon in the Bible to one single entity has succeeded without bending meanings, setting aside certain applications, or torturing the chronology of various prophecies.

It is reasonable to leave open the notion that end-time Babylon takes forms and manifestations at more than one level in prophecy. This view does not deny in any way that all Bible prophecy ultimately culminates in literal fulfillment.

The same challenge on the topic of Babylon may arise as the one that faced the Jews on the question of identifying their Messiah. The mistake made was to assume that only one appearance of the Messiah was to be expected. Though Scriptures said Christ would appear as "mighty...upon on the throne of David" (Isaiah 9:6–7) and as the one "they have pierced" (Zechariah 12:10), the Jews looked for these signs in one event. Partly for this reason, the Jews as a nation rejected Jesus Christ as the Messiah. He did not first appear as the long-awaited king who would free them from the oppressive rule of Rome, as they had imagined.

Today, a similar confusion exists in relation to the expected return of Christ. He will appear again at a time that people think not—a time of "eating and drinking, [and] marrying" (Matthew 24:38), as was the case just prior to the Great Flood during Noah's time. Yet, He also returns at a time marked by great tribulation (Mark 13:24–26). It is the same type of problem. These prophecies cannot be reconciled in one single event. Therefore, many Bible readers conclude that there must be at least two. As our earlier reasons illuminated why America is not Babylon, the notion of a spirit entity behind Babylon or a global, systemic version of a Babylonian trading system cannot be summarily discounted.

As such, it must be admitted that this idea of multiple occurrences, or forms of manifestations, could apply to end-time Babylon. All of its prophetic characteristics, though clearly meant literally, may not take the form of a single-time manifestation or only a localized, physical entity. Certainly, the Babylon (single or plural) described in Revelation 17–18 is shown as an amorphous synthesis of many things that are difficult to separate clearly. We must acknowledge that the Holy

Spirit did not inspire accidental wording in this Scripture. There is a reason these prophecies about the characteristics of future Babylon are shown to be blurry—different, yet connected. In studying these questions, it is helpful to remain open to these possibilities as we return to our examination of the Babylon Occlusion. Our intent here is not to conclusively answer this broader question of Babylon's end-time identity, other than to show that it is not America. Rather, keeping to our objective, we want to focus on one set of its characteristics—its global reach and its commercialism.

THE WESTERN OCCLUSION

Old-time Bible readers could see that one day, when the systemic form of Babylon would stretch its tentacles across the whole earth, it would involve the intertwining of commerce and religion. Embedded in it would be enormous power.

Consider these comments excerpted from Benjamin Wills Newton's writings, penned in 1843.[28]

> When we consider this, we cannot but confess that such a spectacle has never yet been presented in the history of human things. It is the marvelous exhibition of a power yet to be. It is all the more marvelous, because it will be the power not of an individual, but of a system, which, though long prepared in secret [see Zechariah 5:5], will suddenly burst in development upon the eyes of men. "When I saw the woman," says the apostle, "I wondered with a great wonder." (Revelation 17:6)

> What features can be more clearly marked as indicative of the Babylonish period than commercial greatness, the supremacy of

wealth, and the mixing of iron and miry clay in the government of the kingdom?

The supremacy of commercial wealth is an unusual feature in the history of men. I do not mean that there have never been cities like Tyre, Corinth, Carthage, or Venice that have flourished commercially, but their influence has been little felt beyond their immediate spheres. Nor have they by their institutions ever imparted a character to the general system of the nations. Commerce was not supreme either in the early native monarchy of Nimrod or in the Chaldean, Persian, Grecian, or Roman empires. None of these empires was distinctively commercial.

All would have emblazoned the sword rather than the ephah on their banners.

In times past, democrats were wont to assist democrats, and despots to aid despots. But now men have found a new and more efficacious center of union in their commercial interests, and they feel themselves mutually dependent upon each other for the preservation as well as the increase of their riches. When the ruin of one involves the danger of all, men in such circumstances become wonderfully careful of each other's interests. This is the kind of dependence into which nations are being brought, one on the other.

That peace may be promoted in this way is beyond doubt. The sword is not mentioned in all the detail of the greatness of Babylon. Instead, "...merchandise of gold, and silver, and precious stones, and pearls, and fine linen, and purple, and silk, and scarlet, and all thyme wood, and vessels of ivory, and vessels of most precious wood, and of brass, and iron, and marble, and cinnamon, and odors, and ointments, and frankincense, and wine, and oil, and fine flour, and wheat, and beasts, and sheep, and horses, and chariots, and bodies and souls of men" (Revelation 18:12–13) are its stabilizers.

Newton, writing early in the 1800s, realized that the Babylon of Revelation 17–18 was to include a global, commercial "system," though it indeed may eventually find its center in a specific city. He clearly saw the picture of the ephah shown in Zechariah 5:5–11 as being related to end-time, commercial Babylon. Neither the system nor the future city existed in his day. He recognized this, saying that "this system is not as yet developed, so that we must not expect at present to be able fully and accurately to trace its details."[29]

Yet, reading Scripture, he could see that the day would arrive when the enjoining of Mammon would be almost universally accepted as the sure "road to peace" and the basis for world union and power. Rather than Christ guiding "our feet in a straight line into the way of peace" (Luke 1:79), the common interests of money and prosperity are seen as the glue and catalyst for world peace and unity. However, the exact opposite would result—tyranny and an insurrection against God.

Christ at His first coming was not at all about peace. Rather, He said, "Do not suppose that I have come to bring peace to the earth. I did not come to bring peace, but a sword" (Matthew 10:34). Truth and the kingdom of God, in the hearts of believers during the dispensation, would bring turmoil into the world. Only Christ Himself, in the role of Prince of Peace (Isaiah 9:6), brings peace in the Millennium.

CHRISTIANS IN THE BELLY OF BABYLON

Sadly, much of today's church has swallowed the lie that enduring peace among men can only found in the bowels of Mammon—particularly those branches of Christendom that endorse Replacement Theology (the church being substituted for Israel) and aspects of Dominion Theology, which is dominating political circles today, but not exclusively. Even much of North America's premillennial, evangelical community suffers from this Babylonian Occlusion. We think our riches and power—also evangelical, political power—are useful tools for God to disseminate faith in the world. Some Christians may shout judgment on an unsaved world and trumpet their sanctified destiny of blessings and prosperity, yet they do so ensconced and comfortable within the bowels of the most materialistic, pagan societies in the world.

What exactly is this occlusion? It is an optical one, for the most part. Living inside the systemic Babylon now suffusing the world and living in its present hot spots (certainly including North America), we cannot see. Yet, the sliver has become so large it has become a log: "Why do you look at the speck of sawdust in your brother's eye and pay no attention to the plank in your own eye?" (Matthew 7:3).

We cannot see clearly for several reasons. The most crucial is that our point of reference has become the world, not the Bible. The world enjoins us, shouting that the "future is friendly," [30] that peace is attainable through the eradication of poverty (meaning equality and wealth for all), and that the objective of a prosperous heaven on earth is found in religious and commercial Babylon.

A second reason is that the same smugness and confidence found in ancient Babylon is evident today. "Sit in silence, go into darkness, Daughter of the Babylonians…You said, 'I will continue forever—the eternal queen! But you did not consider these things or reflect on what might happen. Now then, listen, you wanton creature, lounging in your security and saying to yourself, I am, and there is none besides me. I will never be a widow or suffer the loss of children. Both of these will overtake you in a moment, on a single day'" (Isaiah 47:5, 7–9). While this prophecy did have a near-term fulfillment, it also speaks of a future event.

Isaiah's words line up with Revelation 18:7, which describes the "great city" of Babylon: "Give her as much torture and grief as the glory and luxury she gave herself. In her heart she boasts, 'I sit as queen; I am not a widow, and I will never mourn.'" Given these characteristics of pride and complacency, we are blinded to the reality of true riches and the world's extreme vulnerability to the judgment and wrath of God.

A third reason we may not be able to see the greater end-time Babylon spirit today is that we may have limiting notions. As mentioned, some prophecy commentators hold the view that Babylon the Great of Revelation 18 is only a city—in other words, a physical place. Indeed, there may be a city considered to be its center. But end-time Babylon the Great is never called a "city" in the Bible. To be technically correct, the "economic" Babylon of Revelation 18 is always called the "great city"—in fact, six times in the Book of Revelation. It is never called a "city," only a "great city." This is significant. Why isn't it referred to as a "city"?

In the Greek, the word combination "great city" is found only ten times in the New Testament—six times for economic Babylon, three times for religious Babylon, and once for the New Jerusalem. Each of its uses leaves open the interpretation that the two-word term "great city" may mean something bigger than just a common city, perhaps a system, organization, or a unique structure. In ancient times, a city was the closest thing there was to an organized economic entity, what we would recognize today as a systemic concept. In fact, ancient Greek had no word for "system" or "organization" as we understand the terms today. We are hard pressed to find words or word combinations anywhere in the Bible that explicitly refer to the idea of a system. The closest word combination that is apparent is "kingdom of nations" (Isaiah 13:1). We do find word combinations in the Old Testament that refer to globalism, but not a specific word that means "system."

As such, Babylon the Great is not necessarily only a physical city, though, as mentioned, it may very well have a city considered to be its center. Rather, it seems more plausible that it is also a system, in this case the economic trade and financial system dominated by the present or future high-income countries of the world, if not the entire world. Moreover, a spiritual entity lurks behind this organized form of end-time Mammon.

The great global commercial system or "city" exists today. A similar concept is still embedded in the English language—the global village. This global economic village has erupted upon the world in very short order.

THE END OF BABYLON

We live during a time of great deception and corruption. Many can't see it. A great trap is being laid for the people of the world.

Many Christians are in that number, particularly those who live in the prosperous West. We have also been duped into believing that, in the end, it is Mammon, not Christ, that will bring peace to the world. Globalization finds a common ground upon the desires for material gain and complacency.

There is one thing all prophecy scholars must agree upon. Babylon—whatever its type or identity—clearly comes to an end. In one day, it falls and is judged—though this may unfold as three separate events of "one hour" duration. The final form of Babylon does not carry through into the Millennium. The great commercial colossus and its embedded religious idolatries are ended. But what does that really mean?

The answer will shock most readers, Virtually all of us are inclined to view Bible prophecy through the lens of what is seen—the conditions of today, the same mistake the Jews made two thousand years ago. We are living in this brief space of time marking the great ascendancy of man's global systems. It is the unprecedented time of the great industrial age of rising wealth and prosperity, though largely an illusion for the majority of the world's citizens; the age of oil; and the age of global capital. It is a time of great arrogance, smugness, and confidence. Mankind thinks its progress will endure forever and that these great global phenomena of the last two hundred years are permanent.

The age of oil, the age of global capital, and globalism will pass and be replaced. Technology will have its pedestal moved as well. It all seems so unthinkable to us at this late, great point of history. And, therein we find a major occlusion. It is a form of blindness and confidence apart from God. That is precisely why it is so easy for us as Christians to say, "I am rich; I have acquired wealth and do not need a thing" (Revelation 3:17), as does the church of Laodicea. The same blindness applied to Sodom and Gomorrah just prior to their judgment—"…pride, fullness of bread, and abundance of idleness" (Ezekiel 16:49–50).

In fact, Bible prophecy about the Millennium does confirm significant changes for the world and mankind.

THOUGHTS TO PONDER

The great Babylon Occlusion: Can you see it?

We are living during the day that the revelator saw…at least with respect to the systemic Babylonian conditions. And, this system has culminated in deep idolatry and is not unassociated with religion, even modern-day Christianity. Said John Wesley, more than two centuries ago, "I fear, wherever riches have increased, the essence of religion has decreased in the same proportion. Therefore, I do not see how it is possible…for any revival of true religion to continue long. For religion, almost necessarily, produces both industry and frugality, and these cannot but produce riches. But as riches increase, so will pride, anger, and love of the world in all its branches." [31]

We need to regain our sight of this fact. For, "How can you say to your brother, 'Let me take the speck out of your eye,' when all the time there is a plank in your own eye? You hypocrite, first take the plank out of your own eye, and then you will see clearly to remove the speck from your brother's eye" (Matthew 7:4–5).

Now is the time to put away the rose-colored glasses through which we peer at our condition today. Christ specifically calls out to us, even as He stands at the door of His imminent return: "Those whom I love I rebuke and discipline. So be earnest, and repent. Here I am! I stand at the door and knock. If anyone hears my voice and opens the door, I will come in and eat with him, and he with me" (Revelation 3:19–20).

Is there a price? We can take the example from Moses: "He chose to be mistreated along with the people of God rather than to enjoy the pleasures of sin for a short time. He regarded disgrace for the sake of Christ as of greater value than the treasures of Egypt, because he was looking ahead to his reward. By faith he left Egypt, not fearing the king's anger; he persevered because he saw him who is invisible" (Hebrews 11:25–27).

Without a doubt, the massive commercial idolatry the world would witness in the last days is evil. Zechariah tells us that this system "…is the iniquity of the people throughout the land" (Zechariah 5:6). In short, "This is wickedness" (verse 8). "This is the iniquity…" (Ezekiel 16:49). In fact, Zechariah's writings independently confirm that these conditions already exist today. Therefore, we next take a closer look at Zechariah Chapter 5. The objective of the next chapters is to open our eyes to the wickedness and pervasiveness of the commercialism of our society and world that we can no longer see.

Figure #8

Increasing Global Economic and Financial Integration

Ratio of Foreign Assets/Liabilities to GDP, 1970 to 2004, Industrial and Emerging Countries

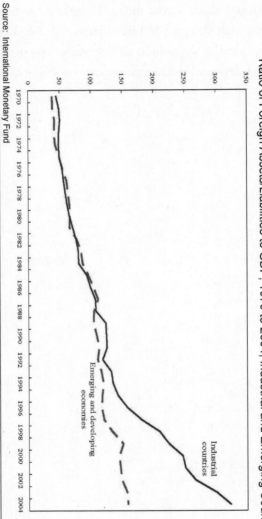

Source: International Monetary Fund

An Increasingly Interconnected Global World. One of the most astoundingly rapid trends of the recent half century has been the process of globalization. Nations have become increasingly inter-connected through merchandise trade, financial flows and consumer tastes. Globalization is process prophesied in the Bible, leading to a time when the entirety of the world can be controlled through commerce. For all practical purposes, such a world is already on the scene. The chart above depicts just one of many hundreds and thousands of indicators of the advance of globalization. It shows the increasing reliance upon foreign assets and indebtedness between countries.

7

RAMPANT AND WICKED:
END-TIME COMMERCIALISM

Remarkable for such a short chapter (only eleven verses), Zechariah 5 contains two separate but important visions of the end times. This text contains the sixth and seventh visions given to the prophet Zechariah. We first read of a giant scroll that is levitating in the air (verses 1 to 4). Right after this, the angel speaking to Zechariah shows him another vision. We then see a strange picture of an ephah (measuring basket) being carried by two women with the wings of storks. What do these visions mean? They reveal incredible prophecies about last-day economic corruption and rampant greed.

Yet, these prophecies have not been well understood. For example, the meaning of the first picture of a flying scroll has been most problematic. While a few expositors have drawn out some meaningful perspectives, I have yet to encounter an interpretation of this vision that meets a common-sense, literal fit with all of its criteria. Attempts at deciphering this flying scroll have surely resulted in some very imaginative interpretations…and not just among laypeople.

Other interpretations include a modern-day satellite revolving around the earth. The argument here is that this large scroll is descriptive of a large cylindrical object that is flying in the air. Others are convinced the scroll is really an ancient attempt at explaining a modern-day intercontinental ballistic missile (ICBM), or is the representation of a binary code that underpins futuristic computers and information technology.

However, there is a very important clue that these more extreme interpretations overlook. The angel speaking to Zechariah reveals that the two visions are in fact linked. They must be taken together, any interpretation applying to both.

If we follow the literal, common-sense meanings of this text, we discover yet another prophecy that uniquely applies to the times in which we live. Moreover, such an interpretation also offers a compelling perspective to the heavily debated question of the identity of future, end-time Babylon. The evidence in Zechariah 5 is rather clear, though mostly overlooked.

THE TWO VISIONS CONNECTED

In tackling this important chapter, we must pursue somewhat of a circuitous route. This stems from the two "unlocking" keys provided in this chapter. Let's review each of the visions as we first draw out these important keys, starting with the first:

Then I turned, and lifted up mine eyes, and looked, and behold a flying roll. And he said unto me, What seest thou? And I answered, I see a flying roll; the length thereof is twenty cubits, and the breadth thereof ten cubits. Then said he unto me, This is the curse that goeth forth over the face of the whole earth: for every one that stealeth shall be cut off as on this side according to it; and every one that sweareth shall be cut off as on that side according to it. I will bring it forth, saith the LORD of hosts, and it shall enter into the house of the thief, and into the house of him that sweareth falsely by my name: and it shall remain in the midst of his house, and shall consume it with the timber thereof and the stones thereof. (Zechariah 5:1–4, KJV)

Just what does this scroll represent? It "enters" houses, flies, consumes timbers, and is inordinately large. Most would agree that in only reading these four verses, one is left perplexed and wondering. There simply aren't many clues that allow us to put this vision into its intended framework and prophetic timeframe. We, therefore, must read further.

Then the angel that talked with me went forth, and said unto me, Lift up now thine eyes, and see what is this that goeth forth. And I said, What is it? And he said, This is an ephah that goeth forth. He said moreover, This is their resemblance through all the earth. And, behold, there was lifted up a talent of lead: and this is a woman that sitteth in the midst of the ephah. And he said, This is wickedness. And he cast it into the midst of the ephah; and he cast the weight of lead upon the mouth thereof. Then lifted I up mine eyes, and looked, and, behold, there came out two women, and the wind was in their wings; for they had wings like the wings of a stork: and they lifted up the ephah between the earth and the heaven. Then said I to the angel that talked with me, Whither do these bear the ephah? And he said unto me, To build it an house in the land of Shinar: and it shall be established, and set there upon her own base. (Zechariah 5:5–11, KJV)

Before delving into the meaning of this vision, we want to isolate the first of the key clues. It is found in verse 6, which says that the wickedness in the ephah is "*their* resemblance through all the earth." To whom does "their" refer? The Amplified Bible brings out this point more clearly:

> And I said, What is it? [What does it symbolize?] And he said, "This that goes forth is an ephah [-sized vessel for separate grains all collected together]. This," he continued, "is the symbol of the sinners mentioned above and is the resemblance of their iniquity throughout the whole land." (Zechariah 5:6, Amplified)

Who are the "sinners" said to be "mentioned above"? They are the same who either "sweareth falsely" or "stealeth," the two groups listed on opposite sides of the opened scroll in the first vision. We will come back to these two groups of people as we delve into the details of this vision more closely. However, for now, we have found the first of the important keys to this chapter. The two visions are clearly linked. Understanding the second vision is necessary before approaching the first vision.

The second key to which we must turn our attention is also clear and logical. Because one vision follows the other, the sequence of the two prophetic visions is significant. In other words, it will make sense that the events surrounding the second vision will follow those of the first, especially since both are related.

Holding on to these two keys, we can now launch our investigation into the meaning of these two visions. We need to start by examining the second vision first. Here, it speaks about judgment and something being relocated to Shinar, an area inside Iraq today. Just what is being moved, and to where? As did Zechariah, we will have to leave these answers to the conclusion.

The Ephah Explained

The ephah Zechariah saw lifted up toward heaven—shown with a lid of lead upon it to contain the iniquity—was a commercial measuring unit for dry goods. It is the approximate equivalent of about eight to nine bushels today. This unit of measure is mentioned more than twice as often as any other in the Bible—the hin, the homer, or the seah, for example. Clearly, the ephah was the primary unit of commerce during the prophet's time, both for measurement and transport. If Zechariah's vision had been given in our day, God may have used the image of a twenty-foot shipping container (the type that is transported on ocean-going ships and tractor trailers) or perhaps even a No. 10 cardboard box. Clearly, the ephah here is used as the symbol for trade and commerce.

Yet, more than this is being represented in this vision. More expressly, it indicts the iniquity and idolatry associated with commercialism—a worldwide orgy of commercialism, as we will show. The woman figure contained in the ephah speaks of idolatry or unfaithfulness, as often symbolized in the female form in prophetic language. All in all, it is a grave allegation. "This is wickedness," says the angel in no uncertain terms (Zechariah 5:8).

But, can we at this point determine the general period during which the prophecies of Zechariah 5 play out? We can conclude that it definitely refers to the last days, most likely the Tribulation period and the worldwide developments leading to this condition. Involved here is a global application and a divine intervention. Such apocalyptic events do not occur in prophecy until the seventieth week or thereabouts. Specifically, the vision of the ephah being transported arguably applies to the time when the Millennium period begins. Several more factors we will yet review line up with this interpretation.

Now that we have the correct framework, timeframe, and sequence, the meaning of the first vision unfolds. We are now ready to examine this vision. And, as we will see, doing so provides further proofs for our interpretation of the second. Most of all, we must remember that we are dealing with the massive idolatry of commercialism in the last days.

The Flying Scroll: What Is It?

What a strange sight: a flying scroll levitating in midair. Yet, Zechariah mentions two times that he sees a flying scroll: "Then I turned, and lifted up mine eyes, and looked, and behold a flying roll. And he said unto me, 'What seest thou?' And I answered, 'I see a flying roll; the length thereof is twenty cubits, and the breadth thereof ten cubits'" (Zechariah 5:1–2, kjv).

The scroll seen here is surely one of odd size. Converting its dimensions into the measures of our day, it is approximately thirty feet wide and fifteen feet high. It is visible as an open book, an open ledger of record. As with most scrolls of that day, writing was on both sides. Zechariah says twice that the flying object he saw was a scroll with writing on both sides. The writing could be clearly seen. Therefore, it was unfurled, rather than rolled up. The Bible uses two Hebrew words for literary documents, *megillah*, (used here) and *siphrah*. Both mean a type of document that can be rolled up. If God meant us to understand that the scroll was to prefigure an object of some type that was cylindrical, or a futuristic technology, Zechariah likely would have explained what he saw quite differently.

Yet this scroll is very large, much larger than can be handled by a single reader. It floats in the air as if it were a banner for all to see across the whole world…having application to "the face of the whole earth." The Bible says it is a scroll that is a record-keeping device for all the world to see; it is a marquee, announcing a curse and a final judgment: "Then said he unto me, 'This is the curse that goeth forth over the face of the whole earth'" (verse 3a).

A Banner Proclaiming a Worldwide Curse

The scroll represents a curse that applies to the whole world. Why a curse? As the Bible shows, a curse is always the result of forsaking God's ordinances. For example, referring to the Hebrews: "'If you do not listen, and if you do not set your heart to honor my name,' says the LORD Almighty, 'I will send a curse upon you, and I will curse your blessings. Yes, I have already cursed them, because you have not set your heart to honor me'" (Malachi 2:2).

The book of Deuteronomy lists numerous curses that would befall Israel if they failed to follow the commands Moses gave them. Joshua summed them up. He "... read all the words of the law—the blessings and the curses—just as it is written in the Book of the Law" (Joshua 8:34).

However, Isaiah mentions a curse that applies not just to Israel, but to the whole world:

The land shall be utterly emptied, and utterly spoiled: for the LORD hath spoken this word. The earth mourneth and fadeth away, the world languisheth and fadeth away, the haughty people of the earth do languish. The earth also is defiled under the inhabitants thereof; because they have transgressed the laws, changed the ordinance, broken the everlasting covenant. Therefore hath the curse devoured the earth, and they that dwell therein are desolate: therefore the inhabitants of the earth are burned, and few men left. (Isaiah 24:3–6, KJV)

There is an argument to be made that this curse applying to the whole world is in fact linked to the curse we are now examining in Zechariah. In this case, why is a curse being pronounced?

The Bible tells us clearly: "...for every one that stealeth shall be cut off as on this side according to it; and every one that sweareth shall be cut off as on that side according to it" (verse 3). Therefore, both those who steal and those who swear falsely are being cut off and cursed. This answer triggers another important question: Why is the world being judged for these two sins? Aren't there ten commandments?

The Ills of Swearing and Stealing

Peculiar is that only two of the Ten Commandments—the fourth and the eighth —are mentioned as the cause of the curse upon the whole world (misusing the Lord's name and stealing). It could be argued that the ninth commandment, "You shall not give false testimony against your neighbor," is also involved (Exodus 20:16).

Whatever the case, why are only three sins mentioned at most? Because the breaking of the other commandments is not directly involved. That is another important clue. However, at this point, we must again recall the first clue—that the vision of the scroll is linked to the ephah of the second vision.

We therefore can know that the false witness and the stealing have to do with the idolatrous commercialism of the last days pointed out in the second vision. Pinpointed are the two sins mainly responsible for the filthy idolatry shown in the flying ephah—the last-day semblance of manmade prosperity, the religion of greed, the intoxicating wine of Babylon the Great mentioned in Revelation 18, and the human quest for the actualization of man on earth through the economics of satiating people's physical and materialistic wants.

In no uncertain terms, we are seeing here the endemic commercialization and financialization of all human life on earth of the last days. Rampant globalization is surely part of this picture…whether in its earlier or later stages. Encompassed here is everything from the elevation of manipulative and global monetary systems, fiat money, capitalism, globalism based on the vested interest of intertwined worldwide trading systems, accounting shenanigans, corporatism, and debt-based wealth. Altogether, it represents that heaving mass of mammonism—a world that has chosen money over God.

The corrosiveness and imbalances of these systems are literally consuming "the timber thereof and the stones thereof" (Zechariah 5:4), symbolizing the structural integrity of man's globalized foundation. For such systems to prosper—prospering here meaning nothing more than giving the semblance of success, though its underpinnings are deceitful and not sustainable—they depend upon two impulses alone. What are these? To no surprise, they are the very two sins of stealing and false witness.

Swearing Falsely and Stealing Up Close

To understand the linkage of these two sins more closely with Zechariah's second vision, let's examine them more closely, beginning with swearing falsely. Swearing here means to take an oath, or to promise something. The translation of the Hebrew word is to "seven oneself,"—in other words, to enter into a contract or declaration by saying it seven times. The issue here has to do with "swearing falsely by my name" (verse 4, KJV). Therefore, this first wicked condition has to do with lying, perjury, and deceit—misusing the Lord's name. It concerns the issue of making a promise without intending to fulfill it.

But how is it that the Lord's name is involved? Well, it must be. After all, "God is not a man, that he should lie, nor a son of man, that he should change his mind" (Numbers 23:19). He is the God of truth (Psalms 31:5, 33:4). Every man may be a liar, but God is true (Romans 3:4). The Bible clearly tells us that God is the personification of truth. Therefore, to swear falsely in the name of truth is to "sweareth falsely by my name" (Zechariah 5:4).

Actually, this type of lying—swearing falsely in the name of truth—is the glue of our world's economic and geopolitical systems. At the highest levels, it is mirrored in the institution of contract law. On the one hand, legions of lawyers are required to establish a rigid framework for world commerce to function. Of course, this wouldn't be required in the first case were there not so many false promises. In fact, for a long time the common law system has included the practice of asking deponents and witnesses to swear upon the Bible so they will "tell nothing but the truth."

Most contracts today are made entirely on the premise of what is legally allowable as opposed to what is right, moral, and a true promise. All that is required to get out of one's obligation is a simple loophole. It is as easy as that for the most part; it is nothing more than a façade of truth.

The same attitude applies to the world of competitive geopolitics. The "lie" is the most deftly used technique in the pursuit of nations' interests. Lying and deceit definitely defines the modus operandi of the entire world today. Christ warned of this murky quagmire of swearing: "Simply let your 'Yes' be 'Yes,' and your 'No,' 'No'; anything beyond this comes from the evil one" (Matthew 5:37).

Hand in Hand with Theft

What about stealing? It is the other side of the coin...or, we should better say, the other side of the flying scroll.

Stealing in our time is probably more prevalent than ever. However, it is much more sophisticated. Numerous types of stealing are institutionalized into world systems. For example, consider the phenomenon of inflation (the price of goods continually rising in currency terms). It is one of the biggest forms of stealing. While there are many complexities to inflation, in reality, it is nothing more than stealing. Yet, every central bank in the world will argue that a little bit of stealing (inflation) is necessary for the smooth and safe functioning of economies and financial systems.

Too much inflation, however, can be disastrous. Therefore, quite a bit of inflation (meaning the stealing from the pocketbooks of the citizenry) is masterfully concealed or lied about so as to not arouse unnecessary suspicion. Officials are swearing falsely about inflation. These are factual statements that can be proven, had we the space. However, we want to continue illustrating how endemic stealing is today.

It is the staple of many other activities, as well. Corporate executives steal from shareholders (like never before), and countries try to steal precious resources from other countries (oil, for example). Such motivations are couched in official policy-speak such as "securing our interests" or "gaining access through free trade." This is all the norm today, though every now and then some people who make this too obvious for comfort will face conviction.

In conclusion, we see that swearing falsely and stealing are at the very root of man's global, end-time edifice. The competitions of modern-day economic pagan man and sovereign countries around the world are typified by "swearing" and "stealing." They come to their apex in the form of the commercial Babylon the Great, ancient Tyre reborn into its final global manifestation.

Two-Sided Meaning

We stop to consider the symbolic significance of the fact that the flying scroll has two sides. On one side thieves are listed; on the other are those who swear falsely. Why are they shown as opposites or as two sides of the coin? Actually, the entire economic system upon earth is defined by these very two symptoms as well as this nature of duality.

Isaiah, prophesying of judgment and wrath in the last days (the same period that Zechariah sees) also emphasizes a duality: "And it shall be—as [what happens] with the people, so with the priest; as with the servant, so with his master; as with the maid, so with her mistress; as with the buyer, so with the seller; as with the lender, so with the borrower; as with the creditor, so with the debtor" (Isaiah 24:2 Amplified).

He lists six sets of pairs that harbor an element of opposites. For example, there can be no maid without a mistress. Interestingly, three of these pairs (50 percent) directly refer to commercial aspects: There is a buyer and a seller; a lender and a borrower; and a creditor and a debtor. Significantly, these are mentioned last. The sequence moves from the highest order of people to the basest. It pretty much fits the evolution of mankind's systems. The last pair pictures the crassest and most brutal world based on the rights of creditors and debtors—of those who "stealeth" and those who "swear falsely."

And, indeed that is the world today—one witnessing an explosion of debt and the widest chasm between lenders and borrowers ever in history. Interestingly, it is a commercial system perched upon the "double-entry" bookkeeping system, its foundational duality.

ZECHARIAH'S CONCLUSION: THE FINAL JUDGMENT

A literal rendering of Zechariah's prophecy speaks of an endpoint—a final judgment. He sees a picture of the world being cursed in its sophisticated perversions of stealing and perjury. Then comes the point when this idolatry is encased in an ephah and moved. The ephah—the filth and wickedness it contains, which is the related condition to the "swearing and stealing" that is upon the whole earth and is therefore under a curse—is sealed off with a heavy lid of lead and removed to a specific location.

The key aspects here are removal and sealing off. We note that Zechariah tells us that after the contents of the ephah are revealed, the angel "pushed her back into the basket and the pushed the lead down over its mouth" (verse 8). This does not reveal a releasing of this wickedness and idolatry to again flourish in some end-time location, but rather a sealing. It is an end.

Next, we are told that the ephah is taken away to be set upon its base, which is a place that has been prepared for it (verse 11). We must ask ourselves why such advance preparations are required, and who is doing the preparing. Of the many answers that can be probed, the only one that relates to the general theme of judgment in this entire chapter is that this removal is one for divinely set purposes.

In other words, the filth and wickedness of a worldwide condition is quarantined and set upon a "resting place" (a base, possibly being a dungeon) somewhere in the land of Shinar.

Iniquity Moved to Its Final Quarantine

What is the significance of Shinar being mentioned as the final resting place for the flying ephah? Consider the significance of this location. It is just outside the eastern extremity of the land promised to the covenantal descendants of Abraham, the Euphrates River (Genesis 15:18). Shinar is on the eastern side of this river, as is Babylon, and therefore is just outside the periphery of the restored, millennial Israel.

Because the ephah contained wickedness (Zechariah 5:8) and the restored land of Israel is considered holy in the millennial period—harboring the holy hill of Zion and holy Jerusalem—it is therefore understandable why this worldwide "wickedness" would be removed to somewhere outside millennial Israel. And since Shinar was the original source of this wickedness, it is most fitting that it is returned to that location.

The Meaning of Shinar

It is significant also that the original Hebrew texts confirm that Zechariah uses the word "Shinar," not "Babylonia," in identifying the future and final location of the ephah. The latter term, Babylonia (which some Bible translations incorrectly use) was the more modern term for this region during this prophet's ministry (after the Babylonian captivity of Judah). The Babylonian kingdom at that time is referred to as Neo-Babylon by Assyriologists (experts in Middle Eastern history and archaeology). Though both terms, "Shinar" and "Babylonia," refer to the same general region, the former is the more ancient term harking back to the days of Nimrod and Semiranus. That was at least two thousand years before the prophet lived, even earlier than Chaldea. This was the era out of which the original post-Flood paganism and commercialism was spawned.

Since Zechariah refers to ancient Shinar, it is reasonable to conclude he must be linking this prophecy to the ending of the ancient pagan beliefs and idolatry that first emanated out of the time of Nimrod, not the Neo-Babylonian empire. It is these that are removed to a dungeon outside the millennial kingdom.

Babylon Rebuilt?

As mentioned in the previous chapter, many respected prophecy scholars see these final verses in Zechariah 5, which refer to the ephah being moved to Shinar, as lining up with a revived, rebuilt Babylon. In fact, some use this reference as proof that this will be the case. They see the ancient commercialism and paganism being returned to its previous eminence in the rebuilt Babylon just before the final Armageddon.

Actually, Zechariah 5 provides no such proof. In fact, over the course of studying this topic, I have also gradually shifted my own views on this point. While other Bible references may be used to support the "rebuilt Babylon" view, verse 11 in Zechariah 5 cannot qualify, for several reasons.

First, Shinar, the location to which the wicked are removed, is a region and not a city. Also, as already shown, the term "Shinar" does not refer to the same era as Babylonia, though they are the same general region. Therefore, to link this prophecy to the city of Babylon and its rebuilding cannot be substantiated. This verse simply does not say this; it refers neither to any rebuilding nor to any city. Furthermore, as we have learned, the prophecies contained in the sixth and seventh visions speak of an end and a judgment, not a period of resurging wickedness.

There are additional problems with the interpretation that the ancient city of Babylon will revive as a great commercial center of the world at the end time. First, those who assume this indeed will occur link it with the great, global, commercial colossus identified as Babylon the Great in Revelation 18. For this to happen, we must expect some monumental changes over a very short time frame. This shift must take place no later than the Tribulation period. Could this really happen?

We recognize, of course, that just because Bible prophecy sometimes speaks of incredible and unlikely developments as humans may see them, this in no way disproves future literal fulfillment. After all, we serve a God of the impossible. Yet, let's consider the possibility of such a development as the city of Babylon reviving and the necessary developments for this to transpire.

UNLIKELY EVENTS MUST BE EXPECTED

As is well known, the ancient city of Babylon is located in Iraq of today. One could not think of a more dysfunctional and unruly country in the present day. Even the world's only superpower cannot bring this region to heel. Are we to believe that this region will be transformed into the center of the globe's trading system by the midpoint of the Tribulation? If so, it would soon have to overshadow the financial and trade centers of New York, London, Frankfurt, Singapore, or Hong Kong. Practically, how long a period would such a transition require, were it possible?

Never before in the history of the world has such an unlikely shift taken place in a period of less than fifty years…even perhaps a hundred years. Not only does Scripture appear to preclude this outcome, but this scenario stretches simple common sense and historical precedent.

To begin, we must remember that we are living in the very generation that Christ said will see the birth pangs of the end-time world. Israel, the fig tree, has come back to life.

We don't exactly know what length of term Christ meant by the phrase, "this generation" (Matthew 24:34), when He said to the Jews—meaning the revived Israel of the future—that "this generation will certainly not pass away until all these things have happened." It may be sixty to seventy years or more, but likely not centuries. If so, there simply isn't enough time for Iraq or the city of Babylon to flower into the world's economic power center. Alone, cultural changes of the type required to allow a Muslim nation such as Iraq to gain the type of broad-based power that determines world potency today requires many decades. This is improbable in itself.

A TREE MUST BE RELATED TO ITS CULTURAL FRUITS

An insightful book by Lawrence E. Harrison[32] concludes how unlikely and difficult it is for societies to change their cultural identities. The entirety of history provides no precedent for such a rapid change as would be required to so suddenly alter its cultural course. When this has happened for any particular society, such changes almost always have occurred from within, requiring many years. Rarely have major cultural changes been forced from outside.

Consider the case of Turkey. It can be argued that this present-day nation and its forerunner, the Ottoman Empire, have been making attempts to westernize for perhaps as much as a century or more, especially under Mustafa Kemal, its founder—Attaturk —since the middle 1920s. Yet, it remains a developing nation with a fundamentally Islamic society. Virtually 100 percent of Turkey's population is Muslim. It is still considered a developing economy by the World Bank and other such transnational agencies.

The type of transformation that is therefore required in Iraq in order for this nation to be able to control and commandeer the world economy would take much more time than could be allowed by Christ's indication of a "generation." Assuredly, as mentioned, what the Bible prophesies will surely happen, no matter how unlikely and impossible it may seem. However, let's be reasonable. At the very earliest, something as unlikely as a revived Babylon would take many, many decades if it is to fit the descriptions found in Revelation 18. On that logical basis, we must conclude that the Tribulation period is still fifty years or more in the future, at the earliest.

Yet, revived Israel is on the scene today. We would then have to agree that a "generation" as mentioned in Matthew 24:34 must be at least one hundred years, if not much more. Also, if a revived Babylon were to occur any sooner, we must then consider that apocalyptic events would be needed to change the order of the world that rapidly. Yet, apocalyptic events of this scope prophesied anywhere in the Bible do not take place any earlier than in the Tribulation period. To suppose that such a transformation could then occur inside a seven-year Tribulation period—a time of enormous economic and geopolitical dislocation—begs incredulity.

THOUGHTS TO PONDER

We conclude our review of the visions of the strange, flying scroll and the transported ephah. If we have followed their literal, common-sense meanings, we may now understand some very important prophecies that in some cases may have been opaque to Bible readers.

Prophecy in the form of symbols is intended to convey a specific meaning, not an allegorical one. Often, prophecy of this type can contain things or concern events that are not understandable to the prophet relative to the conditions of his time. While the two visions do in fact concern concepts that would have been impossible to understand twenty-eight hundred years ago, they do not refer to strange technology, but rather to futuristic, systemic forms. Zechariah is not referring to intercontinental ballistic missiles, satellites, or any other such inventive thing. He is referring to an end-time period of massive and idolatrous commercialism that will envelop the world. Living inside the proverbial fishbowl of Western culture, most people today cannot see this reality. This is again the Babylon Occlusion that we have reviewed.

The ephah of wickedness will indeed be taken to Shinar—the land of Babylonia—and become an astonishment. It speaks of the end, not of a beginning.

It fits hand in glove with the conditions that will be fully realized in the Tribulation period:

> The coming of the lawless one will be in accordance with the work of Satan displayed in all kinds of counterfeit miracles, signs and wonders, and in every sort of evil that deceives those who are perishing. They perish because they refused to love the truth and so be saved. For this reason God sends them a powerful delusion so that they will believe the lie and so that all will be condemned who have not believed the truth but have delighted in wickedness. (2 Thessalonians 2:9–12)

We live during the time when we can see such conditions develop before our eyes. For how long will the Lord tarry? The curse is already upon the land and the world. Economic inequities and injustices are waxing great. Man's wealth and commercial systems are exploding into unstable prominence. Greed is consuming the house, weakening its very timbers.

Yet, we Christians must face this flood of iniquity and stand firm. Admittedly, it is nearly impossible. Even as we strive not to participate in the world's materialistic orgy, we can identify with Jeremiah, who complained, "Alas, my mother, that you gave me birth, a man with whom the whole land strives and contends! I have neither lent nor borrowed, yet everyone curses me" (Jeremiah 15:10). Christians are falling prey to the Babylon Occlusion in great numbers. As has occurred with the global financial crisis, due to this blindness in part, many more find themselves entrapped in the end-time money snare. Many more will likely yet fall into the trap...their faith running cold.

Figure #9

Trends in Gold vs. Inflation

Historical Gold Prices, U.S. Consumer Price Index, Relative Trend, 1800-2008 (1800 Base = 1)

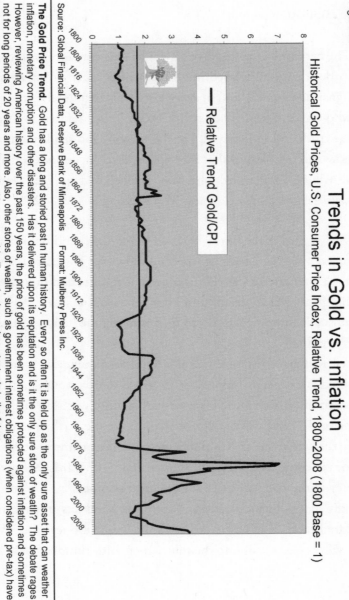

— Relative Trend Gold/CPI

Source: Global Financial Data, Reserve Bank of Minneapolis   Format: Mulberry Press Inc.

The Gold Price Trend. Gold has a long and storied past in human history. Every so often it is held up as the only sure asset that can weather inflation, monetary corruption and other disasters. Has it delivered upon its reputation and is it the only sure store of wealth? The debate rages. However, reviewing American history over the past 150 years, the price of gold has been sometimes protected against inflation and sometimes not for long periods of 20 years and more. Also, other stores of wealth, such as government interest obligations (when considered pre-tax) have delivered much steadier income and growth. However, gold will surely play an important role in the future.

8

666, GOLD, AND OTHER
END-TIME MONEY VIEWS

The number 666 surely is infamous among both Christians and non-Christians alike. However, before we even remotely broach this topic, we should keep in mind biblical scholar Joseph Thayer's comment concerning this number in *The Greek-English Lexicon of the New Testament:* "Six hundred and sixty six, the meaning of which is the basis of much vain speculation."[33] Therefore, we will not entertain any such speculation and will limit ourselves to the Bible's plain meaning.

That said, there assuredly is a lot of nonsensical and ludicrous speculation about the meaning of this number. Even well-known Bible teachers make speculative associations, employing numerology, arbitrary calculations (gematria), and other twists of mathematics. One high-profile prophecy teacher with a large TV audience openly makes associations with the number 666 purely on the basis of the number values of English names. This is so spurious it can hardly bear comment. For one, this practice presumes that the English language must be used to unlock the meaning of a text originally written in Greek. This is the equivalent of saying that all people—whether Chinese or Swahili—must be required to learn English before they can be allowed to read the Holy Scriptures! We forget that the Bible's words were inspired in Hebrew, Aramaic, and Greek. On this theory, we must all first learn these three languages before we can study the Scriptures.

No doubt, many levels of meanings may be taken from the number 666. However, in essence, the Bible provides a fairly straightforward description. Said John the Revelator, "If anyone has insight, let him calculate the number of the beast, for it is man's number. His number is 666" (Revelation 13:18). Clearly, the beast and man are indicted together in this passage. It is man's number…representing his systems, beliefs, and idolatries. These happen to be encouraged by the prince of this world.

It should be noticed that the revelator's mention of the number 666 follows right after the verses that inform us that the False Prophet will attempt to induce everyone to take the mark of the Beast: "And he causeth all, both small and great, rich and poor, free and bond, to receive a mark in their right hand, or in their foreheads: And that no man might buy or sell, save he that had the mark, or the name of the beast, or the number of his name" (Revelation 13:16–17).

There clearly is an obvious economic and financial connection. An idolatrous, man-made system of control is likely indicated, implying self-sufficiency and a reliance upon earthly materialism. Systems such as these are destined for destruction or breakup, like what happened to Solomon's kingdom. In this sense, we may see that a common spirit finds a connection with the later stages of Solomon's reign, the number 666, and the prophetic events. Just how is it possible that Solomon has a connection with the number 666? It is a question worthy of an investigation; it will offer the reader an additional biblical perspective on the urgent and dangerous conditions of our times.

SOLOMON'S GILDED REIGN

To this point in history, the greatest period of power and wealth for Israel was during the reign of King Solomon. During this time, for the most part, Israel was at peace. Its land mass stretched from the Mediterranean and northern Egypt to outposts on the river Babylon. Solomon received tributes and levies from many other kingdoms. First Kings 10 (and 2 Chronicles 9) gives an account of Solomon's Golden Age, including the ostentatious visit by the Queen of Sheba. An excerpt from 1 Kings 10 (verses 21 to 26, NIV) provides an indication of Solomon's grandeur:

> All King Solomon's goblets were gold, and all the household articles in the Palace of the Forest of Lebanon were pure gold. Nothing was made of silver, because silver was considered of little value in Solomon's days. The king had a fleet of trading ships at sea along with the ships of Hiram. Once every three years it returned, carrying gold, silver and ivory, and apes and baboons. King Solomon was greater in riches and wisdom than all the other kings of the earth. The whole world sought audience with Solomon to hear the wisdom God had put in his heart. Year after year, everyone who came brought a gift—articles of silver and gold, robes, weapons and spices, and horses and mules. Solomon accumulated chariots and horses; he had fourteen hundred chariots and twelve thousand horses, which he kept in the chariot cities and also with him in Jerusalem. The king made silver as common in Jerusalem as stones, and cedar as plentiful as sycamore-fig trees in the foothills.

We see that Solomon was wealthy beyond imagination. However, the Bible makes it clear that these riches were not a result of Solomon's works, but rather a blessing from God. When Solomon asked God for understanding, the Lord responded thus:

"Behold...I have given thee a wise and an understanding heart; so that there was none like thee before thee, neither after thee shall any arise like unto thee. And I have also given thee that which thou hast not asked, both riches, and honour, so that there shall not be any among the kings like unto thee all thy days" (1 Kings 3:12–13, KJV).

Yet, we also know that while God surely did deliver His promise, Solomon did not finish his life faithfully. In time, he allowed the blessings themselves to corrupt him. As he gained power, honor, and influence, he began to break many of God's commands. He wandered off to follow his own interests and indulgences. While tragic, it was not surprising. Only two generations earlier, Samuel had warned Israel about the dangers of appointing a king over them. Nevertheless, the people had said: "We want a king over us. Then we will be like all the other nations" (Samuel 8:19–20).

Even earlier, Moses had expressly laid down requirements should Israel ever want a king. The king "must not acquire great numbers of horses for himself" (Deuteronomy 17:16); "He must not take many wives, or his heart will be led astray. He must not accumulate large amounts of silver and gold" (verse 17). Solomon did all of these things. He had hundreds of horses, wives, and concubines. He built himself an immense palace, much larger than the temple he had built for the Lord. Moreover, he built himself an impressive throne (verses 18–20). While God had told Moses never to build steps in front of any altar, Solomon elected to have six steps leading to his throne, with twelve golden lions placed upon them.

And, true to the prophecy of Samuel that the entire nation of Israel would end up being oppressed by its kings economically (1 Samuel 8:10–18), this indeed proved to be the case with Solomon. Jeroboam, appealing to King Rehoboam (Solomon's son), said, "Your father put a heavy yoke on us, but now lighten the harsh labor and the heavy yoke he put on us" (2 Chronicles 10:4). Solomon had raised a levy upon all Israel (1 Kings 5:13). Other extrabiblical sources indicate that high levels of inflation existed during the later stages of Solomon's reign. As a result, the population was in a plaintive mood.

Solomon's Foreshadowing and 666

The account of Solomon's reign holds many lessons, some that we will want to explore here as they align with the themes of this book. Interestingly, Solomon's Golden Age provides a useful type or fore-shadow of another type of Gilded Age...one the world is hankering after today.

First Kings 11 is rather remarkable in several respects. In this one chapter is shown both the rise and fall of Solomon, providing another example of a man (symbolizing all of mankind, in our view) receiving blessings, but ultimately forgetting its source and conditional aspects. And, most curiously, the number 666 is mentioned.

What, if anything, could this infamous number have to do with Solomon's era? This is puzzling. The mention of this number is neither accidental nor circumstantial. The Holy Spirit intended it for reason.

In 1 Kings 10:14–15, we read, "The weight of the gold that Solomon received yearly was 666 talents, not including the revenues from merchants and traders and from all the Arabian kings and the governors of the land." This surely was a large income. Based upon recent gold prices, this would amount to an annual income of about one-half billion dollars in U.S. dollar terms. Based upon the average income of that time, King Solomon would have earned an income equivalent to about two-hundred thousand laborers. In those terms, his annual income would be closer to an equivalent of eight to ten billion dollars per year today. As the Bible confirms, no other king was as rich as he was during that time.

But, let's return to our examination of this curious number—"six hundred threescore and six," as it is phrased in the King James translation. It comes up on only three occasions in the Bible. Most well known is its reference in Revelation 13:18. Another reference is found in Ezra 2:13, where it refers to the number of Adomicam's family that was returning to Jerusalem from Babylon. However, the parallel account in Nehemiah 7:18 counts them differently, at 667. Given this apparent inconsistency, we are best not to attribute any importance to this reference.

However, the first reference in the Bible to the number 666 appears in the two parallel records of the reign of King Solomon (1 Kings 10 and 2 Chronicles 9). In both, the number 666 is specifically mentioned.

But why should its reference here attract further attention? There are at least two reasons. First, the number is incongruous with the rest of these two chapters. It sticks out like a sore thumb. The two almost identical accounts employ many numbers in describing the reign of King Solomon and the opulence of his kingdom and possessions. For example, they mention three hundred concubines, fourteen hundred chariots, three hundred shields, and twelve thousand horses. Among more than fifteen numbers mentioned, we find only one unusual number—666. Of the eleven numbers greater than one hundred employed in this chapter, only one is not rounded to nearest one-hundredth, one-thousandth, or ends in zero. It is the number 666.

Second, the application and context of this number is ill fitting.

King Solomon's annual income in terms of talents of gold "was 666 talents, not including the revenues from merchants and traders and from all the Arabian kings and the governors of the land" (2 Chronicles 9:13–14; 1 Kings 10:14–15). The text clearly tells us that he had much greater revenues than 666 talents per year. Then why is the odd number of 666 used in describing his income? It would be just as strange to express one's hourly wage as "six dollars and sixty-six cents plus a whole lot more." In any case, it would be strange if Solomon's gold income weren't to fluctuate from year to year.

Therefore, we should conclude that this number is also meant to provide a symbolic connection. It may simply alert us to the fact that King Solomon commanded a prosperous and opulent economy that then descended into idolatry and bureaucratic controls, or that it was not a "divine" economy, but an enterprise of man with all its usual defects and troubles. In the end, the bureaucracy under Solomon ended up becoming a type of oppressor. One commentator says, "Solomon's success came at the high price of individual freedom and tribal sovereignty."[34]

CURRENT MISCONCEPTIONS

This "late, great" era of human history—from a commercial point of view, we refer to it as the age of global capital—is marked by worldwide fiat money and sophisticated forms of monetary corruption and theft.

Because of these conditions, many people seek a safe haven for their savings. Investors therefore value gold for what they believe is its property of "real money." Come hyperinflation, perhaps a massive economic depression, monetary debasement by corrupt governments, or any other form of economic theft, gold will reliably hold its value "in season and out of season," they reason. Is this really the case? No… at least, not reliably. We could cite reams of supporting economic and financial history, both ancient and modern, on this point.

The history of the past century alone will dispel all such comfortable notions. Quoting GaveKal, a well-known global economic consulting firm: "Indeed, despite two or three world wars (whether one counts the Cold War), a supposed massive debasement of our currencies (as the gold bugs like to say), hyperinflation, and the recent gold rally, gold has returned a princely [total]—9 percent in real terms in 111 years." Suffice it to say that to this point at least, the supposed financial safe harbor of gold has been a myth.

Before going any further, it is important to settle the point of "false hope." In this present age, gold—as alluring as it may appear—does not offer a sure escape from monetary corruption or judgment. It may be a promising investment from time to time. It may even provide protection from the ravages of inflation during certain periods. But it will not provide assurance against a world "where moth and rust destroy, and where thieves break in and steal" (Matthew 6:20). It cannot. In the first place, we must remember that Jesus Christ remains in heaven, and therefore this world remains thoroughly corrupted. "He must remain in heaven until the time comes for God to restore everything, as he promised long ago through his holy prophets" (Acts 3:21).

Just what does the Bible say about gold today and its future role, especially at the time when God "restore[s] everything"?

To tackle this gilded subject, let's consider gold's role over five different eras: 1.Old Testament times; 2.The last days (beginning with the revealing of the church); 3.The Tribulation period; 4.The Millennium; and finally, 5.The eternal Jerusalem. But first, it will be illuminating to briefly review some facts and history about gold.

GOLD AND ITS FUTURE ROLE

The topic of gold evokes interest today just as it has throughout the millennia. Much of mankind's history has been motivated by possessing this lustrous, fascinating metal. It plays a part in many famous stories—from gold-rich King Solomon and the Greek mythological tale of King Midas, who had the "golden touch," to the New World's Coronado and his quest for the Seven Cities of Cibola (lost cities of gold) and countless others. One would think there must be lots of gold in the world today. Not so.

If all the gold presently existing above ground in the world were put into one place, it would amount to one solid cube the size of a doubles tennis court and forty-five feet high. That glistening block would represent most of the gold ever mined in history. Only about 15 percent of all gold ever produced has been either consumed or lost, it is estimated. The rest of it, whether unearthed from King Solomon's mines more than three thousand years ago or produced from Barrick's (the world's largest gold producer today) Porgora mine in Papua New Guinea last year, all remains accounted for and owned by some person or entity today.

Why the big attraction to gold? It is a rare and special substance; one of its most valued properties is that it does not corrode (under natural conditions). The only other metal that rivals gold's properties is platinum. However, platinum is very difficult to produce...and is much rarer. The timelessness of gold and the fact that it is only found in pure form in nature are qualities much admired. In the Bible, gold is used to express ideas of purity, value, and wealth.

Gold plays a significant role in prophecy. Today's world, with its fiat and corrupt monetary systems, will want to heed what the Scriptures say about gold, especially its "last-day" roles and possibly its use during the millennial period.

Unfortunately, some serious misconceptions and false hopes exist about gold today. Not only do we want to tackle these issues next, but we also will direct our inquiry to the future role of gold—which is a very big future, indeed.

The Biblical Roles of Gold

The Old Testament role gold played was quite straightforward. Gold served as money or adornment. While corruption certainly existed—for example, people would shave gold coins until they ended up as little more than nubs—gold remained physical gold, and its value was not systematically destroyed or manipulated through a fiat financial money system. In a previous section, we briefly reviewed the time of King Solomon who, during the Golden Age of Israel, had lots of gold—bringing in 666 talents of gold per year and more. We concluded that the use of the number 666 in this account was significant.

Next, we turn to the evolution of gold's role in the last days. That is our time—the period during which the "spirit of the antichrist" (1 John 4:3) and the great deceiver are working furiously. Gold plays a relatively minor part of what becomes a highly sophisticated and advanced Babylonian system. James, in fact, prophesies, "Your gold and silver are corroded. Their corrosion will testify against you and eat your flesh like fire. You have hoarded wealth in the last days" (James 5:3). While there is much debate about to whom he is referring and to what period this prophecy applies, we can safely conclude that this process of "corrosion" is well advanced, if not nearly complete. The judgment aspect of James' prophecy (James 5:1–6) likely occurs during the Tribulation period—or perhaps also at the bema seat judgment for Christians.

The Bible shines additional light upon the Tribulation period. Gold holdings will be of little help at that time. The Lord says, "They will throw their silver into the streets, and their gold will be an unclean thing. Their silver and gold will not be able to save them in the day of the Lord's wrath" (Ezekiel 7:19). People will continue to hold on to their materialistic idolatries and corrupt financial systems despite terrible times. "The rest of mankind that were not killed by these plagues still did not repent of the work of their hands; they did not stop worshiping demons, and idols of gold, silver, bronze, stone and wood—idols that cannot see or hear or walk. Nor did they repent of their murders, their magic arts, their sexual immorality or their thefts" (Revelation 5:20–21).

What role will gold have in the millennial period? We know that gold will continue as a form of wealth. Several prophetic verses mention that wealth at that time will flow to Israel from the rest of the world. "Surely the islands look to me; in the lead are the ships of Tarshish, bringing your sons from afar, with their silver and gold, to the honor of the LORD your God, the Holy One of Israel, for he has endowed you with splendor" (Isaiah 60:9; see also Isaiah 60:5, 61:6, 66:12).

Gold may also play a central part of the millennial economic system. However, this aspect of gold would be more of a deductive conclusion. It doesn't seem to be definitively mentioned in the Bible. In any case, such interpretations from several prophetic statements involving gold would depend upon their chronological placement. For example, the account of the war involving Gog (Ezekiel 37–38 and Revelation 20:18) is in this category. At the time of this event, gold is mentioned as being an asset worth plundering: "Sheba and Dedan and the merchants of Tarshish and all her villages will say to you, 'Have you come to plunder? Have you gathered your hordes to loot, to carry off silver and gold, to take away livestock and goods and to seize much plunder?'" (Ezekiel 38:13).

Also, Isaiah mentions gold in relation to Israel. "Their land also is full of silver and gold, neither is there any end of their treasures; their land is also full of horses, neither is there any end of their chariots" (Isaiah 2:7). If the Ezekiel passage refers to the millennial period, then gold can be seen to have a prominent role at that time. On the other hand, if these two Scriptures are to be placed before that time, Israel can be expected to become quite prosperous before the final events of the Tribulation come to a close. There is much debate on these points. However, Israel is certainly becoming prosperous today, and is a nexus point for significant financial wealth around the globe. (We certainly cannot determine whether Israelis are in fact hoarding gold and silver today.)

Finally, after the Millennium, the holy city of Jerusalem will descend to earth (Revelation 21:10). It is a majestic edifice: "The wall was made of jasper, and the city of pure gold, as pure as glass" (Revelation 21:19). "The great street of the city was of pure gold, like transparent glass" (Revelation 21: 21). Gold will be one of its main structural materials. Given the holy city's dimensions—for example, twelve thousand stadia (fourteen hundred miles) square and tall, its walls 144 cubits thick (over two hundred feet)—it will require perhaps more than a thousand times as much gold as exists above ground today. After all, only a little more than 150,000 tons of gold are known to exist presently (and remember, all of it fits on a doubles tennis court).

GOLDEN IDOLATRY IS MISPLACED

Back to the present. An extreme idolatry—even a pseudo-religion—has grown up around gold, especially in North America. Indeed, a sizable industry likes to hawk gold bullion and numismatic investments (rare coins) as if gold were God's very own money and the perfect way to run a monetary system. Such claims are surely overstated. Gold is not the be-all and end-all to the world's problem of corruption and sin.

Often, the age of the gold standard of the late 1800s—when Britain was at the center of global finance and the kingpin of the Gilded Age as the world's strongest reserve currency—is held up as the great age of money stability. Actually, this era had its problems and accidents, too. The success of this period is heavily mythologized. There were problems, inflation, and financial collapses during that period, as there are today. Writes Guilo Gallarotti, "Widely considered the crowning achievement in the history of international monetary relations, the classical gold standard (1880–1914) has long been treated like a holy relic."[35]

We must also recognize that it was a different world then. Today, given the interconnectedness and explosion of financial wealth, gold only plays a bit role in the world's financial shenanigans. The entire value of all existing gold (a little over three trillion dollars in U.S. dollar terms) amounts to only about one-half of 1 percent of the total financial "position value" of the world today. This is despite the fact that fifty percent of all gold in existence has been mined since 1960.

There are numerous conspiracy theories about the fate of gold. One expert, Dr. Antal Fekete, an intellectual heavyweight when it comes to monetary theory and the roles of gold, currently argues that almost half of all gold has been siphoned off into private hands over the past fifty years (meaning, moved outside the official monetary system).[36] At one point, gold was mainly in the possession of sovereigns, nation states, and their central banks. Where did all this gold go? Who specifically accumulated these amounts? It could be wealthy individuals or simply many thousands of ordinary investors. Could this development play a role in the near future? Dr. Fekete claims that a similar phenomenon occurred in the latter stages of the Roman Empire just before its collapse.

On this point, the Bible agrees. Man's monetary systems will collapse. "...man will be brought low and mankind humbled.... The LORD Almighty has a day in store for all the proud and lofty, for all that is exalted and they will be humbled...for all the towering mountains and all the high hills, for every lofty tower and every fortified wall, for every trading ship. The arrogance of man will be brought low and the pride of men humbled" (Isaiah 2:9, 12–17).

Surely, a world monetary system based upon gold, which many advocate, would be better than the reckless systems that prevail at present. After all, money today is nothing more than a paper or digital electronic figment. Central banks around the world are again furiously creating fictitious money following the global financial crisis. Wall Street and its sister financial centers around the world may exult in this financial debauchery as they are being rescued and offered new, profitable opportunities. Today, we observe that the business of making money from money—the basest form of human organizational systems—has become the largest industry in the world in recent decades though significantly downsized due to the fallout of the GFC.

Yet, gold would certainly not solve the problems of the world that results from mankind's penchant for the "love of money" (1 Timothy 6:10) and greed. Gold was never the solution to such problems in the past, and will not be in the future. The "... cravings of sinful man, the lust of his eyes and the boasting of what he has and does" (1 John 2:16) remain the key propulsion of history and geopolitics. This hasn't changed, and will not until "all things are restored."

POINTS TO PONDER

No doubt, today, the world is experiencing a remarkable era. Around the globe, a new unified belief is gaining strength: Mankind's materialistic systems and globalism—in its simplest form, symbolized by the number 666—is unstoppable...or so most people think. A grand, new, gilded era of peace and economic prosperity seems assured. It would be tempting to agree.

Nowhere is this confidence currently more evident than in the fields of global finance, economics, and globalism. The popular and celebrated view is that globalization is leading to another golden age for mankind...the best and biggest ever...far better than the previous time that a similar confidence emerged. That period was referred to as the Gilded Age, occurring between 1880 and 1914. It also was a period of rapid technological progress and advances in globalization. Unfortunately, it ended horribly when the First World War erupted.

Solomon's later reign of self-reliant commercialism and dependence upon a prosperous economy ended badly. So will the current one. The only difference is that today's "gilded" confidence was and will be once again more swaggering, unified, and globally pervasive than ever. Its treacheries and deceits are therefore also much larger and more dangerous. We are surely experiencing now the systemic rise of the 666 system that will very soon intersect with the literal prophecies found in Revelation 13.

All of this may not sound very uplifting and optimistic. However, we can choose to view our current epoch from either of two perspectives: as did Abraham, "longing for a better country—a heavenly one" (Hebrews 11:16); or, as "friends of the world" (James 4:4). Actually, the former is an optimistic view; the latter a pessimistic one. It is only "friends of the world"—who have both feet firmly staked to hopes of a better and more comfortable place upon earth for a season—who will likely view the perspectives of a literally interpreted Bible as pessimistic.

What is the outlook for gold? According to the Bible, indeed, gold will someday again have a prominent role—very possibly in the millennial period, and surely during eternity. It seems sure that the gold in existence now will pass into the Millennium, remaining intact. Of course, that information will be of no practical use for Christians living today.

Still ahead is the period in which, "Violence has grown into a rod to punish wickedness; none of the people will be left, none of that crowd—no wealth, nothing of value" (Ezekiel 7:11). All the while, "'The silver is mine and the gold is mine,' declares the LORD Almighty" (Haggai 2:8).

For now, it is best to remember one fact: Gold has not yet assumed its millennial or eternal role. Therefore beware. We live in a time of great deception and corruption. And, try as the righteous might to make their way on this earth, the Bible says such conditions will continue to heighten until judgment. On this side of the Millennium, gold will remain manipulated, as everything else is in the financial realm. Continuing as before, "thieves break in and steal" (Matthew 6:19).

But, one day the restoration will come. Quoting Nathanael West, "And only when the Antichrist is overthrown, and the future temple built to Christ from all 'the precious things of all the nations,' will the whole world's wealth—the treasure of the world, its '666 talents of the gold of Ophir' be consecrated to His Service."[37]

We will see that future restoration, probably looking down from above. In the meantime, we turn from all the false idols of gold that the world may flaunt, instead seeking "purses for [ourselves] that will not wear out, a treasure in heaven that will not be exhausted, where no thief comes near and no moth destroys" (Luke 12:33). We "rejoice, though now for a little while [we] may have had to suffer grief in all kinds of trials. These have come so that [our] faith—of greater worth than gold, which perishes even though refined by fire—may be proved genuine and may result in praise, glory and honor when Jesus Christ is revealed" (1 Peter 1:6–7).

Figure #10

Prosperous Christian Money World
World GDP and Population Share of Christian Nations, %, 2007

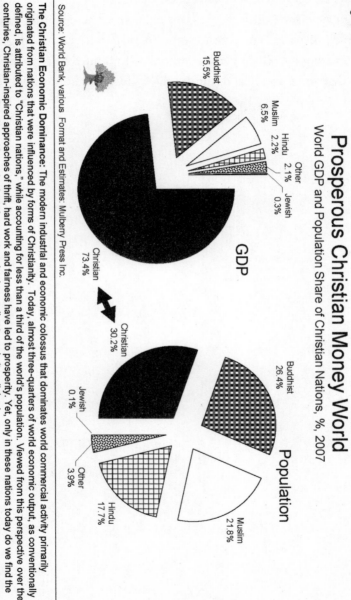

Source: World Bank, various Format and Estimates: Mulberry Press Inc.

The Christian Economic Dominance: The modern industrial and economic colossus that dominates world commercial activity primarily originated from nations that were influenced by forms of Christianity. Today, almost three-quarters of world economic output, as conventionally defined, is attributed to "Christian nations," while accounting for less than a third of the world's population. Viewed from this perspective over the centuries, Christian-inspired approaches of thrift, hard work and fairness have led to prosperity. Yet, only in these nations today do we find the influence of Prosperity Theology. (Countries have been categorized according to majority religion.)

9

THE CHRISTIAN
PROSPERITY CRISIS:
A DEFICIT OF TRUTH

Researchers point out that one of the main differences between the U.S. financial crash and others—for example, that of Japan in the 1990s—was that it was households (individuals and families) that became heavily overindebted. This was not the case in Japan, during the Asian crisis of the late 1990s, or in Scandinavia in the early 1990s. It was more the actions of companies and governments that led to these crises.

But why, in the case of America's situation, did people become so easily seduced into taking on such huge amounts of debt and into accepting the vain predictions of perpetual prosperity? Debt levels relative to household disposable income rose relentlessly to all-time highs in recent years. It appeared as if accountability and steward-ship were thrown to the wind. The sanguine belief that everlasting prosperity and ever-rising housing prices could be relied upon to bail everyone out of their debts and bills became widespread, as if divinely mandated.

Apparently, the Sugar Plum Fairy was dancing in many people's heads. Refinancing mortgages and cashing out equity became an annual exercise for some households. Wealth was an effortless prospect never to be constrained by budgets or insufficient income. Now, after the GFC has razed housing prices, the average American household- ers with mortgages find themselves with record-low equity in their homes. It is remarkable that so many families in the most prosperous nation in the world could become so impoverished so quickly.

Why did this happen? It may have to do with another main differ- ence between America and other countries. Without a doubt, America is the most Christian-professing, major nation in the world. It is also the only nation in the world that has been so profoundly infused with a post-modern, utilitarian aberration of biblical Christianity. This may seem a harsh statement; however, the facts well support it, as we will show.

But how could this be connected with the GFC? Actually, that reli- gious belief and philosophy have an impact on economies and financial markets is a well-established fact. After all, economies are nothing more than human beings acting upon their wants and beliefs. For example, why do Chinese households save so much? Could it be that their Confucian culture is predisposed to such behavior? Why did nations inspired by Christianity produce the Industrial Age of the 1800s? Or, why are Latin American countries so often vulnerable to inflationary collapse and corruption? Max Weber (see *The Protestant Work Ethic and the Spirit of Capitalism*[38]) and other social economists such as R. H. Tawney (who wrote *Religion and the Rise of Capitalism*[39]) studied these religious/economic connections. Beliefs do drive actions.

Only in North America do we find such a significant influence of the Prosperity Theology. It should not be surprising, then, that this teaching will have played a contributing (perhaps causal) role in America's late slide into financial crisis and decline. We want to examine this connection further by investigating some of the doctrinal distortions behind this movement that merges Christianity and money into the eschatological timeline.

Crucially, it can be shown that beliefs and behaviors allowed under the influences of Prosperity Theology align with developments that the Bible indicates will take place in the last days, right into the Great Tribulation.

DEEPLY ROOTED, FALSE PROSPERITY BELIEFS

While Prosperity Theology tends to be more associated with the charismatic segment of Protestant Christianity, it could be said that virtually all of North American Christianity has been infected with its influences. This perspective coexists comfortably with the ideology of the American dream. For centuries, the "Christian" nation of America has been a land of opportunity, espousing freedom, upward mobility, and success for all who seek it.

Prosperity thinking is therefore subtly embedded in the psyche of North American Christians. It is almost considered an entitlement in some circles. Of course, most will perhaps not swallow the extreme teachings and techniques of the likes of Benny Hinn, Kenneth Copeland, Creflo Dollar, and Peter Popoff—he of the "divine transfer"—and many others. After all, some of these more extreme teachers in this community even go as far as to claim that if you have much faith, you can "get wealth"—just send in your seed faith offering and you may get a "divine wealth transfer" or "a hundred-fold" return.

In this bartering system with the Most High, promoted by the above-mentioned teachers, one is taught to expect that God will reciprocate—actually multiply one's seed offering with a monetary or material blessing of some kind. It could be a sizable check arriving in your mailbox from a mysterious source or some other lucky happenstance. If you believe and have true faith, it is a sure payout, backed by a God who has the unlimited capability of redirecting money and earthy wealth upon Christians.

If this really is the case, then we have discovered a heaven-ordained Ponzi scheme. What is this? This fraudulent scheme was named after Charles Ponzi, one of the most famous American swindlers of all time. He promised people high returns on their investments by paying them with other people's new, incoming investment money. This is how Bernie Madoff amazingly managed to misappropriate over sixty billion dollars in recent years. As long as people were investing more in his fund than he was paying out, his actions went undetected.

Let's conservatively check out the math on the promises of the more extreme Prosperity Theology teachers. A favorite verse is found in Matthew 19:29, which reads: "And everyone who has left houses or brothers or sisters or father or mother or children or fields for my sake will receive a hundred times as much and will inherit eternal life." This indeed is a wonderful promise. However, it does not refer to earthly riches, as is taught by the more extreme prosperity promoters; rather, it refers to eternal reward.

For the purposes of illustration, let's assume that there are one hundred million real, "in-spirit-and-truth" Christians on earth (this being approximately 1.5 percent of the world's population), and that they will conservatively get a ten-fold return (not one hundred-fold). Next, if we take these one hundred million Christians from North America, where the average person has about $166,000 in net worth,[40] we quickly discover that such a promise can only apply to a select few. After all, with this kind of a guaranteed return, everyone would surely give the prosperity preacher everything he or she has. If donors then were to get a ten-fold payback on their contribution, it would amount to $16.5 trillion. How much is that? That is more than half of all the money deposits in all the banks of the world. How then could this work? It doesn't.

Think of the consequences if this and other similar teachings really were true. The world would have the greatest money inflation in history, and North America would have the most hedonistic Christians imaginable. Perhaps this result is not so far from the truth. Indeed, hedonism is a susceptible characteristic of this teaching.

THEOLOGICAL WEALTH DISTORTIONS EVERYWHERE

False gospels—no matter how subtle—are deadly, their heresies distorting virtually every doctrine, worldview, and eschatological perspective. In like manner, Prosperity Theology radiates its destruction into many doctrines and perspectives. If the case for its destructive contributions to America's recent demise is already not provocative enough, there is even more to consider.

A sure sign of all false gospels is their perspective on money. Every single false teaching or heresy mentioned in the New Testament epistles (and there are many) was associated with greed or an inordinate affection of money and wealth. This is as evident today as it was then. If anything is different, it is that some of these heretical perspectives have become much more systemized and sophisticated than they were in New Testament times.

Though beliefs held by certain Christian sects may appear rooted in scriptural teaching, it is disturbing to discover how subjective and unfounded these are. These beliefs simply do not hold up under the scrutiny of all Scripture. However, these do find good company in pagan and New Age religions. An entry on the Wikipedia online encyclopedia under the topic of "Prosperity Theology" points out that this "somewhat similar (yet strikingly different) belief appears in most 'New Thought' religions, Unity, Religious Science, and Divine Science denominations."[41] It should seem strange that such commonality is found with these other religions. It is not coincidental.

As we have already shown, Prosperity Theology does not even pass the test of common sense. Yet, one would at least expect to discover that if the promises of Prosperity Theology were legitimate and observable, its adherents indeed would be wealthier than the general population. Yet, the opposite is true.

According to the surveys of the Pew Forum on Religion & Public Life,[42] the average income level of all Christians is less than that of other faiths. For instance, the percentage of protestant Christians with incomes over one hundred thousand dollars per annum is 15 percent. This is less than Muslims (16 percent), Jews (46 percent), Buddhists (43 percent) and Hindus (43 percent).

Drilling down into comparisons between Christian denominations themselves, the same lack of confirmation is evident. If one assumes that Prosperity teaching is most prevalent in evangelical Pentecostal sects, the falsehood of this teaching is found to be most fraudulent. The Pentecostal demographic is the poorest of all, with the exception of Baptists in the Historically Black Tradition.[43] Forty-eight percent of Pentecostals have incomes less than thirty thousand dollars; only 7 percent have greater than one hundred thousand dollars per annum. That compares to 31 percent and 18 percent in the Christian population overall, respectively.

Clearly, the promises of Prosperity Theology are a hoax. Much worse allegations could be made. It would be considered a financial sham were its promoters seen to be preying on the hopelessness of its congregants. In that sense, it would not be much different than the consumer credit business. Just which demographic segment of society has historically proven to be the most profitable credit market for financial institutions…at least up until the global financial crisis? The poor. These people are required to pay high loan fees and interest rates, and they tend to run high balances on their credit cards with exorbitant charges. In like manner, this gospel is certainly not "releasing the oppressed," as was Christ's mission (Luke 4:18).

Why is it that Christians are so gullible? It may be for the same reason that the thickest complaint file of the Council of Better Business Bureaus in America is the category of religiously associated fraud. When con artists or teachers imply a relationship with God or make a purported scriptural reference promising prosperity, the wallets are opened unthinkingly. Why is it that charismatic churches time and again have proven themselves most vulnerable to the flimsiest of Ponzi schemes? It is both astounding and explainable.

Unfortunately, the false teachings about money and its roles in the world do not stop there.

MONEY, CHURCH AND THE END TIMES

A more recent theological invention with designs on money holds that the church will soon inherit great wealth here on earth. Apparently, not only are wealth and health the sure proof of the Christian life, the church will also yet have a great economic footprint in the world. Such ideas can only breed from the same general mist and non-literal perspectives of Scripture that give rise to Prosperity Theology.

Proponents of the expectation that the church will gain great wealth claim that the Bible supports this view. A key foundational reference is found in Proverbs 13:22, which states, "A good man leaves an inheritance for his children's children, but a sinner's wealth is stored up for the righteous." It is mainly from this single verse that the "wealth of the wicked" is conjured up for divine distribution to Christians and the church.

But really, what does this verse mean and to whom does it apply? A number of answers have gained popular support in recent years. Representing a growing view, C. Peter Wagner says, "...the body of Christ needs to come into alignment with God's declared purpose to release unprecedented amounts of wealth for the extension of His kingdom on earth."[44] Wagner is one of the key proponents of the view that the transfer of the "wealth of the wicked" is a premillennial event and is specifically meant for the church...more precisely, his own association of churches, which is under his senior apostolic authority. Dr. Wagner, who was also a major impetus behind the "Church Growth Movement" and the "Third Wave," has much influence. Supposedly, this wealth transfer is a glorious development of the last days that energizes and honors the church.

There are quite a number of loose interpretations of Proverbs 13:22. Applied to the church, this concept is also often linked with the teaching that a massive, worldwide, last-day ingathering of souls will yet occur. It is also well known that Prosperity Gospel preachers like to hang their theology on this verse in Proverbs, though they apply it to the individual Christian.

Can any of these ideas be broadly supported in Scripture? Will the church soon be showered with the wealth of the unrighteous, thus being able to fund the last, great global harvest of souls? We will investigate further.

UNDOCUMENTED TRANSFERS

Again quoting Dr. Wagner, "I think the time is ripe for those of us who are apostles to begin to understand the crucial role we have in

God's plan to release the wealth of the wicked for the advance of the kingdom of God."[45]

But what does the Bible say? Pursuing a historical-grammatical interpretation—in other words, interpreting the Bible as it reads—try as we might, we cannot find this view supported in the Bible.

Dealing first with the "wealth transfer" notion, indeed, we do find that there is a great wealth transfer prophesied in Scripture. However, it has nothing to do with the church, but rather applies to Israel and the millennial period. Many more Scripture verses connect this event to Israel, rather than with the church. Here are six:

1. "You will feed on the wealth of nations, and in their riches you will boast" (Isaiah 61:6).
2. "Then you will look and be radiant, your heart will throb and swell with joy; the wealth on the seas will be brought to you, to you the riches of the nations will come" (Isaiah 60:5).
3. "I will extend peace to her like a river, and the wealth of nations like a flooding stream" (Isaiah 66:12).
4. "Rise and thresh, O Daughter of Zion, for I will give you horns of iron; I will give you hoofs of bronze and you will break to pieces many nations. You will devote their ill-gotten gains to the LORD, their wealth to the Lord of all the earth" (Micah 4:13).
5. "Your gates will always stand open, they will never be shut, day or night, so that men may bring you the wealth of the nations—their kings led in triumphal procession" (Isaiah 60:11).
6. "The wealth of all the surrounding nations will be collected—great quantities of gold and silver and clothing" (Zechariah 14:14).

Additional indications of a great wealth transfer are also prophesied in the Old Testament. Their context refers to the same general time—late in the Tribulation and early millennial period. For example, a prophecy applying to Tyre—this city prefiguring the godless commercial systems that align with the Babylon the Great of Revelation 18—speaks of wealth being set aside for "those who live before the Lord":

> At the end of seventy years, the LORD will deal with Tyre. She will return to her hire as a prostitute and will ply her trade with all the kingdoms on the face of the earth. Yet her profit and her earnings will be set apart for the LORD; they will not be stored up or hoarded. Her profits will go to those who live before the LORD, for abundant food and fine clothes. (Isaiah 23:17–18)

While this is not an exhaustive list of references, we have at least established broad, scriptural support for Israel being the recipient. Interestingly, we cannot find one verse in the New Testament that even indirectly refers to a great, end-time wealth transfer to the church. Even the book of Revelation is silent on this topic, though it refers to the destruction of the wealth of Babylon the Great, which will "never be recovered" (Revelation 18:14). That event plays a defining role in the final global financial apocalypse, which we will outline in Chapter 14. Assuredly, if such massive wealth were to be transferred to the church, support for this concept would have been found in the New Testament. Instead, there we only find admonishments about the deceitfulness of wealth and how the faith of many will grow cold due to the cares of this life. It requires a new band of so-called apostolic prophets to supply new revelation to support such scripturally unfounded ideas.

THE EFFECTS ARE SUBTLE BUT DANGEROUS

Our review of the more extreme aspects of Prosperity Teaching and related misconceptions is not meant to attack anyone personally. Rather, we seek to stand up for truth and contest dangerous teaching. Yes, many prosperity teachers may preach inspiring sermons, be of good character, and not even realize that they are influenced by Prosperity Theology. But that still would not be sufficient excuse or render this teaching harmless.

In the physical world, purity is highly prized. Were we to purchase a bar of twenty-four-carat gold, we would expect it to be 100-percent pure. When we buy gasoline for our cars or are prescribed penicillin tablets, we expect the contents to meet the specifications on the label. Anything else is fraud and deliberate deception. The same is true of any teaching that does not meet the exact specifications of the gospel and the Bible.

Satan, the Bible tells us, is a cunning deceiver (John 8:44) and masquerader (2 Corinthians 11:5). If we devised a plan to poison someone with arsenic, we would surely know how to secret its ingestion. We might hide it in a slice of sweet apple pie covered with ice cream. Effective rat poison is designed the same way. It is deliberately manufactured to be tasty and nutritious. Even though only a very small percentage of its content is poison, it is enough to kill the rodent. The fact that the other 99 percent of its ingredients is life-sustaining food—or that that the other 99 percent of teaching is sound—does not prevent bad consequences.

Then what are the evil consequences of Prosperity Theology, and why does it fit into the eschatological timeline? There are a number of answers to those questions, some of which are deviously subtle. First, Prosperity Theology that overly focuses upon material riches and physical well-being acclimatizes Christians to feel comfortable in the realm of Mammon…in the worldly kingdom that will one day pass away and that only offers fleeting pleasures. The risks and rewards of the material realm are put onto a spiritual level. The opposing kingdoms of God and Money are confused. Monetary fortunes—the ups and downs of the bank account and investment portfolios—are interpreted as the omens of God. For example, if people were to lose their jobs, God is punishing them. On the other hand, if one were to receive an inheritance from a distant relative, then that person is being divinely blessed. That perspective is not biblical…it's certainly not found in the New Testament.

This teaching about money promotes the erroneous idea that the Lord operates the way many humans do—with an eye only on money and material things. Nothing could be farther from the truth; God never "bribes" Christians to love or obey Him with financial abundance or material gifts. They confuse the domain of Mammon for the kingdom of God. The danger of this perspective is amply evidenced by the recent, disastrous global financial crisis. Because stock markets and housing prices were soaring, people who were entranced by the Mammon spirit uncritically received it as a blessing. To them, it was a sign of God's favor upon America. In reality, it was a deliberate and deceptive trap. Today, as a consequence, America is weakened.

Prosperity Theology also can lead to slovenly stewardship. Why practice sensible budgeting if I have a few divine lottery tickets soon to pay off with a big win? With a hundred-fold return promised, why not spend the money in advance? Or, if a finance company approves an option mortgage with no money down, is it really a blessed intervention by God to provide a house that is bigger than I need and cannot afford? With this kind of undisciplined thinking, personal accountability can go out the window. Such teaching in spirit does not promote sensible stewardship.

CONSEQUENCES INTERTWINE WITH
END-TIME DEVELOPMENTS

The deadly mindset of Prosperity Theology promotes at least three other dangers, the worst of all. First, it greases the slide to the final grand ecumenism—the perversion that merges the worship of God and Mammon. Did Christ really say that we cannot serve two masters? Yes, of course. Matthew 6:24 and Luke 16:13 say we can serve either Mammon or God, but not both. But if we redefine wealth and money as the sure manifestation of God's blessing; if we redefine a massive commercialization and globalization of the world as godly because its goal is to free the world of poverty; and if we consider "capitalism" and other "-isms" biblically endorsed concepts, then it only follows that manipulated global wealth booms must be the sure working of a pleased God. That is precisely the type of world shown in Revelation 17 and 18, which depicts a worldwide marriage of religion and commerce.

The second disaster of America's collision with the effortless prosperity pipe dream is that it is now reduced and ridiculed in the world's geopolitical sphere. This is not a good sign for Israel. Political leadership will not have much difficulty abandoning Israel if this facilitates the nation's return to bubbly prosperity.

Finally, we know that a time will come when the entire world will fall for the "prosperity teaching" ruse. An Antichrist will stand up and deliver what appear to be the promise of prosperity and perhaps even the eradication of poverty. It will sound good to the "mammonish" mind. Take the "mark" and you will be assured of prosperous future.

WHINING, SUCKLING CHRISTIANS

The implicit message of Prosperity Theology is that the evidence of God's blessing—yes, even the validation of one's salvation—is a high standard of living as defined by the world's dominant humanist perspective. This view does not stand up to any scriptural scrutiny. It is not biblical. Not one mention or even an indirect statement supporting this doctrine is found in the New Testament. If that were so, we must conclude that Jesus Christ, all the apostles, and most first-century Christians were unsuccessful "under comers." They had not discovered the Prosperity Gospel and never entered into its blessings. One wonders why one of the first names for Christians in the first century was "Ebionite," meaning "the poor ones."

Prosperity Theology is an errant belief system heavily laced with paganism and candy-coated with Christian form and words. It is a heresy that has played a role in bringing America to its ruin, turning cold the faith of many. It may eventually reveal that many of America's progressive Christians never had a true conversion in the first place. It is not a gospel but rather an idolatry.

While we may decry the hedonism of elites and the fraudulent thefts of Wall Street captains, a special blame must be reserved for the false shepherds who have crept into the pulpits this past half century. They did not storm the pulpits by accident. What was not preached was self denial (Matthew 16:24), that "we are not our own" (Romans 14:7), or that the ultimate purpose of our existence is the glorification of God, not the satisfaction of fleshly stomachs and glands.

As a result, high-income countries such as the U.S., Canada, and others are full of baby Christians, still dieting on milk, who cannot deal with the "meat" of reality and responsibility. Paul thought such Christians contemptible, saying: "You need milk, not solid food!" (Hebrews 5:12); "You are worldly" (1 Corinthians 3:3); and "...solid food is for the mature, who by constant use have trained themselves to distinguish good from evil" (Hebrew 5:14).

The greatest tragedy is that many of these "baby Christians" will give up on their faith and begin to hate God during current and coming tough economic times. The "different" God, they had been taught, was the proverbial big sugar daddy who showered baubles, toys, success, and acceptance upon them every time He was called on the cell phone. To them, God was a means, not an end.

And now, just because a "Darwinian" world economic system has preyed upon and destroyed their earthly wealth, they no longer want treasures in heaven. Could it be that some people were never interested in eternal wealth in the first place? Letting go of everlasting riches for a bit of temporal luxury is bad investment policy in the extreme. At such times as this, we must be resolute not to look to the left or right, but toward our never-ending destinies and promises.

What Christians might not be tempted to think that God and country have abandoned them? Instead of the American dream or the soothing promises of the preacher, disappointing hardships and troubles are being experienced.

Many Christians would be inclined to whine to God, as Jeremiah did: "Will you be to me like a deceptive brook, like a spring that fails?" (Jeremiah 15:18). Jeremiah figured that since he was walking with God and answering His calling, he deserved special treatment. He bargained with God, saying, "I never sat in the company of revelers, never made merry with them; I sat alone because your hand was on me, and you had filled me with indignation. Why is my pain unending and my wound grievous and incurable?" (Jeremiah 15:17–18).

How did God respond? He didn't even acknowledge the complaint. He simply said this: "If you repent, I will restore you that you may serve me" (Jeremiah 15:19).

No doubt, all twelve of the New Testament apostles settled this same issue in a satisfactory manner. They were doing the Lord's will and as a result were all blessed with rich robes and fine foods…or were they? Actually, directly to the contrary. Eleven of them died an unnatural death. All of them physically suffered for their beliefs. Was this just? Paul said, "Rather, as servants of God we commend ourselves in every way: in great endurance; in troubles, hardships and distresses; in beatings, imprisonments and riots; in hard work, sleepless nights and hunger; in purity, understanding, patience and kindness; in the Holy Spirit and in sincere love…" (2 Corinthians 6:4–6).

THOUGHTS TO PONDER

The apostate church and its many daughters, shown as Mystery Babylon the whore in Revelation 17, are well on their way to a full union with commercial Babylon of Revelation 17. The grand, last-day ecumenical lie of serving both God and Mammon is far advanced. Since this is an impossibility—we "cannot serve both God and Money" (Matthew 6:24)—it is really a movement in which Mammon has robed itself in the garb of religion and apparent "Christian godliness."

The true church of the last days, if anything, is more of a remnant than it is resplendent with wealth. Revelation 3:8 says that the church of the "open door" is weak and feeble, far from being imbued with worldly power and wealth. This little Philadelphian band of believers is promised, "Since you have kept my command to endure patiently, I will also keep you from the hour of trial that is going to come upon the whole world to test those who live on the earth" (Revelation 3:10). If the Third Wave movements are correct, one wonders why it is the rich Laodicean church that is being reprimanded by Christ.

There is great eternal value to be found in the privilege of serving Him: the undeserved promise of eternal life and the indescribable prospect of being in His presence forevermore. However, admittedly, this is not a very consumer-friendly interpretation of the gospel. The modern pagan we unveiled in an earlier chapter would not be interested. This person is instead looking for temporal benefits and payoffs in the here and now. Such people have no concept of eternal riches or a commitment to the inviolability of biblical truth. Their point of reference is earthly and their timeframe very short.

Seen from this set of values, Christianity is indeed more attractive if it provides sanctification of human esteem and a self-help regimen to personal betterment and prosperity in this life. In this view, eternity gets short shrift because it is not seen as real, or as promising sufficient gratification to the earth-bound consumer. This brand of Christianity requires no sacrifice and finds a comfortable friendship with the world. Christianity then becomes a personal entitlement contract to prosperity in the here and now, and nothing more.

As we have shown, gospels have been invented or bent to serve the lust for temporal comforts and wealth. Where there is demand, a product will soon be created. There is no caution, no fear of the dangers of wealth the Bible so clearly lays out. According to these new revelations, not only are individual Christians fated to be healthy, wealthy, and wise, but the church itself, whose kingdom is not to be of this world, will come into great earthly wealth. We see that some churches today do hanker after worldly power and have set their eyes upon monetary wealth. Apparently, without laying one's life down for Christ and taking up a personal cross, one can just use the principles in the Bible to become prosperous and lead a well-adjusted life in every way. This is one of the biggest and sorriest misinterpretations ever perpetrated. It is a major reason real faith is running cold.

That is exactly why the present juncture in America is so terrifying. The GFC will reveal the conditionality of many people's faith and its connection to prosperity. Just what will be the response to the deep economic troubles that have come upon America (now and in the future)? Will there be rebellion and anarchy as people jettison their faith in an untrustworthy God? Or, will there be repentance and contrition, as people respond maturely to economic disciplining? It can only be one or the other. There can be no middle position.

We have to admit that either outcome is possible. It is not scare-mongering to suggest that anarchy will occur if trends do not change. After all, it would be understandable. Hasn't society ingrained in us the right to prosperity…the good life…and effortless, endless progress toward greater wealth, indulgence, and satiation? Haven't countless pastors told us that prosperity is the emblem and purpose of our Chris-tian faith? It would be no surprise, therefore, if many "fair-weather" Christians turned on God, accusing Him of not having kept His end of the bargain following the calamities of the GFC.

What God would allow such economic hardships and prove to be such a "false brook" of prosperity? Contractual Christians and most others would reject such a God, and instead turn to the promises of government or some future demagogue. And, if in turn these don't end the economic sufferings, would not some resort to rioting and pillaging? One would certainly hope not, although some are actu-ally predicting such an outcome. One reputable trend watcher, Gerald Celente, chief executive officer of Trend Research Institute, goes so far as to predict that America will "plunge to the status of an undeveloped nation" and that "America's going through a transition the likes of which no one is prepared for."[46] He predicts that by December 2012, a consumer Christmas will only be a memory, since getting food on the table—not exchanging gifts—will be the priority. This outcome is certainly possible. People who become angry with God, abandoning eternal perspectives and the ideas of sin and judgment, will be vulner-able to fall into such anarchy and lawlessness.

Like the earth dwellers during the Tribulation period, according to the Bible, these people put their idolatries ahead of obedience and repentance. On four separate occasions, we read in the book of Revelation that despite the wrath and punishment suffered for their idolatries, earth dwellers will not let go of their idols (Revelation 9:20–21; 16:9, 11, 21). While that time is in the future and only relates to those who refuse to recognize and acknowledge the lordship of Jesus Christ, an inverse form of this trial is occurring now. The faith of Christians who have been tainted by the prosperity teachings is now under vicious attack. In a sense, it is indeed, as I mentioned earlier, "Apocalypse Now" for Western Christians.

JEWS:
OUR BROTHERS

Figure #11

World Jewish Population & Diaspora

Population Distribution by Country (2006)

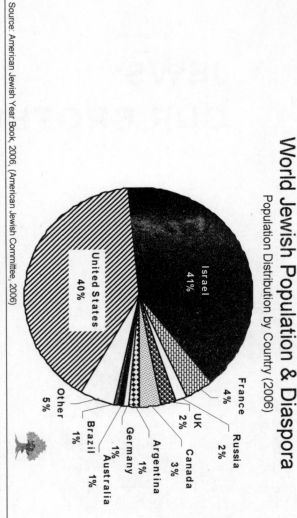

Israel
41%

United States
40%

France
4%

Russia
2%

UK
2%

Canada
3%

Argentina
1%

Germany
1%

Australia
1%

Brazil
1%

Other
5%

Source: American Jewish Year Book, 2006, (American Jewish Committee, 2006)

The Shrinking Jew. As of the end of 2006, for the first time since the country Israel was reborn, the largest number of Jews worldwide lived in that country. Up to that time in the Post WWII period, the greatest number of world Jewry lived in the US. Significantly, this shift is attributable more to out-marriage and slower population growth within the Diaspora Jews than immigration. Also, Jews living in Israel have a higher population growth and a low rate of out-marriage. The world's Jewish population continues to shrink relative to the rest of the world. While there were 7.5 Jews per 1,000 people in the world in 1938, today there are only 3.5.

10

JEWS, GENTILES, AND MONEY: AGAIN AT THE CROSSROADS OF HISTORY?

It happened again just recently. A supposedly mature, evangelical Christian spewed an anti-Semitic remark during a conversation. The comment was something to the effect that Jews are despicable because they are in positions of control and wealth in the world today. I was deeply grieved. Yet, knowing the history of the Jews and the Bible, I was not shocked. Once again, God's sentence upon this special people more than twenty-five hundred years ago found a willing participant among the Christian Gentiles.

Many anti-Semitic Christian Gentiles there remain. In fact, in one form or another—anti-Zionism being just one form—there is a surge of anti-Semitism today. Sadly, this is also true among supposed Christians, both individually and institutionally.

It is a topic to take very seriously. Why? Because the Bible clearly warns of serious consequences. This is sufficient reason for Christians—in fact, for everyone—to take heed about participating in any form of this heinous sin. But there is one other urgent reason. It has to do with money, as the title of this chapter indicates. As we observed in the conclusions to Chapter 3, the many and atrocious persecutions of this people over the centuries have had an alarming correlation with the aftermath of financial and economic crisis. It is therefore an extremely important topic. As we will see, it likely also intersects with the fate of America.

Before we tackle this topic, however, a word of warning to Gentiles: Approach the subject with great humility. For He is the Judge, the One who says, "It is mine to avenge; I will repay" (Deuteronomy 32:35). For all will fall under judgment—Jew, Gentile, and Christian.

WHY THE JEWS? ACCORDING TO SCRIPTURE

To ensure that we address our topic from a firm foundation, we must begin with Scripture. After all, it is a document written exclusively by the Jews. We must first remember who it was that made a covenant with Abraham and issued the pronouncements upon all of his children and heirs. It was Jehovah who inspired all the prophecies of the Hebrew prophets.

These prophecies applying to the Hebrews—almost all of them very plain and clear—are true and reliable, no matter what modern theologians may think or what preferential positions or vested interests some denominations may like to appropriate for themselves. Just as all of the prophecies concerning the Jews have been accurately fulfilled to date, we can be assured that those applying to the future will be fully fulfilled as well.

The early prophets clearly outlined the consequences of disobedience for Israel and Judah ahead of the fact, demonstrating God's fore-knowledge of their choice, as well as their promised and yet-to-come millennial role.

Seemingly countless times—in fact, many tens of times—the Israelites were warned that they would be scattered to the four corners and all nations of the world. God's punishment and discipline for this servant people would be severe: "I will pursue them with the sword, famine and plague and will make them abhorrent to all the kingdoms of the earth and an object of cursing and horror, of scorn and reproach, among all the nations where I drive them" (Jeremiah 29:18–19). Judah would be scattered, its people facing conditions of scorn and persecution during that time of dispersion.

But, crucially, something else was also prophesied: the Jews would be restored. This wouldn't be simply a restoration to Old Testament primacy. No, the Jews would be placed at the head of the nations—in other words, at the head of the entire world. Because of this, we know the Jews will surely one day rule the world and reign from Zion. The conditional blessings set down by Moses, which the Jewish people effectively disowned, would be superseded by a gracious God who would remain faithful to His promises to the patriarchs.

For Gentiles who have oppressed the Israelites, there is one more prophecy to acknowledge: "May the praise of God be in their mouths and a double-edged sword in their hands, to inflict vengeance on the nations and punishment on the peoples, to bind their kings with fetters, their nobles with shackles of iron, to carry out the sentence written against them" (Psalm 149:6–9). Just as played out in the book of Esther, the Jews themselves will be used as the instruments of God's vengeance.

These developments—all of which will come to pass in the future—hold some great admonitions for all people—Christians, Jews, and Gentiles alike.

Why the Chosen People

Why did God choose the Hebrews as His people? This topic is a stumbling block for many. Why did He make one people superior…superior in the sense that they might be "super humans"? To begin with, this question reveals an incorrect perspective.

God did not choose the Hebrews for their greatness or superiority in any sense. Moses said, "The Lord did not set his affection on you and choose you because you were more numerous than other peoples, for you were the fewest of all peoples" (Deuteronomy 7:7).

To believe God needs superior numbers, great populations, or mighty armies contradicts Scripture. Paul said: "But God chose the foolish things of the world to shame the wise; God chose the weak things of the world to shame the strong. He chose the lowly things of this world and the despised things—and the things that are not—to nullify the things that are, so that no one may boast before him" (1 Corinthians 1:27–29).

Most Christians who have received undeserved grace would identify with this perspective of the "lowly things of this world," having no reason to boast. The same applies to the Hebrew. Therefore, the question of selection may never be answered or understood. For the Lord says, "I will have mercy on whom I will have mercy, and I will have compassion on whom I will have compassion" (Exodus 3:19).

A point to recognize in the case of the Hebrews is made by Michael Medved, a high-profile talk-show host and author who is a Jew. "According to Scripture, the Jews have been chosen for distinct responsibilities, not for unique privileges: we accept special obligations, rather than claiming special power."[47] The Hebrews were not chosen to have special privileges or might to take over the world, but rather were given a task. "I will also make you a light for the Gentiles, that you may bring my salvation to the ends of the earth" (Isaiah 49:6).

Many times throughout Scripture, Israel is referred to as "My servant" for the very reason that the Hebrews were selected—in fact, a people taken out and formed—to be servants of God. "But you Israel, are My servant, Jacob, whom I have chosen, the descendants of Abraham My friend" (Isaiah 41:8, KJV). God referred to Abraham, the progenitor of all Hebrews, as "my servant Abraham" (Genesis 26:24). In contrast, believers in Christ (whether Gentile or Jew) become God's spiritual children. "Yet to all who received him, to those who believed in his name, he gave the right to become children of God—children born not of natural descent, nor of human decision or a husband's will, but born of God" (John 1:12-13). According to Scripture, therefore, it will be the Jews who finally spread the gospel to the entire world after the church is gone.

THE BLESSINGS OF THE JEWS

The Bible clearly says that the Jew will be a blessing to the world in many ways, also during the Diaspora. "As you have been an object of cursing among the nations, O Judah and Israel, so will I save you, and you will be a blessing" (Zechariah 8:13).

Possibly without major exception, every nation that has given harbor to the Jews has eventually prospered and risen in prominence. For example, during the Golden Age of Poland of the mid-1800s, approximately 30 percent of all Jewry was estimated to be living in that country at that time. Later, this successful population of Jews was severely persecuted. Not surprisingly, it has been a long time since Poland has played a significant role in the world. This same observation applies to Spain after the 1400s. Before that time, Jews were a large reason for the prosperity and progress of Spain. Spain rapidly declined after 1492, the year the Jews were expelled.

Indeed, the Jew has brought great blessings to the world in many ways, just as the Bible said: "The remnant of Jacob will be in the midst of many peoples like dew from the LORD, like showers on the grass, which do not wait for man or linger for mankind" (Micah 5:7).

Other examples could be cited, including Russia and even the Ottoman Empire, a Muslim empire that at one time allowed a great deal of freedom to the Jews (however, not at other times, or hardly so in Turkey today). But how does this observation reflect upon the contemporary world ? Frankly, it begs the question of the role of the Jew in America, where approximately 60 percent of the Diaspora Jews live. Consider that the period since the 1950s has been dubbed by some as the "Golden Age of the American Jew." We will come back to examine the significance of that observation. But first, it is crucial that we understand the impact of God's decree of dispersal upon this people and its connection to the Jews' cycle of success and persecution.

THE GREAT DYSFUNCTIONAL BLESSING

The Jews' state of separateness, combined with cycles of oppression and their fervent belief that they have a future, contributed to the crucible out of which were forged great achievements. This incredible state that God has cast upon them—in a sense, ensuring their survival and the fulfillment of the prophecies—brings to mind Johnny Cash's famous song, "A Boy Named Sue."

Not at all attempting to belittle this topic, consider the song's central message. The story is told of a father who would not be around to raise his son, so he named him "Sue." Because of the ridicule and trouble this name would bring the boy, the father was sure his son would develop the strength and resilience it would take to survive.

In this sense, God has also marked the Jew. After He divorced and abandoned them to the Diaspora and they continued to stay separate and practice the Sabbath, the factors contributing to their persecution has pressured them to excel and survive. Albert Einstein is reported to have said, "It may be thanks to anti-Semitism that we are able to preserve our existence as a race; that at any rate is my belief."

So we see that a repetitive and chronically depressing cycle has played out over the millennia. Throughout their long history of oppression and abandonment, wherever and whenever Jews have been allowed an environment to do so, they have prospered. The nations in which they have resided have also prospered. Then, usually after a period of success and conspicuous prominence, jealousy or some other type of loathing has set in and the Jews have been again expelled, suppressed, and murdered. There are many reasons for this, but one factor has certainly always played a role.

MONEY AND THE JEW

The world is thankful for the many achievements of the Jewish people, the many Nobel Prize laureates they have produced (about one-fifth have been Jewish), the great inventions, and the arts. We see that the Jews have excelled in almost every category of achievement for which Gentiles laud them. Few would feel jealous that many of the greatest violin soloists have been Jewish, or that an outsized number of the Boston Symphonic Orchestra members may be Jews.

Yet, one area has almost always unleashed a renewed hatred of the Jews—"the love of money." It would be more apt to term this the "jealousy of the Gentile." Why is it that Jews are legendarily connected to the topic of money in the world's eyes? Is this reputation deserved? Much lore perpetuates this image from the earliest times. For instance, the Koran (written in the seventh century) makes this claim about the

Jews: "They delight in twisting words and distort even the word of God. They break their contracts and are treacherous. They hound the people for money. They boast of special privileges in the life to come, yet cling tenaciously to life on this earth."

We now are treading on a charged topic and therefore need to proceed with great care. Before considering this issue any further, a review of history and hard facts is necessary to ensure that we present a balanced answer.

To begin with, that money should be an effective instrument for inciting the persecution of the Jews or any people should be no surprise. It is important to understand the diabolic and dark dynamics at play here so as not to fall prey to this satanic scheme. Remember that the love of money strikes to the very core of mankind's susceptibly corrupt nature. According to the apostle Paul, "the love of money is the root of all kinds of evil" (1 Timothy 6:10). An improper attitude toward money, whether through jealousy or obsession, is an extremely potent lure to destruction for both Jew and Gentile.

The second point to realize is that there is no mystery to the basic task of accumulating capital. Simply viewed, it takes time, disciplined saving, and only a little bit of extra effort. If you were to save only 2 percent more of your earnings than your neighbor every year, and work only 2 percent harder (everything else being equal), it would take only twenty-five to thirty-five years for you to become twice as wealthy as your neighbor. That is a significant difference achieved over a relatively short time. Yet this illustration has been upon conservative assumptions. It is not unusual to see immigrants work harder—in fact, much harder. Why? They may feel a more urgent need to establish themselves. Imagine how much more disciplined and striving would be a people that throughout history had been persecuted, often on the move, striving for survival. It is no surprise that such people would be inclined to become wealthy if allowed the opportunity.

Though Jews in America have become wealthier than the general population in the past half century, the difference is exaggerated to the point of an anti-Semitic caricature. Many immigrant groups have risen to prominence and levels of above-average achievement in one sense or another. This is true for Asians, Chinese, and others, particularly for Hindus. They have higher incomes as a group on average; greater concentration in professional job categories such as medicine and academia; and higher education. Quoting a report from the Pew Foundation, "Nearly half of Hindus in the U.S., one-third of Jews, and a quarter of Buddhists have obtained post-graduate education, compared with only about one in ten of the adult population overall."[48] Then why is it so accepted to demonize the Jews in this respect?

Even in public life, Jewish people are commonly vilified. While many people believe various Jewish lobby groups have a significant influence upon the American government, their impact is certainly debatable. It could just as easily be said and proven that Arabs have an even greater influence upon America. There is no contesting the fact that the United States, for example, has a very special relationship with Saudi Arabia and even Kuwait. We have sent a number of armies into the Middle East to protect the interests of these countries. However, for some reason, the influence of Arabian oil does not elicit as many howls of protest.

We come back to this main point: Whenever the Jews have been allowed to prosper, eventually money has usually played a role in a following persecution. Invariably, the Gentiles took great pleasure in stripping the Jews of their homes and wealth. Even governments and kings would participate in these confiscations. For example, the king of France, Philip Augustus, during the expulsion of the Jews in 1182 AD, confiscated Jewish wealth, ransoming their release from imprisonment and allowing Christians to repudiate their debts to Jews.

Another example was King Ferdinand of Spain, who during the eviction of the Jews in1492, similarly required that 20 percent of all debt repudiation to Jews accrue to him.

THE JEW: PROOF OF GOD'S EXISTENCE

King Louis XIV is said to have asked Blaise Pascal, the renowned French philosopher, to provide him with proof of the existence of God. Apparently without any hesitation, Pascal replied, "Why, the Jews, your Majesty—the Jews." The Bible-believing Christian would agree. How can one not see any Jew today as living proof of God's existence and faithfulness?

Yet, even as the history of the Hebrews testifies to the glory of God, He set them aside for a time. According to the Bible, a final "time of the Gentiles" was decreed. Jesus Himself identified this time, saying, "They will fall by the sword and will be taken as prisoners to all the nations. Jerusalem will be trampled on by the Gentiles until the times of the Gentiles are fulfilled" (Luke 21:24).

That era certainly came to pass and continues today. Nebuchadnezzar, the Babylonian king, destroyed Jerusalem and the Temple, and deported a large number of the Jewish population to Babylon. From that time on (although some might argue that the inception of this period was with the church), it would be the time of the Gentiles. The world would be ruled by the non-Hebrew nations.

According to Sir Robert Anderson, the famed nineteenth-century author of *The Coming Prince*, now is the sixth, final, and longest period that the Hebrews or their descendants have been under the domination of the Gentiles—the Diaspora.[49] Anderson points out that the Hebrews had been dominated by Gentiles five specific and separate periods before this present age. "They became slaves to king of Mesopotamia for eight years, to the king of Moab for eighteen years, to the king of Canaan for twenty years, to the Midianites for seven years and finally to the Philistines for forty years," he noted.

Yet, despite the Bible's clear testimony that it remains the era of the Gentiles at this very time, one of the most nefarious and stubborn beliefs about Jews around the world is that they are colluding to control the world. How could this possibly be true?

JEWS: RUNNING THE WORLD TODAY?

The biblical book of Esther is prophetic, though in a different form than the spoken foretellings of the prophets. The entire book is an allegory (better said, a foreshadowing) of what the Jews would face during the Diaspora. The story takes place only two generations after the time when the Jews were given the freedom to resettle and rebuild Jerusalem. The vast majority (probably nine-tenths) chose to stay in Babylon. Later, some moved elsewhere, including Susa. In the book of Esther we see them prospering in this Persian city under King Xerxes. Esther and Mordecai, the main Jewish players in this account, both pierce into the highest echelons of that society. Extra-biblical records of that era in Susa count many Jews as prosperous merchants, traders, and bankers at that time.

In the Esther account, we see that the Jews were seen as separate, yet "Jewishness" was not necessarily a religious identification, as with many Jews today. (Interestingly, no reference to God is made in the entire book of Esther.) We also note that Jews were prone to persecution. An important perspective of the story is that while the Jews would indeed prosper and gain great influence during times of the

Diaspora, they would still be subject to the Gentile. Xerxes, a Gentile, was still very much in charge. So it is today in the world, even in the United States, with its relatively large population of Jews.

While many Jews have had influential positions in government (for example, Henry Kissinger, or Paul Wolfowitz) and may have an outsized presence on Wall Street or in Hollywood, it nevertheless remains the times of the Gentiles. The Jews remain small in number (a little more than one-fifth of 1 percent of the world population). True to Scripture, "The LORD will scatter you among the peoples, and only a few of you will survive among the nations to which the LORD will drive you" (Deuteronomy 4:27).

It is also true that many Jews have been prominent or in the forefront of both good and perhaps controversial movements. Because Jews could be found at the edge of change and of major world trends, whether social, moral, or economic, they may be perceived as influential beyond their numbers. But the aspect to see is that while influential, they have usually been on both sides of any debate. Think of the late 1800s, before two million Jews left Russia. Jews made up a large portion of the two main opposition parties of that time, both the Bolshevik and the Menshevik parties. We see this division of the Jews today in America. Jews actively exercise their opinions and influence on both sides of any spectrum.

These are some of the reasons we can ignore the conspiracy theories that are claimed to be commandeered by Jews. As Bible-believing Christians, we have every reason to believe in another conspiratorial agenda, one that the Bible lays out. In the end, God acting in wrath will cause the Jews to finally recognize the Messiah, "the one that they have pierced" (Zechariah 12:10). Then, indeed, He will place the Jew at the head of the world. However, this will not happen before the time of the Gentiles has ended.

SMUG CHRISTIANITY

Jews have been horribly persecuted by the Gentiles. Of this there can be no doubt. But what of the Christians? Sadly, history records that many so-called Christians have assumed a supposedly righteous role in persecuting the Jews. Here also, the atrocities are beyond count.

For example, most infamously, the Crusades produced incredible horrors against Jews in the name of Christ. Heinous acts were endorsed from high up, from the Vicars of Christ (the popes) to the state or the opportunist soldier. Typically, according to Emico the Wicked, a German noble who led a rabble of crusaders (German and French) to slaughter defenseless Jews in Mainz in 1096 AD, "Now let us avenge the blood of 'the hanged one.'" Or, consider this declared cause of a statewide action, as recorded in a royal decree, "We, in requital for their crimes and for the honor of the Crucified, have banished them from our realm as traitors." [50]

Countless other statements could be quoted that are equally misguided and self serving. The question is begged: If the oppressions of the Gentiles will some day be punished (see Psalms 149:6–9), then what of the crimes of so-called Christians? Could it be possible that parts of the true church have a hand in these sins? Here, too, prophecy provides some understanding.

THE JEW AND THE TRAVESTY OF THE FALSE CHURCH

The prophet Micah uttered a puzzling prophecy:

> Do not gloat over me, my enemy! Though I have fallen, I
> will rise. Though I sit in darkness, the LORD will be my

light. Because I have sinned against him, I will bear the Lord's wrath, until he pleads my case and establishes my right. He will bring me out into the light; I will see his righteousness. Then my enemy will see it and will be covered with shame, she who said to me, "Where is the LORD your God?" My eyes will see her downfall; even now she will be trampled underfoot like mire in the streets. (Micah 7:9–10)

Who is the enemy here, the entity addressed as "she" in this verse? Nowhere in this chapter is "she" identified. By deduction, however, we propose an easy identity for her. It cannot be Israel itself, nor can it be the church (which, at the point of fulfillment of this prophecy, is already gone). There is only one other female candidate the Bible mentions at the time of the Tribulation: the harlot, the apostate global religion depicted in Revelation 17.

We therefore know that persecution of the Jews, in whatever form, is a mark of the false church (though surely, some individual Christians have erred in this way). While this persecution has already occurred over thousands of years, the capstone of this insurrection still lies ahead. And, the precedent and mindset for this taking place is already well set.

Many church denominations endorse the idea of Replacement Theology, the notion that the church has replaced the Jews and thus all the promises to the Jews have been transferred to the church. This essentially dubs the Jews as of no more consequence. Because God is finished with them, this thinking goes, the Gentiles can do to them as they wish, for there is no more eternal consequence.

Suffice it to say that this view "distort[s] the words of the living God, the LORD Almighty, our God" (Jeremiah 23:6).

JEWISH TIMELINE NOW BECOMES INTERESTING

Following the miraculous reestablishment of the land of Israel in 1948, the Jewish people have been in the process of returning to their land. The *aliyah* (homecoming) is still underway, to be fully completed after "Jacob's trouble." In this regard, a significant milestone occurred in recent years. Did you notice it?

For the first time in more than twenty-six hundred years, more Jews are living in Israel than in any other nation. Think of the significance of this for a moment. For the first time in well over two millennia, the number of Jews in Israel has surpassed the number of Jews living in any other nation. Forty-one percent of world Jewry now lives in Israel. The next-largest group, representing another 40 percent, is living in America.

This would be celebratory news if it weren't for the reasons this has occurred. While the country of Israel is experiencing healthy natural population growth (now numbering 5.4 million Jews), Diaspora Jewry is declining not for reasons of *aliyah*, but because of secularization and "outmarriage"—Jews marrying people who are not Jewish. According to one study, whereas outmarriage rates were generally below 5 percent for the majority of Diaspora populations in 1930, today it is in excess of 45 percent.[51] In America, fewer Jews report having two parents of Jewish origin. Less than 40 percent of the 18–34-year-old age group who identify themselves as Jewish has two Jewish parents today.[52] In fact, a major point of debate today is the very definition of Jewish identity.

For this and other reasons, Jews are becoming ever less numerous in the world. While the Jewish people represented 7.5 out of every one thousand people in the world in 1938, today this figure is less than half—only 3.5 per thousand.[53]

This declining trend will continue, according to some researchers. Others talk of the "Hansen's Principle" phenomenon—"What the son wishes to forget, the grandson wishes to remember." But such a renaissance of Jewish culture in America seems unlikely, given that evidence indicates extremely high rates of unmarried cohabitation with non-Jewish partners.[54] If that is the case, the assimilation of North American Jews will rapidly continue.

But would it seem likely that more than one-half of Diaspora Jews in the world will remain outside of Israel? According to Scriptures, it is certain that the *aliyah* is not yet complete; this will fully occur only after the Tribulation. Could it be that American Jews will simply assimilate and eventually wither away?

Hopefully, the Messiah will come first and America will never be the handmaiden to another occurrence of Jewish persecution. We can be sure of one thing: When the Jews leave America, it will be the harbinger of the final downfall of the U.S.A. For, to repeat, "I will bless those who bless you," said the Lord Jehovah (Genesis 12:3).

THE COMING PROTOCOLS OF GOD

Ultimately, once the Jews repent and recognize their Messiah, they will be forgiven. "'In those days, at that time,' declares the LORD, 'search will be made for Israel's guilt, but there will be none, and for the sins of Judah, but none will be found, or I will forgive the remnant I spare'" (Jeremiah 50:20).

The next uppermost fact to realize is that the times of the Gentiles will end. In the not-too-distant future, the tables will be turned. The Israelites will reign, preeminent upon earth; Jesus Christ Himself will be in the seat of David; and justice and law will go forth out of Jerusalem (Isaiah 2:3).

In this seat of God-given power and wealth, will Israel be forgiving and non-retaliatory to the nations that have persecuted its peoples through the ages? Scripture is clear about the fate that will befall nations:

> This is what the LORD says: "As for all my wicked neighbors who seize the inheritance I gave my people Israel, I will uproot them from their lands and I will uproot the house of Judah from among them. But after I uproot them, I will again have compassion and will bring each of them back to his own inheritance and his own country. But if any nation does not listen, I will completely uproot and destroy it," declares the LORD. (Jeremiah 12:14, 17)

At the end of the Tribulation, the Jews indeed will recognize their Messiah. Then the Millennium will begin—the seventh, final, and greatest period when Israel will again flourish unmolested and free of international interference in its own land. Once the tribes of Jacob are restored, says the Lord, "I will also make you a light for the Gentiles, that you may bring my salvation to the ends of the earth" (Isaiah 49:6). "...once again he will choose Israel" (Isaiah 14:1).

THOUGHTS TO PONDER

We want to come back to the role of the Gentiles throughout history in relation to the Hebrews. It would be at their hands that the Jew would suffer. The history books are full of unspeakable atrocities and injustices. A Gentile can only utter graven silence at the specter of this gargantuan evil.

Jesus Christ says of Himself through the prophet Zechariah,

"After he has honored me and has sent me against the nations that have plundered you—for whoever touches you touches the apple of his eye—I will surely raise my hand against them so that their slaves will plunder them. Then you will know that the LORD Almighty has sent me" (Zechariah 2:8–9).

We are alerted to understand that just because God has decreed a disciplining or punishment upon His people, it does not absolve Gentile people and nations He might use as His instruments to do so. The example of Babylon's role in the Old Testament in this regard illustrates this point clearly. While the prophets far in advance identified Babylon as the tool God would use to bring His judgment against Judah, it was still counted as evil that this nation would touch Jacob. "But when the seventy years [of captivity] are fulfilled, I will punish the king of Babylon and his nation, the land of the Babylonians, for their guilt" (Jeremiah 25:12).

It was the same of the Edomites, the descendants of Esau. Though Esau was the brother of Jacob, his progeny were punished for their adversity and plundering of the Jews. (See Joel 3:19 and Amos 1:6–2:1). If this was the case for these bloodline relatives of the Jews, we can be sure that members of the church, part of the olive tree, will surely be accountable for their deeds and thoughts against them.

While God has been the author of the Jews' sentence into the Diaspora, both the Gentile and Jew have been complicit in its carrying out and completion. However, a Christian need not—must not—be part of these injustices though God may have allowed the Gentile a role in this manner.

Though God decreed this time upon our brothers, the Jews, we still individually have a choice in the matter. We dare not be part of this sin, for it indeed is something that will be severely punished. For the Bible says, "I will bless those who bless you, and whoever curses you I will curse; and all peoples on earth will be blessed through you" (Genesis 12:3).

This is an important message at this time in America after the advent of the global financial crisis. Economic dislocations are hardly over for America. In my view, the most difficult stages are still ahead. In time, an angry citizenry will look for scapegoats—and corrupt, weak governments will supply them. If history is any guide to the future, it has always been true that the largest population of Jews—specifically in those countries where they reached prominence and contributed to a Golden Age—eventually were persecuted and displaced. May it not be so. As Bible-believing Christians, we must be warned to pray and work against this demonic spirit of anti-Semitism.

In doing so, we should also refrain from meddling in the affairs of Israel. We do not need to be apologists for the Jews or condone every action of the modern state of Israel. However, there are several things we must do: First, "If some of the branches have been broken off, and you, though a wild olive shoot, have been grafted in among the others and now share in the nourishing sap from the olive root, do not boast over those branches. If you do, consider this: You do not support the root, but the root supports you" (Romans 11:17–18).

Next, "Do not be arrogant, but be afraid. For if God did not spare the natural branches, he will not spare you either" (Romans 11:20–21). While judgment and restoration have been set for the Jews, the Gentiles best remember that judgment awaits them also. For the Christian, the bema seat still lies ahead. Thanks to the Jew—Jesus Christ, in the flesh—we (and also the house of Jacob) are spared eternal damnation, but we do not escape judgment. Oh, may the severity God has shown the Jews pass over us! How many countless times have we been disobedient, as were Israel and Judah…yet, Jesus Christ has been faithful to forgive us.

According to the prophet Hosea, this restoration surely draws near. Hosea was inspired to say, "After two days he will revive us; on the third day he will restore us, that we may live in his presence" (Hosea 6:2). As a "day is as a thousand years" (Psalms 90:4, 2 Peter 3:8), it is now well into the second half of the third day for the Jews. If we count from 606 BC, the time from which the servitude to Babylonia began, 612 years of this third day have already passed. Given this reference point, we can know that this third day is here.

As God's plan decrees, one day there will be a Jewish, global confederacy. It will be the Millennium...and not as the result of the "Protocols of the Elders of Zion" or any other contrived conspiracy theory. Gentiles will then be thankful that Jews are not the evil they are often made out to be. "In those days ten men from all languages and nations will take firm hold of one Jew by the hem of his robe and say, 'Let us go with you, because we have heard that God is with you'" (Zechariah 8:23).

God will restore the Jews for the sake of His promises to the patriarchs (see Romans 11:28). This is such wonderful news for Jews and Christians alike. For if God is willing to go to such lengths to keep His promise for "David's sake," how much more so on behalf of Jesus Christ, His own Son.

Could it only be so soon. As the Jewish people have said at Passover for thousands of years: "Next year, in Jerusalem."

WHAT LIES
AHEAD

Figure #12

World Share of Economic Value: Advanced vs. Emerging

Gross Domestic Product, Purchasing-Power Parity (PPP) 1990 to 2007, 2009 to 2014 Forecast

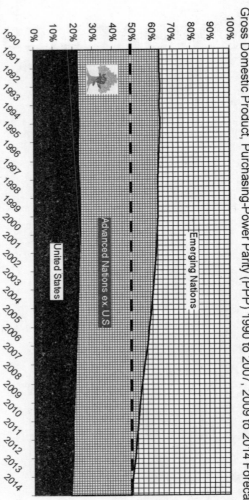

Emerging Nations

Advanced Nations ex U.S.

United States

Source: International Monetary Fund, WEO Database, April 2009   Format: Mulberry Press Inc.

America on the Decline: Many more factors than just economic statistics are required to even attempt to predict the long-term rise and fall of nations. Yet, a certain unwise path taken over the short-term, if not redirected, will eventually lead to dire consequences over the longer-term. In this sense, it can be noted that that the advanced nations of the world, including the United States, have been shrinking in terms of their economic size in the world. According to recent IMF estimates, for the first time in many centuries, the advanced nations (largely the historic Christian West but also including Japan), will soon be the minority economic power on earth. Emerging nations will dominate.

11

END-TIME SHOES: FITTING THE WORLD FOR TEN TOES

That America and the world's financial systems were vulnerable to shattering meltdowns had long been obvious. Yet, now that calamitous events have occurred and difficult times are obvious to everyone, most of the world remains asleep as to what really is underfoot behind the scenes. What's ahead, especially for America?

We need not speculate. We know where this global rebellion against God is headed, because the Bible tells us the future in advance. While it is true that we cannot know the exact timing and the minute details of future events, at the same time, by reading the Bible we do know what the general world order will look like nearer the time when the Tribulation period begins. We can discern developments today that are fulfilling a rapid progression towards that prophesied time.

Unlike the Rapture, which is signless, the Tribulation period is not. Observers should surely be able to recognize its forerunning developments. Many Bible scholars take the view that its inception will be signaled by the advent of a peace treaty that Israel will make with a world leader the Bible clearly identifies as the Antichrist.

One other condition that helps us certifiably diagnose that the Tribulation period has not yet begun—yet is nearing—is that the "end-time shoe" does not yet fit the time of the ten kings. The ten kings must exist before Antichrist is revealed. Because of this, we can know that the world will experience some great geopolitical and economic power shifts before the final, end-time events described in the Bible can occur.

Despite the many "signs of the times," the "Day of the Lord," is said to come "as a thief in the night" (1 Thessalonians 5:2; 2 Peter 3:10). It will sneak up on humanity.

ULTIMATE DOOM AND GLOOM DEFERRED

Prospects looked so grim to some analysts following the eruption of the GFC that they predicted the world would soon return to the Dark Ages. They reasoned that during difficult times, individual sovereign countries will resort to protecting their own narrow interests. They would therefore no longer comply with global organizations and institutions, abandoning multilateral relationships and retreating to the principle of "every man for himself." Even globalism might be abandoned, some speculated.

Also, the unprecedented collapse in world merchandise trade signified to some that global commerce is doomed. They concluded that globalization must therefore be dead. However, though the globe may be facing unprecedented and calamitous times, a total collapse in world trade and globalism is not imminent. Predictions of terminal doom occurring now are wrong. The Bible indicates otherwise.

There are two more reasons we can be sure of this conclusion in addition to the argument that a working global financial system is a prerequisite for the Antichrist and the False Prophet to carry our their prophesied deeds (see Chapter 2). For one, we know that the world will have many sea captains at the time Babylon is judged (Revelation 18:17). How otherwise would it be possible for "all who had ships on the sea [to become] rich through [the great city Babylon's] wealth" (Revelation 18:19)? Because of this, we know shipping captains will experience a time of prosperity in the future.

Views that the world will face a permanent reversal with respect to globalism are also likely to be wrong. It is much too late for this to occur, because the world is already too interconnected through global trade. The fortunes of every country are so mutually dependent that very few, if any, can risk being recklessly independent. In this sense, the road back from globalism is more horrible to policy makers than the one forward.

Said differently, ever more sovereignty will be bartered for the sake of grain, just as foreshadowed by the Bible's account of Joseph's policies in Egypt's time of crisis thousands of years ago. "And all the countries came to Egypt to buy grain from Joseph, because the famine was severe in all the world" (Genesis 41:57). The world is resolute upon achieving prosperity and its popular comforts its own way, without first seeking the kingdom of God.

PURPOSE OF THE LATEST CRISIS: A SHOE HORN

We can make one other deduction from the Bible that proves the Tribulation is not yet upon the world, though it is near. A condition of global multipolarism does not exist. Multipolarism is a situation of global interrelationships in which the world's key nations are relatively balanced in terms of power and influence. Let's examine this more closely, because it is very significant, and it also connects to the question of America's fate.

Scripture outlines that a ten-king power coalition will take form near the start of the Tribulation period. At least five separate visions depict these kings. (See Daniel 2:41–42 [in the form of ten toes], 7:20, 24; and Revelation 12:3, 13:1, 17:3, 12, 16). This group is referenced as ten horns, ten toes, or ten kings exactly ten times. This end-time power coalition is a significant prophecy—most certainly for the earth dwellers who will not be raptured away—for at least one other reason that is worth repeating. The Bible expressly indicates that these ten kings must appear before the Antichrist is revealed. These kings would be the equivalent to ten male leaders or kings of sovereign nations today. The reference verse, Daniel 7:24, was quoted in Chapter 2. Here we see that only "after" the ten kings are on the scene, "another king"—the Antichrist—will arise. The Antichrist's rule at first is borne on the strength of ten kings, and then he becomes the eighth. "The ten horns you saw are ten kings who have not yet received a kingdom, but who for one hour will receive authority as kings along with the beast. They have one purpose and will give their power and authority to the beast" (Revelation 17:12–13). Effectively, this power configuration comes into existence for a very short duration, and gives rise to the world's eighth kingdom. In Revelation 17, the beast with seven heads and crowns is again shown. The heads portray the past Gentile kingdoms that have suppressed Israel—from Egypt to the second revived Roman-based organization of countries existing at the time of Israel's reemergence as a nation. As is well known, Israel indeed was reborn as a nation in 1948.

Many characteristics are revealed about this group of world leaders. In fact, the Bible reveals thirteen sets of factors that apply to this future alliance of kings. This development of a ten-nation coalition is one of the most important and early signs of the times. While the world will not know the exact configuration of this assembly until the Antichrist achieves a peace accord with Israel, a general trend toward world governance will be evident long before. This progression is playing out before our very eyes.

It is essential to understand the uniqueness of the arrangement in which ten kings will pool their power and agree to place it at the disposal of the Antichrist. There are two reasons this is so unusual: First, the general pattern throughout history has been that only one nation would dominate the known world or its regions. Even in our modern age, this has been the case. It has been a long, long time since the world has not been dominated by one prominent and powerful country. Second, the world has never before been ruled by a voluntary coalition of countries. That is not even the case today, although the European Union, NATO, the United Nations, and many other international organizations have broad country memberships. That's because at least one or more geopolitical nation-state is too powerful or independent to be ruled by a voluntary association of smaller countries. There can be no real multipolarism if a superpower exists. Therefore, we can know that the prophetic "glass slipper" has not yet found the ten-king Cinderella.

TEN TOES PICTURED AS TEN KINGS

In Daniel 2:41–42, we see that an end-time "power coalition" of ten kings is portrayed as ten toes. In this chapter, we read the account of Nebuchadnezzar's famous vision, in which he saw a tall statue made of various materials, from a head of gold down to ten toes of iron and clay. This vision outlined the future kingdoms and power structures of the Gentiles, right to the time of the return of Jesus Christ, when He establishes His millennial reign upon earth.

Nebuchadnezzar's vision of the toes contains a very important clue, as it represents the last power structure that extends into the Tribulation period. Studying this picture, it would be reasonable to conclude that the world is already very near a last world power structure comprised of ten kings. But, here we discover an ill-fitting fact. Were Nebuchadnezzar's vision to apply exactly to our day, the feet would be lopsided and deformed. Why? They would only have one big toe. In fact, this toe would look grossly oversized relative to both feet.

Every indication the Bible gives about the last-day, ten-king power coalition is that the kingdoms are roughly proportionate in size. In Daniel 2, these kings are shown as a normal set of ten toes (verses 41–42), and in Daniel 7 and Revelation 12, 13, and 17, they are shown as ten horns. In the "horn" imagery, the ten are compared in size only once, and this to an emerging eleventh horn, a "small horn" that then uproots three of the existing horns (Daniel 7:8). If it is to be small relative to the ten kings, then these cannot be small. This statement implies that the kings are a league roughly of equals—some likely smaller, others more powerful—just as the big toe is normally bigger than the smallest of the toes.

The ill-fitting condition we see today is that there has only been one big toe—a hugely outsized one at that—that does not yet fit into the shoe. Walter Russell Meade, an analyst with the Council on Foreign Relations, points out that the Anglo-Saxon countries of Britain and America have been on top of the world for three centuries, though sometimes fighting each other.[55] The world has really only had one "big toe" these past three hundred years or so, and it's been a hugely disproportionate toe at that.

For the time being, the U.S. is still the most powerful nation in the world. It represents a very big toe...so big, in fact, that it still can render any other coalition of ten kings ineffective. Not only is the

U.S. an economic giant, the annual military budget of the U.S. alone still exceeds the combined spending of the rest of the world. As such, we recognize that a resizing of the relative powers of ten major nations must happen before the prophesied time of the ten kings will occur.

Will America fit into the shoe or not? In other words, will it be a member or not? The recent GFC and America's seemingly rapid economic fall make this a timely question. Are we now seeing the necessary changes beginning to occur...the big toe stubbed?

RESIZING NEEDED TO FIT INTO THE END-TIME SHOE

Since Bible prophecy clearly outlines that there will be a ten-nation power coalition, and not a foot with one big toe, we can conclude that this big toe must then become comparatively smaller. While the British Empire has already fallen from the pinnacle of world power over the past century or so, its younger cousin, the U.S., now undoubtedly also faces a relative decline. Of course, we cannot be sure of the exact timeline, whether this will happen quickly or gradually. But, by whatever means—the Rapture, self-inflicted policy disasters, consequences deserved or divinely willed—this has to happen if the Bible is correct. In fact, viewed against the pace of past human history, a downward shift for America could happen extremely suddenly. While some see a Rapture having this effect upon America, this is not the only plausible scenario.

Less than five years ago, though the seeds of America's moral and economic decline had long been evident, the U.S. was still seen as an invincible, world-dominating power in every sense. At the time, geopolitical analysts were still actively debating the question of whether the United States should really be considered an empire in the classical sense. Many analysts ridiculed notions that America's preeminence might be vulnerable, maintaining that the twenty-first century would belong to the U.S., as did the twentieth. While one should not be too hasty in predicting America's demise on the world scene, trends of relative deterioration have indeed been very rapid in recent years, particularly as a result of the GFC.

Joseph Stiglitz, former chief economist of the World Bank, observed that in the space of the two terms of the former Bush government, the federal budget went from a surplus of $128 billion to a certain legacy of a $1 trillion deficit for the next president. Says Stiglitz, "The national debt has increased by 65 percent, by nearly $10 trillion to which the debts of Freddie Mac and Fannie Mae [the nations' largest mortgage providers] must be added. Meanwhile, we are saddled with the cost of two wars. The price tag for the one in Iraq alone will…ultimately exceed $3 trillion."[56]

Mr. Stiglitz was too optimistic even at the time he made this comment. Events since then indicate even much greater challenges in future years. Given the scale of financial and economic crises, total government debt in America is sure to at least double over the next five years.

To be sure, economic and financial strength is only one measure of global power, though a most important one in this present age of global capital. On these measures, other nations of the world are now superseding the U.S. For example, for the first time in perhaps fifty years, another nation—China—accounted for the most global economic growth in 2007. While America is now by far the world's greatest debtor nation, it is Asia that now houses two-thirds of the world's international financial reserves. While no trend is likely to be safely predictable, these are indeed new signs of the times. Many others could be cited.

SHARED GLOBALISM GOING FORWARD

Now that the contagion of the GFC has rocked the entire world, the calls for greater global coordination are becoming shrill. For example, Miguel Angel Ordonez, Spain's European Central Bank (ECB) governor, said: "We've got to get together on both sides of the Atlantic. It is absolutely essential to coordinate everything, including monetary policy."[57]

According to one global financial analyst, "A global conference (along the lines of Bretton Woods) under a respected chairman must be convened. It would bring together all the major players including the vital creditor nations—China, Japan…etc.—to develop a framework for the major economic reforms (currency policies, fiscal disciplines and trade barriers) to work towards a resolution of the crisis."[58]

To that end, world meeting forums of countries and global leaders continue to be held. Progress has been modest in view of the severity of the GFC. Yet, some geopolitical analysts are encouraged by the spirit of multipolarism that is apparently galvanizing a new participative spirit for these meetings.

Even formerly non-aligned nations have indicated a cooperative sentiment. China's Premier, Wen Jiabao, is keenly aware of the direct connection his country has to America's recent financial troubles, saying, "If anything goes wrong in the U.S. financial sector, we are anxious about the safety and security of Chinese capital."[59]

Even the money mavens of the Islamic world see reason to participate in global collaboration. Quoting an article from *Emirates Business 24-7* magazine:

> Adnan Ahmed Yousuf, Chairman of the Union of the Arab
> Banks (UAB), said all countries are expected to contribute to

the evolution of the new global system adding the recent trips by British Prime Minister Gordon Brown and other officials to the Gulf illustrated the important part it can play in this field. "All countries are expected to participate in the new world financial order, including the Arab states. The trips to the Gulf by Gordon Brown and other officials represent a clear recognition of the role of regional states in tackling the current crisis. In recognition of such a role, they should be involved in forging the new global economic order on par with other nations," Yousuf wrote in the Arabic magazine for the Beirut-based UAB. Yousuf, whose group comprises most of the Arab world's 470 banks, said acting as a single bloc would largely strengthen Arab bands and allow them to face the current crisis given their massive resources of nearly $117 trillion.[60]

PULLING TOGETHER IN TIMES OF CRISIS

All in all, what appears as global disorder at present—a time of financial and economic near-collapse—likely will act as a catalyst in the rapid metamorphosis to a ten-king global power coalition. There is a broad consensus that a group of nations needs to come together to find economic and financial solutions for the world. How many nations? Some argue that twenty is too many, and others that the G7 (Group of Seven) is not enough. Could a group of ten emerge? The Bible confirms this, though the final form is not fully clear.

We can draw several firm conclusions. First, whatever new global organization emerges, its powers will be shared more equally in the future. Multipolarism must eventually gain ground, according to Bible prophecy. The United States will eventually lose its outsized number of votes and vetoes in such organizations as the International Monetary Fund (IMF) and others. The second conclusion we can safely draw is that we live in a time when an alignment of ten kings could be on our very doorstep.

REASONABLE VOICES HAVE CONCERNS

Thomas Friedman, the high-profile opinion columnist, says, "America still has the right stuff to thrive. We still have the most creative, diverse, innovative culture and open society—in a world where the ability to imagine and generate new ideas with speed and to implement them through global collaborations is the most important competitive advantage.... the twenty-first century is still up for grabs."[61] This is surely a hope-filled thought. But it is hubris. With respect to the U.S. and the future power balances in the world, we are better advised listening to the Bible than to Mr. Friedman.

Other worldly observers have different opinions. Peer Steinbrück, the German finance minister, was quoted to have said that the world's financial crisis prefigures the end of Wall Street's—and, by extension, America's—hegemony and the emergence of a multipolar world. He now sees a world where power is distributed a little more evenly. If he is right that this will happen—whether sooner or later—it surely meets an end-time condition the Bible prophesies.

Many serious American analysts also have grave concerns about America's future. Here are two representative voices that are widely respected. Mr. Leslie Gelb, president emeritus of the Council on Foreign Relations, writes:

> The United States is declining as a nation and a world power, with mostly sighs and shrugs to mark this seismic event. Astonishingly, some people do not appear to realize that the

situation is all that serious. A few say it is serious and hopeless. I count myself among those who think it is most serious yet reversible, if Americans are clear-eyed about the causes and courageous about implementing the cures. The United States is in danger of becoming merely first among major powers and heading to a level somewhere between its current still-exalted position and that of China today. This would be bad news for both the United States and the world...[62]

Roger C. Altman, former deputy Treasury secretary of the U.S., weighs in with an opinion that clearly links the economic rash of 2008 with America's slipping world power and a needed new "global approach":

Much of the world is turning a historic corner and heading into a period in which the role of the state will be larger and that of the private sector will be smaller.... If Obama inherits a $1 trillion deficit, and temporarily enlarges it to $1.3 trillion with a stimulus program, there will not be much of a constituency calling for increased U.S. spending on endeavors abroad. Indeed, the country may be entering a period of forced restraint not seen since the 1930s.... This historic crisis raises the question of whether a new global approach to controlling currencies and banking and financial systems is needed.[63]

THOUGHTS TO PONDER

For the last three centuries, there has only been one big toe. But this cannot continue if prophecy is to be fulfilled. This change is very likely already underfoot, greatly accelerated by the GFC. The economic and financial destruction revealed by these crises likely play a significant role in the geopolitical "birth pangs" and "earthquakes" of an emerging global power distribution the Bible describes as taking form in the very last days. The rise of other nations such as China, India, Brazil, Russia, and perhaps oil-exporting nations must be seen as part of this rebalancing process, though not yet in its final form.

The times of the ten kings could come upon the world very suddenly. In fact, it would not be a far-fetched speculation to believe that some, if not all, of these nations may already be on the world stage.

Surely, the implications of the facts outlined for America will not be received as inspiring much hope. But, to conclude that the doom of America is a near-term certainty could also be wrong. It is not prophetically necessary for America to accelerate the fulfillment of prophecy by collapsing into a toothless tiger or an immoral, tyrannical state right now. It is never too late for a nation to repent until God decides to no longer strive with it. Do we know for certain that America has already come to this point of condemnation?

God said to Israel, "…if my people, who are called by my name, will humble themselves and pray and seek my face and turn from their wicked ways, then will I hear from heaven and will forgive their sin and will heal their land" (2 Chronicles 7:14). We see here that repentance remains an option…provided that it is not past the point when God refuses to listen.

In this view, we must also not make the mistake of Jonah. He was upset with God when the citizens of Nineveh chose to heed his message of judgment. They repented and changed their ways…at least for a little while. As a result, Nineveh's demise was delayed for another 150 years or so. Could such an outcome still be open for America and other Western nations? Our Lord, for the most part, allows people the freedom to choose to follow His precepts and ways voluntarily. Yes, God foreknows what our choices will be, but that is not the same as predestining our willful actions.

Yet, according to Bible prophecy, America must decline relative to the ten kings in one way or another. Prophecy in this case can be fulfilled in a number of ways. For example, ten other kings could increase in power enough to supersede the geopolitical position of the U.S. Or conversely, America could be disastrously downsized…either becoming one of the ten kings or not at all. Which will it be?

The jury is out. America's destiny is up to the nation's leaders and citizens. However, to date, the signs are not encouraging. Most certainly, the world will rush together into new alliances, reforming its economic and financial policies in a coordinated fashion—something that is only possible in a multipolar world.

The current GFC is not likely disastrous enough to drive the world into the arms of a ten-king power coalition. At least another, more serious, phase to the GFC or other crises will be needed to achieve this state. As explained, these crises encourage the world and America to look for new financial and economic solutions. Any person who can deliver such policies will be accepted as a type of savior.

Even secular analysts, without reference to Bible prophecy, theorize that ultimately a single powerful entity must arise. This could be a coalition of states or even a single person who is invested with "hegemon" powers.

Interestingly, just such a theory was deduced by Charles Kindleberger in the dark days of the Great Depression. A writer from *Yale-Global* comments:

> Decades ago, Charles Kindleberger, in his analysis of the
> Great Depression, announced that the smooth operation of
> a liberal international economic order requires the existence

of a hegemon or, at the very least, a multilateral institution capable of functioning in such a capacity. By Kindleberger's so-called Hegemonic Stability Theory, a sustainable international economy requires an international leader that can and will enforce the rules of the game. The Great Depression, therefore, sprung from an ability-motivation gap in which the United States could, but was not willing, to provide the necessary common goods to maintain economic order, while the United Kingdom was willing, but could not fill this role.[64]

The Bible confirms that the world's progression towards the prophesied global conditions of the last days will continue. Along with the prophesied signs of apostasy, false christs, wealth extremes, hoarding, dissipation, indulgence, globalism, and globalization—all of which are far advanced—a hegemonic power structure will emerge with one man at its apex. It will not be the United States or its leader.

Figure #13

World Currency? One-World Currency System Already Here

Most Active Currencies, Cumulative % Totals, (Buy & Sells Combined), April 2007

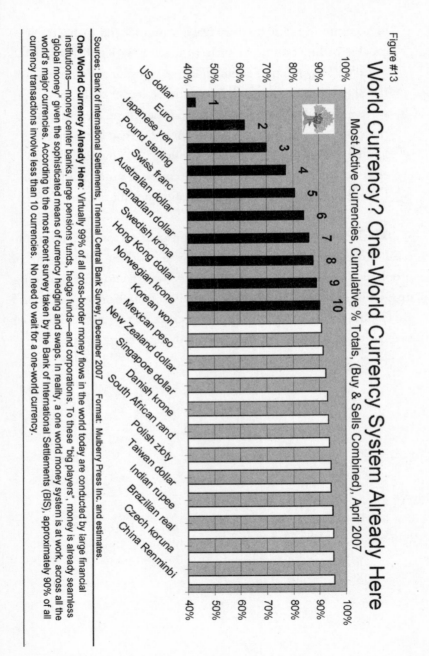

Sources: Bank of international Settlements, Triennial Central Bank Survey, December 2007   Format: Mulberry Press Inc. and estimates.

One World Currency Already Here: Virtually 99% of all cross-border money flows in the world today are conducted by large financial institutions—money center banks, large pensions funds, hedge funds—and corporations. To these "big players", money is already seamless "global money" given the sophisticated means of currency hedging and swaps. In reality, a one world money system is at work, across all the world's major currencies. According to the most recent survey taken by the Bank of International Settlements (BIS), approximately 90% of all currency transactions involve less than 10 currencies. No need to wait for a one-world currency.

12

ONE WORLD, ONE CRISIS, ONE CURRENCY

Huge developments are sweeping the entire world in recent times like a tidal wave, broaching money, power, and geopolitics all at once. First, a "globalization bubble" spread out over the past several decades—one that was popularly thought would never end. Then came the biggest and most rapid bust of world financial and real estate wealth since the 1930s. Next, the most invasive and coordinated intervention of governments and global non-governmental agencies occurred around the world as they sought to resuscitate plunging economies and bail out failing companies. In tandem, a desperate and unprecedented bout of money manipulation has unfolded.

While these interventions are likely to forestall further financial and economic collapses for a time, they at the same time sow the seeds for the next crises that are sure to come, the next and perhaps final stages to the ultimate global financial apocalypse. These developments are likely to cause challenges even more destructive than what was witnessed with the GFC to date. While most people are still smarting from what has happened in the past—in other words, looking at losses of wealth in the rearview mirror—they stand exposed, unobserving, and unprepared for the next oncoming freight train. For more than one reason, many more people stand to fall trapped into the progressing global, end-time money snare.

None of the disruptive developments of the GFC was expected by the world's policy makers or societies at large even as little as a year before their occurrence. It all happened rapidly…like a trap.

SIGNS OF THE TIMES

No doubt, we have witnessed treacherous times when the unsuspecting are being herded from one disaster to another. Just how can the average household anticipate or navigate through such seesaw conditions? It can be seen as a sign of the end times…the global period of trouble and anxiety when faith runs cold (Matthew 24:12).

Consider that never before—even during the two world wars of the past century—has global opinion been so galvanized and unified to a common view. From Iceland to Vietnam, from rural China to downtown Zürich, whether businesspeople or consumers, the GFC caused virtually the entire world to respond in the same way…by battening down the hatches in response to the global "financial heart attack."

These shakings of the false gods of global prosperity struck fear into the remotest parts of the globe. Filipino guest workers in the Arab Emirates were flocking home, running away from debts and obligations. Possibly as many as thirty million Chinese lost their jobs in the early stages of the GFC. Evidence of fear was everywhere. In international policy-making circles, hurried meetings were held, even with enemy nations, to find solutions to economic and financial ails. We witnessed something very remarkable: Never before has the entire world behaved so much as one monolithic culture.

To illustrate, according to a first-ever, worldwide poll[65] on the current financial crisis, 49 percent of the respondents said they believed the economic situation would worsen in the next three months. In Canada and the United States, 61 percent and 46 percent, respectively, felt that it would get worse. Only 8 percent of citizens in G8 (Group of Eight) countries thought things might get better. Such a one-sided consensus of opinion is extremely rare—let alone when it applies to a greater part of the world. This is significant. It shows that the entire globe has been affected as one. The unified responses of international policy makers, consumers, and businesses (at least to this point) are unprecedented.

We now recognize that current economic and financial conditions have reached the point that man-made events can impact the sentiment of the entire world almost instantaneously. This is new. It would be one thing if the mood of mankind were to suddenly change in response to a nuclear winter or something universally cataclysmic such as the blotting out of the sun. However, a massive global response to an economically related occurrence is of a different order in several ways. For one, it is generated by the non-physical actions of humanity itself. It is largely an emotional event, not a physically induced impulse. Secondly, it reveals a common set of affections…a universal reliance upon the prosperity of mankind's global commercial systems.

This alone is a realization of one of the expected "signs of the times" of the last days. From Scripture, we already know that certain economic conditions—from food affordability or supply problems (Revelation 6:6) to systemic collapses (Chapter 18), commercial controls (13:17), and other phenomena—will affect the entire world. We see this potentiality at work today. The entire world, from peasant to king, is under the influence of common commercial developments. None can escape its influence.

UNIFIED FOR GLOBAL JUDGMENT

In Isaiah's Apocalypse (Isaiah 24–27), we read of the "globality" of God's final judgments and punishments. Though much of these chapters refer directly to Israel and the Jews, many apply to the entire world. For example, "The earth will be completely laid waste and totally plundered" (Isaiah 24:3). Also, "The earth reels like a drunkard, it sways like a hut in the wind; so heavy upon it is the guilt of its rebellion that it falls—never to rise again" (verse 20). In fact, emphasizing the global span of these events, the word "earth" is mentioned seventeen times in Chapter 24 alone.

Of course, it only follows that a global judgment will apply to a "globalized" mankind, one characterized by a unified rebellion against God. If that were not so, why would the entire world be judged, and no nations spared? God, who is compassionate and just, was even willing to spare Sodom if only ten godly people could be found. Therefore, as revealed prophetically, mankind will choose to move to an ever-more-global, monolithic culture of godlessness. This culture, we contend, is already upon the world.

In that vein, note the current longing expressed by many leaders and policy makers to build and pursue global organization and solutions. It is a natural extension of "...the cravings of sinful man, the lust of his eyes and the boasting of what he has and does" (1 John 2:16). One doesn't need to spin great conspiracy theories involving cabals of demon-possessed people to bring about this result. We see this innate human impulse to pursue greatness and power at work everywhere. In the corporate world, firms conglomerate into ever-larger entities seeking a broader global footprint in their respective industries—executives aspiring to be big fish in an ever-smaller global pond.

The same hegemonic impulse is shared by politicians, church leaders, and global policy makers. There is a natural, fleshly appeal to greater celebrity; to ruling over ever-larger domains...even the entire world. Interestingly, all of these corporate captains, policy makers, and Christian reconstructionists see times of world crisis as signaling great global opportunity. To them, it is an opportune moment to satisfy the "lust of the eyes." Recognizing the timely facility of a crisis, the reputedly profane chief of staff of the Obama administration, Rahm Emanuel, said, "You never want a serious crisis to go to waste. And what I mean by that is an opportunity to do things you think you could not do before."[66]

Documenting this hegemonic yearning, here are several excerpts from comments of selected global policy makers and thinkers.

What is needed is a large worldwide fiscal stimulus to counteract falling private demand.... The world must also build the institutions for the twenty-first century economy. Any crisis is an opportunity. This crisis has demonstrated that the destinies of countries around the world are linked. Policy coordination and a global strategy that instills confidence and creates hope will bring a quicker and stronger recovery to us all.[67] (Kemal Dervi and Juan Somavia of the United Nations Development Program)

What I am saying is that a crisis is an event which can force democratic governments to make difficult decision like those that will be required to create a North American Community. It's not that I want another 9/11 crisis, but having a crisis would force decisions that otherwise might not get made.[68] (Dr. Robert A. Pastor)

[The year] 2009 will be a year of learning the lessons of the financial crisis; a year where its reach in terms of time and scope becomes more evident; a year that calls for a new financial architecture to be shaped. At the same time, it will be a year that will test the resolve and willingness of world leaders to collaborate and take action to move beyond this crisis. [The year] 2008 has proven the extent to which the world is subject to global risks; let 2009 be the year where the world finds a common agenda to begin mitigating their impact.[69] (Klaus Schwab, founder of the World Economic Forum)

...the very unsettled nature of the international system generates a unique opportunity for creative diplomacy. The nadir of the existing international financial system coincides with simultaneous political crises around the globe. Never have so many transformations occurred at the same time in so many different parts of the world and been made globally accessible via instantaneous communication. The alternative to a new international order is chaos. An international order can be permanent only if its participants have a share not only in building but also in securing it. In this manner, America and its potential partners have a unique opportunity to transform a moment of crisis into a vision of hope.[70] (Henry Kissinger)

Countless more such comments could be quoted. The philosophical ferment of the aftermath of the GFC has convinced many more thinkers that global solutions are the hope of mankind. And so, these times of crisis are seen as an ideal environment to hasten the resolve and necessary changes to build a global ark of man.

GLOBAL ARROGANCE REVEALED

Even in view of the apparent chaos and fears resulting from the GFC, we still see the pride and self-determination of mankind on display. This is evident at both national and global levels. Despite the clear and painful repercussions of past follies—including materialism, unbridled greed, economic oppression, poor stewardship, and consumption excesses—one does not discern even a hint of contrition being reported in the popular media. Actually, quite the opposite is true. While overpaid bankers and Wall Street executives are the object of much blame these days, conveniently ignoring the complicity of politicians and many others, the general idea still prevails that there need not be any consequence for past sins, economic or otherwise.

Considering that macroeconomists and policy makers have yet to offer any apologies for the massive failure of their theories, these really are not any different from sorceries. As pointed out in Chapter 3, with very few exceptions, none foresaw or warned that the world's enormous financial imbalances would lead to a systemic "heart attack." They were all blind guides, more greedy for gain than honest and forthright. Yet, they are not shy to offer new solutions today. It reveals that macroeconomics is not a science, but rather a fraudulent religion. It is not capable of dealing with the heart of man. The Bible is clear on that matter: "The heart is deceitful above all things, and desperately wicked: who can know it?" (Jeremiah 17:9).

Yet, the world is resolute in healing its problems without recognizing the underlying spiritual diseases. The Bible gives us clear evidence as to the outcome of such human arrogance. Not only are the experiences of Israel and other nations documented in the Old Testament for our benefit in this case, the consequences of the future choices of "global man" are also foretold. A willful rebellion against God is revealed...a stiff-necked independence and spirit of humanist self-determination. A brief review of some Old Testament prophecies will testify to these future indications. But first, we should be reminded of the original indictments against Israel and the reasons for their disciplining.

MANY ECONOMIC SINS

About Israel, Scripture tells us: "...Because you have rejected this message, relied on oppression and depended on deceit, this sin will become for you like a high wall, cracked and bulging, that collapses suddenly, in an instant" (Isaiah 30:12–13). A point often overlooked is that "economic sins" feature prominently in the list of allegations against Israel. There are seemingly countless references to these in the Scriptures. But, what was Israel's response? It was similar to what we observe today.

"...Ephraim and the inhabitants of Samaria—who say with pride and arrogance of heart, 'The bricks have fallen down, but we will rebuild with dressed stone; the fig trees have been felled, but we will replace them with cedars'" (Isaiah 9:9–10). Edom also betrayed a similar humanist defiance: "'Though we have been crushed, we will rebuild the ruins.' But this is what the LORD Almighty says: 'They may build, but I will demolish'" (Malachi 1:4).

A similar attitude prevails today, but applying to global mankind: The world is effectively saying: "Hah! We will not be reprimanded or reproved. We will rebuild bigger and better! We will not accept that the GFC is the result of our humanist folly."

Paul Volcker, the chairman of the U.S. Federal Reserve from

1979–1987, in a prominent article[71] claimed that the world has the tools to overcome the financial excesses of the past. "Fortunately, there is also good reason to believe that the means are now available to turn the tide," he said. "Financial authorities, in the U.S. and elsewhere, are now in a position to take needed and convincing action to stabilize markets and to restore trust...the needed tools to restore and maintain functioning markets are there. Now is the time to use them."

All the same, though a respected central banker, Mr. Volcker's ideas reflect humanist self-determination. These "propping-up" policies may indeed prove to hold up financial systems for a time—even leading to what will seem to be global solutions—yet in the end they will not solve the problem of the corrupt human heart and the rebelliousness of mankind.

SOLUTIONS SOUGHT WORLDWIDE

Indeed, mankind is in a position where global solutions seem possible. Therefore, rather than stopping to consider the ways and counsels of the Lord, the "global arm of man" is invoked. "We will rise above God...we will make our own future," reflects the sentiment of our times. A similar spirit sometimes appeared evident in speeches given by the previous president, George Bush, following the terrorist attacks on September 11, 2001, and Hurricane Katrina in August of 2005. For example, after the New Orleans flood, he said: "Every time, the people of this land have come back from fire, flood, and storm to build anew—and to build better than what we had before. Americans have never left our destiny to the whims of nature, and we will not start now."[72] President Obama affirmed the same spirit, declaring, "We will rebuild, we will recover, and the United States of America will emerge stronger than before."[73]

What does God think of such an attitude? To Israel, He said: "Cursed is the one who trusts in man, who depends on flesh for his strength and whose heart turns away from the LORD" (Jeremiah 17:5).

Though God has made man in His image and has given him the power of creativity, we are still counseled to put our trust in God, not in armies or the "arm of man." There is no lack of guidance about where our real confidence should rest. "Blessed is that man that maketh the LORD his trust, and respecteth not the proud, nor such as turn aside to lies" (Psalms 40:4, KJV). "Put not your trust in princes, nor in the son of man, in whom there is no help" (Psalms 146:3).

WORLD ORDER DELAYED OR A DIVERSION?

A new world order? It would hardly seem that way. Admittedly, the globe has appeared rather disorderly. Panic and desperate actions better define the times throughout, not order, rank, and file. At points, one might have wondered whether that prophesied day had arrived when people will throw their silver into the streets (Isaiah 2:20, Ezekiel 7:19). However, that prophesied final collapse is not here yet. The prophecies of Ezekiel and Isaiah refer to conditions that will occur in the later stages of the Tribulation…likely nearer the time of the sixth seal.

As I've already expressed, in my opinion, the GFC will be an important stepping stone to the future ten-king coalition that will for one hour give authority to the Antichrist. This is the ultimate end point and the diabolical objective of globalism the Bible prophesies. Mankind's intent on pursuing a materialist "heaven on earth" must come to this end. This conclusion is also ineluctable to religion. If material prosperity is the agreed route to global peace—this being the humanist agenda—then everything else will be compromised to this one end. Great global crises surely are expedient in forcing consensus and accelerating the speed to that destination point.

This being the basic cosmology of Bible prophecy with respect to globalism, we must stop to comment on the "Christian" hysteria that so often is directed to this topic.

THE FUTURE ONE WORLD ORDER

Mountains of paper and oceans of ink have been spent on the speculations of the minute details, persons, and future agendas of global elites who are driving the process of world globalism. This writer has preferred to stay clear of these speculations and the frequent hysteria associated with this general topic. It isn't necessary or profitable. Of course, if you like fiction novels, or simply have a fascination for conspiracy theories, you are free to indulge this taste. As far as the final, ten-king world power coalition is concerned, nothing more needs to happen other than ten key nations coming together with sufficient power to give to the Antichrist, allowing him to subjugate world affairs and initially put into effect peace proposals. Though it is true that the general "signs of the times" with respect to the rapid trend of globalism are clearly observable today, it is not likely that we will find a nice and neat organizational chart defining the workings of a developing one world order or the emergence of the final ten kings.

In that sense, much about the coming one world order written today is contrived and sensational, and may lure us into dangerous error. Why? Consider the identity and nature of the enemy. He is no mere human. We do well to recall that "our struggle is not against flesh and blood, but against the rulers, against the authorities, against the powers of this dark world and against the spiritual forces of evil in the heavenly realms" (Ephesians 6:12). To fail to take account of this organized hierarchy of spiritual adversaries in the affairs of people and the world would misleadingly block our view. Simply analyzing what is seen or read in the newspapers will not produce a correct conclusion, either. After all, it is this refusal to look past the three-dimensional physical realm that underpins the blindness we see today in most fields of human activity, especially economics and geopolitics. Therefore, the world's movers and shakers "…do not know the thoughts of the LORD; they do not understand his plan" (Micah 4:12).

Next, we recognize that there is an elaborate, last-day trap underway—one that has been unfolding over a long period of time and driven forward incrementally by countless thousands of smaller antichrists over the centuries (1 John 2:18, 4:3). And, indeed, if a trap is being set, there must then both be a trapper and a "trappee." "Does a bird fall into a trap on the ground where no snare has been set? Does a trap spring up from the earth when there is nothing to catch?" (Amos 3:5). Amos makes a simple point that if a trap is laid, then there must be an intended quarry. We've already established that there is a trap. Who is the prey? The Bible clearly informs us there are two separate (but interrelated) recipients of God's promises—the church and Israel. These two, both corporately and its members as individuals, are the target.

We finally must acknowledge a grand intelligence, a diabolical schemer, an accuser of the brethren, a persecutor of the faithful, a foe of Jesus Christ at work—the master adversary, who is the Devil himself. Therefore, deflection, diversion, and deception are key strategies that must be anticipated. If nefarious and evil agendas were allowed to be so obvious or blatantly evil, Satan could not as easily lay a deceptive and effective trap for the world.

This fits the general character of the last days…namely, our times.

The Bible says the whole world is overtaken by darkness during the last days—particularly so during the Tribulation period. A number of prophecies alert us to this characteristic of the end-time period. "See, darkness covers the earth and thick darkness is over the peoples" (Isaiah 60:2). "Will not the day of the LORD be darkness, not light—pitch-dark, without a ray of brightness?" (Amos 5:20). Darkness and evil are a mark of these times. Evil lurks under the cover of darkness, and it is the character of evil to work in darkness. "Everyone who does evil hates the light, and will not come into the light for fear that his deeds will be exposed" (John 3:19–20).

Given such end-time conditions, it is doubtful that we would be able to clearly see a ten-nation coalition forming, certainly not anything as obvious as a monolithic, global government structure or a one-world currency. Even though Europe has unified itself in a remarkable fashion over the past fifty years, the final, ten-nation coalition is still not obvious…certainly not identifiable in exact detail. While we may feel pressured to seize and declare a sure answer to the many open questions that still remain with respect to end-time prophecy, we must not do so. Wrong conclusions can lead to even greater error and, worst of all, to serious vulnerability and lethal blindness to ongoing developments that may be right under our very noses. It is better to keep watching, discerning the season, and remaining open to proven facts, both new and old, and what Scripture actually reveals, and no more.

Potentially the most misleading interpretations of end-time prophecies are those that conclude that certain events or developments must yet occur, therefore, focusing the Christian on the future and not on present preparedness for Christ's return. It may be a subtle point, yet it is an important one. Global conspiracy theories, the coming one world order, and a one-world currency are all themes that can be played to invoke hysteria, diverting our proper focus.

The One-World Currency
Actually Has Debuted

It is already very late in the last days. We need not be distracted by expected events with respect to prophecy. The Lord's imminent return is not hindered by any prerequisite future development. While the concept of imminency means that the Lord can appear at any time, though not technically correct, we can say that His coming is even more imminent than ever!

Yet, it's likely that the eschatological timeline is much later than we may believe. In this sense, there is a strong case to be made that globalism has already advanced much farther than may be realized— even far enough that the Tribulation could start at any time.

However, one prominent development many observers argue is necessary to precipitate certain end-time events is the emergence of one-world currency. This is a red herring. Effectively, a one-world, common currency already exists. You may be surprised to read this last comment: The world already operates as if on a single currency standard. How so? Consider that virtually 99.9 percent of all cross-border money flows in the world today are conducted by large financial institutions, money center banks, large pension funds, secretive hedge funds, and corporations. To these "big players," money is already seamless and frictionless "global money." To those outside this system, it may look confusing and complicated. But, in reality, a tightly interconnected, worldwide financial system works across virtually all currencies. There are still separate currencies in name, but it's all part of one global money system. It is worthwhile to briefly explain its workings.

According to a survey taken by the Bank of International Settlements (BIS), approximately 90 percent of all currency transactions involve only ten currencies. All of these currencies can be hedged, swapped, or fixed far into the future using various sophisticated financial instruments. For instance, these facilities allow multinational corporations to move their monetary chess pieces around the world as if there is only one currency.

Where is the evidence? Some excellent sources are available to the public. Several such reports are provided by the BIS. For example, once every three years, this agency publishes a report on world currency trading. What do these reports reveal? First, that foreign exchange is the most enormous financial activity of any type in the entire world. In 2004, more than $1.9 trillion in currencies were exchanged every work day. It has surely increased hugely since then.

Yet, in the early 1970s, these transactions only amounted to $18 billion per year. Imagine! Today, at most only thirty-five years later, this much currency is exchanged every thirteen minutes—a volume that has risen 27,500 times in little more than three decades. (This is an amount equivalent to more than twelve times the entire annual world economic output!)

What we see operative in international exchange markets today has taken form very rapidly, accelerating markedly after 1970. As a young director of research for a major Wall Street firm, I was alerted to these trends very early by simply reading the reports made available by the BIS and other transnational organizations. Already in the mid-1980s, the grand architecture taking form could be discerned. Observing these rapid trends, I remember how amazed I was. What has happened since that time is simply spectacular, making the trends of those early days little more than drops in the sea.

DISCERNING THE MONEY FOREST FROM THE TREES

Is the world likely to ever see a one-world currency, meaning an obvious one that we can name and deposit in an ATM machine around the world? In my view, it is certainly possible, but it is not necessary. A globalized financial system already is interconnected as if operating on a single currency standard. Therefore, to become fixated on the idea of one-world currency and to sound the fire alarms every time there is a report of a currency unification plan cause deflection from the most important issue.

One can make the argument that a single currency is much too obvious an indicator of the lateness of end-time processes. Would Satan allow his deceitful ruses to be so transparent, even to undiscerning, unspiritual people? In this view, a single currency would be much too obvious, as it is not needed in any case. Yet, one can certainly travel around the world as if there were a single currency. Simply go to an automatic teller machine (or automated banking machine) in Tokyo or Tel Aviv (or almost any other major city in the world) and it will conveniently issue to you yen or shekel notes, respectively, debiting your account in local currency. Effectively, your debit or credit card already acts as a common currency.

For the most part, the "big" financial participants like the system the way it is now. Exchange transactions between the existing currencies generate rich revenues for the financial institutions. More importantly, a system of many currencies allows much greater leeway for manipulation and nefarious games to be played around the globe.

Will we see continuing convergence in the number of currencies in the world? That is very possible. Many new currencies are on the drawing board. For example, the six members of the Gulf Cooperation Council (GCC) have wanted to form a single currency, the khaliji, although of late the United Arab Emirates has pulled its support. They have since found it necessary to defer these plans. Also, a number of Asian nations have agreed to accelerate their plans to form a common currency. We could dedicate many pages to documenting other similar plans or the supportive viewpoints of various global policy makers or economists. Perhaps of greater significance in recent times is the initiative of the G20 (Group of Twenty) nations to expand the use of the SDR (special drawing right). This is an accounting unit of the International Monetary Fund that has long represented a type of single currency. Could this be the world's new single currency? In a sense, it already was, having been first introduced in its present form in 1969.

Despite the apparent push to a harmonize currencies, today there are actually more currencies and central banks in the world than there were fifty years ago. Nearly two hundred different currencies still exist. But, is there a system that works as a de facto one-world currency? Very definitely. There is an operating, one-world currency system that is more than adequate as a tool for a ten-nation coalition to bludgeon the world with.

Everything in this respect that might be required for last-day events is already operative right now. If you are expecting a mono-lithic one world order or a single currency, your eyes may be off the real action. You need not be like Didi and Gogo of the famous Beckett play, hopelessly waiting for Godot to arrive. These developments are not only specifically unnecessary prophetically, but the real develop-ments of importance may be in an entirely different form than most people are expecting. As it is our hope in any case, we are waiting for something very different—the return of Jesus Christ, which remains imminent.

HYSTERICAL DEFLECTION

It is sometimes tragic to see how a flimsy article published by an obscure newspaper without any substantiated sources will set off a flurry of misguided interpretations among "end-time" watchers. I sometimes imagine an editor somewhere having a chuckle tantalizing this community, watching these Christians taking the bait hook, line, and sinker. They know exactly how to wave a red flag. We need to be careful. Satan is very familiar with Scripture, too.

Also, not everything said by important elites or people of position should be taken as an inside tip on an emerging one-world-order development. There are a lot of bright people with many vain, imaginative, and foolish ideas. Nor is it always easy to understand the agenda behind the statements such people might make. For example, when George Soros (the famous billionaire hedge fund manager) makes a public statement, it should be asked: Is he buying or selling? What is his real agenda? It is not always as it may seem. Likewise, the comments of other influential people should be tested before taking them as clear evidence of some prophetic fulfillment or distraction.

THOUGHTS TO PONDER

God will never allow humanity the excuse of not having known the truth of His existence. He reveals more to those who seek Him and search for truth. It is God's good pleasure that these additional nuggets of truth are partially hidden. They are precious pearls reserved for seekers and Bereans, and they are not to be thrown before careless skimmers and thinkers.

The exciting fact is that all the information needed to understand our times is more available today than ever before. All that is required is a bit of sleuthing and common sense. And, we have the biblical imperative to do so: "Have nothing to do with the fruitless deeds of darkness, but rather expose them" (Ephesians 5:11).

The world doggedly clings to a belief in godless human progress despite the setbacks of recurring world wars, natural disasters, repeated human atrocities, and the toppling idols of monetary and economic systems.

All of man's achievements—technology (techniques of production, increases in productivity) and heaping of wealth—are not of our own making and determination alone. God is the author of all creation, its cycles, its natural properties, both what is in the world and under the earth, and all the possibilities of technology. Technology and financial systems have their good uses. Rather, the heart of man is the problem—the idolatrous attitude of self-determination and independence from God.

Ultimately, mankind's choices will be judged. A period of tribulation lies ahead. After that comes restoration. Isaiah confirms some of the conditions after that time. For example, the Babylonian-based money system will be destroyed and "will never be inhabited or lived in through all generations" (Isaiah 13:20); the rule of elites and the wicked will be finished (Isaiah 14:5); peaceful conditions will prevail (Isaiah 14:7); and no rapacious industry will raze the earth in its quest for profits (Isaiah 14:8).

Those who believe in the God of Israel and accept the gift of salvation through His Son will sing in loud voices: "Worthy is the Lamb, who was slain, to receive power and wealth and wisdom and strength and honor and glory and praise!" (Revelation 5:12).

And, very definitely, the world is looking for a champion savior right now. Shouts the title of a recent economic report, "China: Savior of the World!"[74] The cover of *Forbes* magazine recently blared the title, "Capitalism Will Save Us." A prominent journalist recently wrote, "We are saved. Amid the rubble of the world's financial markets, we can catch sight of the foundations of a new international order. The big lesson of the crisis has been learnt: we cannot escape our mutual dependence."[75] These comments betray that the world is looking for an economic savior, not the eternal One.

We look for our Savior elsewhere. The apostle Paul said to the Philippians: "But our citizenship is in heaven. And we eagerly await a Savior from there, the Lord Jesus Christ, who, by the power that enables him to bring everything under his control, will transform our lowly bodies so that they will be like his glorious body" (Philippians 3:20–21).

While the world stampedes into greater global interconnectedness and hyper-states of commercial idolatry in its quest for the security of grain and bread, it completely ignores the real bread. "For the bread of God is he who comes down from heaven and gives life to the world" (John 6:33). "I am the living bread that came down from heaven. If anyone eats of this bread, he will live forever" (John 6:51).

URGENCY OF
OUR TIMES

Figure #14

World Oil Reserves: Islamic Pre-eminence

Islamic Nations: 74.9%, Israel: 0.000001%

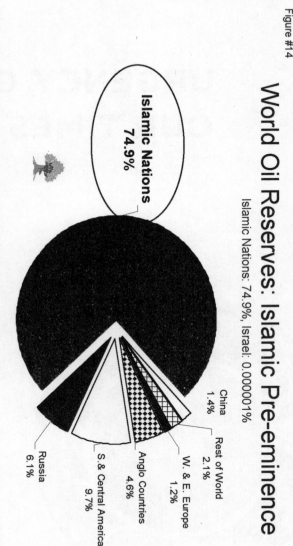

China
1.4%

Rest of World
2.1%

W. & E. Europe
1.2%

Anglo Countries
4.6%

S. & Central America
9.7%

Russia
6.1%

Islamic Nations
74.9%

Source: US, Energy Information Administration. Based upon BP Statistical Review, Dec. 31, 2004

Islam and Oil: How is it that Islamic nations today control approximately three-quarters of world oil reserves — the very commodity that the high-income nations of the world (most of which happen to be countries with historical associations to Christianity) use very intensely? Based on the World Oil survey of 2004, the Islamic share (members of the 57 nations of the Organization of Islamic Countries (OIC) is 74.9%. Various natural gas estimates place between 54.7% to 55.5% of world reserves among OIC members. Although no Bible reference substantiates that oil has an end-time role, the world oil situation evident today could not have happened by chance.

13

FOR ALL THE WORLD TO SEE: EARTH COUNTING DOWN

To this point, our views have mostly centered on the roles of mankind's economic and financial systems on the cosmological timeline. Scripture is clear as to the results of the choices of mankind —a final confrontation with the Creator. Contrary to popular depiction, He is not the menace of malice, therefore disqualifying him as a loving God. Yet, humanity, both as individuals and corporately, chooses to persist in its own ways…to deny Him the glory He deserves and the reward of the suffering of the Lamb that was slain. What should such a God do, who has given His creation the powers of decision and choice? A just ruler is forced to an end point to preserve his authority. There are many signs that this end point is near. In this chapter, we want to review some of the more obvious proofs of this outcome. Here we seek to appeal to the logical mind not only of Christians but also of non-believers.

SIGNS AVAILABLE FOR EVERYONE

Just what are the signs of the last days and the Lord's coming? It is true that some of these indicators are among the most contested questions in Christianity, also among evangelicals who believe in a premillennial return of Jesus Christ and a pretribulational Rapture. Even in this latter group of believers—which is a small minority in Christianity these days—one hears of schisms and breaking of fellowship over various interpretations of these signs of the Lord's coming. Do certain signs only relate to the Jews, or do they also apply to the "times of the Gentiles" and the dispensation of the Church? Is there a distinction between prophetic fulfillment of certain events and the conditions or processes that must take place before these can actually occur?

These questions are surely the subject of important study and discussion. But the practical focus for Christians is relatively straightforward. We are to be watching, looking to His coming, recognizing the season, and being "prepared in season and out of season" (2 Timothy 4:2). After all, "This same Jesus, who has been taken from you into heaven, will come back in the same way you have seen him go into heaven" (Acts 1:11).Yet, the sad reality is that only a small portion of those who call themselves "Christian" believes that the Lord Jesus Christ will soon return, or that the very last of the last-days events, namely the Tribulation period, is fast approaching. The paradox of this situation is this: Christians, the very people who possess the Bible and its prophecies, represent many of the scoffers who protest, saying: "Where is this 'coming' he promised? Ever since our fathers died, everything goes on as it has since the beginning of creation" (2 Peter 3:4). This attitude itself is a prophetic sign of the last-day season. Christ asked, "...when the Son of Man comes, will he find faith on the earth?" (Luke 18:8).

This situation is really more incredible than it seems. Why? Because one doesn't have to be a Bible-reading Christian to recognize that the world is heading for troubles and that many of today's trends are simply not sustainable. If Christians stand accused of ignoring the Bible and obvious world trends and events today, would then a non-Christian have any excuse for ignorance? The evidence says no.

THE SECULAR OBSERVER OF THE WORLD

Any person, in the course of reviewing world developments, must be struck with the many monumental, non-sustainable changes under-foot across the globe today. Of course, the Bible-believing analyst will quickly recognize that all of these factors are in alignment with Bible prophecy, even if not mentioned specifically. To them, it is a com-pelling conclusion that the last-day events of the Tribulation are fast approaching.

Yet, even the secular, non-Bible-believing analyst must conclude that dire times are ahead, if the present course of the world is not soon changed. Many world trends on the scene today are not sustainable. In other words, they either point to an end or to major worldwide dislocations that certainly could be apocalyptic in scale. To prove that the evidence is available for all to see, let's take the perspective of a non-Christian and do a bit of common-sense analysis.

Let's put on an analyst's hat and attempt some forecasts, just as any policy or economics specialist would. Doing so, we of course realize that forecasting is a treacherous endeavor at the best of times. By inter-preting "the appearance of the sky" (Matthew 16:2), in no way are we attempting to prophesy. That's the domain of the biblical prophets. In any case, "Prophecy is not given to enable us to prophesy," quoting Sir

Robert Anderson.[76] We are simply wishing to show that the "last-day season" should be sensed by the entire world and that the "financial signs of the times" are just one such emblem.

In no particular order, let's review ten such possible indicators.

1. Skewing of Wealth between Rich and Poor

The chasm between the world's rich and its poor continues to widen. The only major debate that concerns this topic has to do with its cause. The International Monetary Fund (IMF) profiled an in-depth study titled "Globalization and Inequality,"[77] observing that "inequality has risen in all but the low-income country aggregates over the past two decades." Of greater significance is a groundbreaking report entitled, "The Worldwide Distribution of Household Wealth,"[78] which was released in December 2006. This was the first-ever wealth survey of the entire world. Its conclusions were much more sobering than had been previously indicated by other studies that only surveyed income. James' prophecy in James 5:6, "Now, listen your rich people…you have hoarded wealth in the last days," which speaks of huge wealth inequalities in the last days, surely fits our time.

Secular analysts wonder where these trends are heading. At the present rate of this development, any one of two outcomes, or both, could occur: 1) The world will be controlled by a small cabal of rich overlords; or 2) it will experience anarchy and societal breakdown. It would not be overstating the case to say that today's wealth imbalances in the world exceed those during the late stages of the past Roman Empire. This condition is sure to play a role in future financial market scenarios, as it already has in the GFC. Wealthy people respond very differently in their attempts to preserve the value of their assets than do people with modest wealth.

2. Islam, Europe, and the Catholic Church

In 2006, Pope Benedict XVI faced quite a backlash from Muslims in response to a quote he used in a speech: "Show me just what Muhammad brought that was new and there you will find things only evil and inhuman."[79] It raises the question of whether a major clash lies ahead between Islam and Europe. Also that year, Libyan leader Mu'ammar Al-Qadhafi said, "We have fifty million Muslims in Europe. There are signs that Allah will grant Islam victory in Europe—without swords, without guns, without conquests. The fifty million Muslims of Europe will turn it into a Muslim continent within a few decades." [80]

Some prophecy scholars in fact think Islam will be part of a worldwide religious ecumenism at some point. This, however, seems unlikely. True Islam does not compromise and never has, other than for short-term advantage. In fact, Arabs—Islam, after all, is an Arab religion—cannot even agree among themselves, a characteristic the Bible itself documents. The Bible says of Ishmael, the father of the Arabs, "He will be a wild donkey of a man; his hand will be against everyone and everyone's hand against him, and he will live in hostility toward all his brothers" (Genesis 16:12). If Islam does not become part of the Babylon the Great, Mother of Prostitutes, we have another dilemma that will be sure to heighten in the next ten to twenty years.

Al-Qadhafi's comment points to a dynamic our secular observer would not miss. Arab and Islamic populations are growing much faster than that of Europe and the rest of the world. Compared to overall world population growth of 1.2 percent, the average growth of Middle Eastern countries is 1.7 percent while the European Union's growth rate is only 0.1 percent.[81] Today, it is estimated that there are approximately 1.5 billion Muslims in the world versus 1.2 billion Roman Catholics and perhaps a total of 2 billion people who broadly identify themselves as Christians (inclusive of Roman Catholicism). If present trends are any indication, to the secular analyst it is inevitable that Europe or a broader number of Christian countries will either clash with Islam or become subservient to it.

The Christian would be alerted to these additional perspectives. The prostitute shown in Revelation 17 is not subservient, but rather sits as a queen (Revelation 18:7) and rules over the kings of the earth (Revelation 17:18). We could conclude that the prostitute must already be here, or will emerge in the very near future. In view of the world population growth rate trends we have just reviewed, in perhaps one or two decades, she may no longer have the undisputed position of where she sits as an uncontested queen upon world affairs. This suggests that Tribulation events must begin before that time, if trends do not change.

3. Materialism and Financial Pyramiding

Seen over history, western society (now also including much of the rest of the world) has been living in the "five pillars of P" window for only a very brief time. These five pillars stand for petroleum, penicillin, population, productivity, and pyramiding, the five major factors behind today's end-time modernity. This five-pillar window spans a time space of only a century or so, a fraction of mankind's sojourn on earth. During this late period, mankind has become exceedingly proud of recent achievements. These have contributed to a fertile breeding ground for humanism, mankind's confidence and self-determination without God. Yet it is overlooked that all five pillars are subject to reversal. For example, mankind may lose the battle with microbes due to resistance to antibiotics, and the age of oil will pass, perhaps sooner than expected.

However, none of these factors is more vulnerable than the last two on the list—productivity and pyramiding. The advent of the GFC makes this clear. These relate to the economic and financial growth explosion over this period, involving globalization, technology, the increasingly invasive role of money, and the unstable system of monetarism. It has created a lustrous, intoxicating apparition of wealth…albeit mostly false wealth. While the advance of technology itself likely will not be lost, the huge financial colossus that has emerged in recent years is extremely vulnerable to collapse, as recent tremors testify. Even secular analysts can see this. One does not need the Bible to understand this, though the Scriptures surely are in line with this view. Given the greed, corruption, and rapaciousness that are part of this trend, it is only a matter of time.

Just how long can the world's shaky "financialization boom" last? Keep in mind that we are referring to the centuries-long process that has been underway and is likely to continue after the passing of the current GFC, should the Lord tarry. While it is impossible to be precise about such matters, the current pace of developments cannot continue indefinitely. Simple mathematics and classical monetary theory prove this view. The rate of changes in financial developments and debt are just too astounding. For example, consider that in the space of decade prior to the 2007 peak before the GFC ensued, total world financial value has risen by a factor of ten. Is this sustainable? If not, what will be the ultimate outcome?

Actually, of all the ten indicators we review here, this one qualifies as the most imminent. Technically, it can occur at any time and quite suddenly. While world monetary authorities and governments can buy some time by way of temporary manipulations, it remains very possible that the global financial crisis in fact may serve as the catalyst to the foundational launch point for the final conditions that will culminate in the final disasters in the Tribulation period. The sad truth, however, is that while many non-Christian analysts can see the writing on the wall, a large part of North American Christianity remains deluded, clinging to Prosperity Theology and the idea that God will not judge the materialism and greed that are the very underpinnings of our society.

4. Diseases, Pandemics, Biodiversity

One of the "five pillars of P" was represented by penicillin. The discovery of penicillin and the development of antibiotics that it spawned have had a remarkable impact upon modern civilization. For this and other reasons, death rates dropped sharply and life spans increased significantly over the last century. For example, in 1900, the average life expectancy at birth of a male in America was only forty-eight years. Today? A male can expect to live more than seventy-five years.[82] That has been a welcome trend, but can it continue?

Some disturbing developments suggest that the advances of medicine with respect to germs and microbes may only be temporary. One of these is the emergence of the superbug—bacterium that have mutated to resist multiple types of antibiotics. Infectious disease physicians are becoming increasingly alarmed that the development of new antibiotics will lose pace with this threat. They have good reason for their concerns. For one, pharmaceutical companies are falling behind in the development of new antibiotics. Secondly, antibiotic resistance spreads fast. For example, consider this observation from a study by the Food and Drug Administration:

"Between 1979 and 1987...only 0.02 percent of pneumococcus strains infecting a large number of patients surveyed by the national Centers for Disease Control and Prevention were penicillin-resistant. ...Today, 6.6 percent of pneumococcus strains are resistant, according to a report in the June 15, 1994."[83]

Other developments—in biology, biodiversity, nanotechnology...etc.—are cause for concern and point to possible severe challenges ahead. We can also include the rising vulnerability that arises from genetic engineering and pandemics. A common-sense analyst observing all of these trends can only conclude that the rising risks in this respect point to certain disastrous outcomes someday.

5. Israel and Jews in the World

Even if our secular analyst did not know that the world's time line circumnavigates the Jews and that they are destined to return to their homeland, he would surely make a few notable observations about the Jews. Without a doubt, he would conclude that the Jews must be a special people.

For one, it would have been noticed—as mentioned in Chapter 10—that for the first time in over twenty-five hundred years, the world's largest population of Jews now lives in Israel. That is a recent bellwether. Up until 2006 or so, the U.S. held this distinction. An understanding of probabilities and world history would further highlight the significance of Jewish developments in the world today. What people have ever been restored to their homeland after this long? In fact, what people have ever survived that long with their identity so documented and intact after the point that they have lost their country? What probabilities are defied by the fact that Hebrew, a language that fell out of common usage, would again become a spoken language?

The non-religious analyst would be amazed at such developments, thinking them beyond reason. Yet, astoundingly, there are people who do have knowledge of the Bible and its prophecies who still believe the modern-day events surrounding the world and the Jews are nothing more than circumstantial!

In fact, people who identify themselves as Christians seem to make up the majority of those who scoff at the Bible's prophecies and the doctrine of the imminent return of Jesus Christ. Among many Scriptures, they overlook that at His ascension, two men dressed in white (angels) said, "This same Jesus, who has been taken from you into heaven, will come back in the same way you have seen him go into heaven" (Acts 1:11). That time point becomes ever more unlikely to be delayed. The earth indeed has begun to display "birth pains" (Matthew 24:8) with respect to an unbelieving, end-time world as well as the Jewish people. Just as advancing age forcefully signifies our mortality and a coming end to our corrupt physical bodies, so does the created order under mankind's misappropriated dominion.

6. World Energy Supplies

In recent times, energy prices have been soaring, then crashing. What could this have to do with the end times? A broader analysis of the world's hydrocarbon supplies would certainly lead to the conclusion that the world will some day run out of cheap oil. In that sense, we have in view here an eventual end at least of one type—the end of the oil age. Our secular observer of this development—whether an energy expert or geopolitical strategist—would not disagree that oil supplies will assuredly run down based upon present-day trends. Moreover, the observer will also surmise that this will have a destabilizing effect upon the world. But, from the evidence, could he also conclude something more apocalyptic even without reading the Bible?

Consider these facts: Roughly three-quarters of world oil reserves are found in countries that are either predominantly Islamic or members of the fifty-seven-country member organization of the Islamic Conference. Muslim nations have 3.4 times as much oil per person than the world average and almost 7.7 times as much as major Chris-

tian nations—a group that we have categorized as the "Top-10-X" countries.[84]

Of the ten countries with the largest amount of oil (accounting for 65 percent of total world reserves), eight are Islamic. Of the fifteen countries with the largest natural gas reserves (accounting for a 50 percent of total world reserves), eleven are predominantly Islamic.

Moreover, it is interesting to note that with so much energy resources, these same nations should use so little of it themselves. The average Muslim in the world uses only 15 percent as much energy as citizens of the Top-10-X nations.

These facts and many improbable others relating to the world's hydrocarbon situation today beg incredulity and statistical probabilities. Observing all of these facts, a geopolitical analyst today would be alerted to a cosmic time plan that is indeed headed for a likely flashpoint.

Christians will note additional curiosities. According to experts on world religions, there are perhaps as many as twenty major, separate, sets of religions in the world today. Only one—Islam—specifically mandates in its writings that Jews should be killed. Today, it is even believed among Muslims that the "last day" of the world cannot come before Israel is first annihilated.[85]

The world's other major resources seem to be distributed among nations and religious groups with much less potential for spiritually inspired agendas against Israel. Indeed some nations are rich in certain resources—such as Chile, with one-third of world copper reserves, or Russia and South Africa in palladium. But none of these commodities uniquely fits an end-time role as only oil can. Considering all these perspectives, are we to believe that a random twist of fate has positioned the world supply of oil against Israel's future national interests?

7. Populations and Pensions

Without a doubt, a population-related crisis is underway in the world today the likes of which has never before occurred. Though potential problems have been anticipated by some experts, most people are unaware of its implications. In some respects, its impending manifestations are already evident, impacting financial and income trends around the globe.

What kind of crisis is expected? Not a population explosion, as has been feared in recent decades, but rather an implosion. Where it once was feared that the world would soon be overburdened by too many people, world population growth has since slowed dramatically from the peak rates of the 1960s. Demographic experts are already predicting that the world's population may actually decline twenty-five to fifty years from now. Crucially, world population trends have moved from one extreme to another in less than one century—a relatively short span on the human timeline.

At the turn of the last century, world population growth began to double every twenty-five years or so, an unprecedented development. Yet, by the start of the millennium only one hundred years later, population growth rates around the world had declined sharply. Never before has such a slowdown occurred voluntarily across the broad populace. Usually, sharp population declines in the past have been the result of war, famine, or plague. As such, two unprecedented developments have happened back to back. First, the fastest increase on record; then, a sharp deceleration quickly followed.

The concern is that there will be too many old people and not enough young workers. This and the feared consequence that pension systems—both governmental and private—will become bankrupt threaten to seriously disrupt economies. As such, the potential fallout of the dramatic population swings over the past century will play an integral role in the worldwide financial and economic crises clearly prophesied during the Great Tribulation. In fact, its impact is already evident. Many pension funds and government retirement support systems are grossly underfunded today. The GFC has exposed this situation clearly. Secular analysts all see that these trends will wreak havoc upon world economies, some predicting these effects to come to pass over the next twenty years. This situation, in our view, is a significant determinant of future financial trends.

The issues surrounding population growth are complex and must not be underestimated. The fact that population growth plays such an important role in end-time affairs is itself a logical result of God's created order...a matter of reaping what societies have sown. A recent study by the IMF reveals just how monumental this issue is in terms of future economic trends. Its authors estimate that the cost of the world's "aging crisis" will be approximately five times that of the net-present-value cost of the global financial crisis.[86] Shockingly, we therefore recognize that financial troubles witnessed to date are small by comparison. Figure 15 illustrates the estimated impact that the "aging crisis" will have upon world government debt levels. These are forecast to rise inexorably to levels three times that of today in relative terms by the year 2050.

8. Geopolitics and Human Conflict

Many observers conclude that the world is headed for a geopolitical crisis. For example, the famous Nobel Laureate Buckminster Fuller once wrote: "Humanity is moving every deeper into crisis—a crisis without precedent."[87] An atheist, he therefore errantly believed that this crisis was intended by the universe to transform humanity into a "completely integrated, comprehensively, interconsiderate, harmonious whole." Other analysts theorize that a World War III is inevitable. There are different reasons for this conclusion. To some, it appears certain that "religious fundamentalism" will bring the world to this state. Or, it could simply be the warlike characteristic of man in an age of advanced weaponry and geopolitics that must lead to such an outcome. In recent years, comments about a possible World War III have been popularized in relation to Iran's purported nuclear buildup. World wars are a modern invention, the first two of which have only occurred in the last one hundred years. Whatever the case or the cause for a WW III, the secular analysts must conclude that it could soon hold dire implications for the world.

9. Environmental Concerns

Is the earth wearing out? Despite the contested debate about global warming and various other environmental issues today, the Bible says that the world will run down. "Lift up your eyes to the heavens, look at the earth beneath; the heavens will vanish like smoke, the earth will wear out like a garment and its inhabitants die like flies" (Isaiah 51:6). No matter that globalists might want to use such issues as global warming to further their humanist agenda, the world is being indelibly changed in our day. Pollution has had an indisputable impact in many ways. Forests are disappearing at a rate that is not sustainable. Fish stocks in the world's oceans are being gradually depleted. There are other developments observable in the world, as the wearing out of a garment. Indeed, some effects can be reversed. But all the same, the logical analyst would still be faced with this question: How long can such trends continue before deeper crises impact the world?

10. Technology Signs

Finally, in our abbreviated list of ten indicators of unsustainability, we touch upon technology. It is of interest for at least two reasons.

In some ways, it is the capstone of humanistic hubris. What can mankind not achieve with present and future technology? Man has been to the moon and back, and is contemplating soon setting up habitations elsewhere in the universe. Scientists talk about the day when human life and consciousness will slip the bounds of the human body. Humans might even become nothing more than energy fields in cyberspace, according to the speculations of some so-called scholars. These fanciful dreams apparently pass for informed opinions among scientists. Without a doubt, technology has advanced enormously over the past several centuries, resulting in many conveniences and benefits. But where does it all lead? Some analysts argue that the pace of change can only slow, because the rate of change we are witnessing simply is not sustainable.

But there is a paradox in all this. Consider that two thousand years ago, the apostle Paul could write this: "For since the creation of the world God's invisible qualities—his eternal power and divine nature—have been clearly seen, being understood from what has been made, so that men are without excuse" (Romans 1:20).

If Paul at that time—pre-technology and pre-modern science—could deduce that God must exist based upon knowledge about the physical universe, why not moreso today, given the increase in knowledge? That should be the logical conclusion. Yet, modern man has taken the opposite posture. He chooses to worship mankind itself rather that the original Creator of all this know-how in the first place.

END-TIME TECHNOLOGICAL ALIGNMENTS

We will now leave our secular experts and next appeal to Bible believers. We have touched upon ten trends and observations that point to an end...or at least to an end of sustainability. We have shown that it would reasonable for a non-Christian analyst to be concerned about the future and to believe, as did Buckminster Fuller, in an ultimate crisis.

Christians have even less excuse. There are twenty-five-hundred-year-old Bible prophecies that can only take place in an advanced technological age such as today. For example, the statement about the two witnesses who, "for three and a half days men from every people, tribe, language and nation will gaze on their bodies and refuse them burial" (Revelation 11:9), has obvious implications. This could only occur as of this last half-century—the era of communications satellites. What nation, language, or kindred peoples today would not have access to the Internet or television over a three-and-a-half-day period?

Here is another such technological time stamp of future prophetic fulfillment: Isaiah says one of the modes of the return of the Jews to Israel would be flying. "Who are these that fly along like clouds, like doves to their nests? Surely the islands look to me; in the lead are the ships of Tarshish, bringing your sons from afar" (Isaiah 60:8).

Here we are given at least two significant indications. First, the final return of the Jews to Israel would not occur until manned flight is possible. We can be reasonably sure of this because the Hebrew word for "flying" in the Bible is generally only used in relation to the flight of birds or insects. All of its allegorical applications relates only to concepts (such as age "flying away"), but never to people actually flying. The quoted verse clearly refers to people flying like doves and clouds. Also, consider that the symbolism of a cloud extends beyond flight, as clouds are also thought of as containers…i.e., emptying themselves of their contents, such as rain (Ecclesiastes 11:3).

The second deduction we can make from this prophecy is that mankind will not be traveling in UFO-type saucers or by teleporters in the future, but in planes…machines that look like doves. That puts this prophecy into our era of international air travel, neither into the past nor far into the future. Interestingly, the new Boeing 787 Dreamliner has been widely admired for its remarkable, "bird-like," appearance.

POINTS TO PONDER

The world today shows numerous trends and developments that, should they continue, assuredly point to an end or at least to severe dislocation and troubles. Even secular, non-Bible-believing observers must conclude dire times are ahead if the present course of the world is not soon changed.

One does not have to be a Christian today to sense that the earth indeed has begun its last-day "groanings." Mankind, whether Bible-believing or not, remains without excuse, and not only because a logical analysis of our times must lead to the question of an end. The testimony of the Bible says so—some of its writings originating as much as three thousand years ago and more. The first verified appearance of the prophesied Christ has already occurred, and if He "…had not come and spoken to them, they would not be guilty of sin. Now, however, they have no excuse for their sin" (John 15:22). Moreover, God "has given proof of this to all men by raising him from the dead" (Acts 17:31).

Yet, one also does not need to be familiar with Bible prophecy to sense the season and the times. Mercifully, God has allowed even non-believers and nations—at least, unbiased analysts who can see the obvious, and nations that do not rage against Him (Psalms 2:1)—to see that the current course of the world is not sustainable. An honest, analytical mind alone can sense the many challenging conditions the world is and will be facing. Whether in the fields of religion, economics, geopolitics, or any other, we see developments that, based upon assumptions drawn from present patterns, must either come to a crisis point or at least a turning point, if not an end.

Even more urgent is the observation that almost all of the developments we have reviewed could be headed for crisis points no later than within a ten-to-twenty-year window. We can also draw this tentative conclusion: Never before have all these conditions—all of which stand to have global impact—intersected at the same time in history. The world needs the return of the Messiah, who will restore all things (Acts 3:21).

Of course, the forecasting of any trend is subject to much imprecision and error. After all, only God knows the future precisely. As it was, the objective of this chapter was not our prediction, but rather to show that even non-Bible readers should be able to identify the signs of the times.

What did Christ say to the first unbelieving generation to which He appeared? "When evening comes, you say, 'It will be fair weather, for the sky is red,' and in the morning, 'Today it will be stormy, for the sky is red and overcast.' You know how to interpret the appearance of the sky, but you cannot interpret the signs of the times" (Matthew 16:2). Today, as then, a wicked generation chooses to ignore the prophesied signs.

We have a more sure word of hope. Jesus Christ will restore all things, and we who are in Christ will be taken up to be with Him.

Figure #15

Rising Government Debt – Advanced G-20 Nations
Government Debt as % of Gross Domestic Product

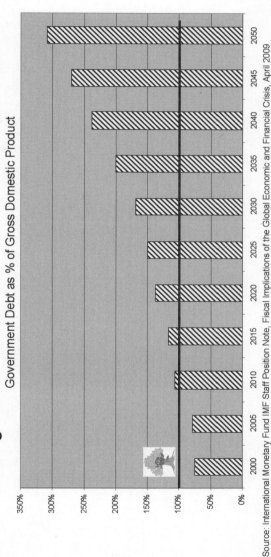

Source: International Monetary Fund IMF Staff Position Note, Fiscal Implications of the Global Economic and Financial Crisis, April 2009

Bigger Troubles Yet Ahead. The debt of most governments of advanced nations has spiraled as a result of the global financial crisis (GFC). The bail-outs of the financial sectors as well stimulative budgetary spending will cause government debt to double and more relative to the size of their economies in some countries. This is an unfortunate development. But, it is not the worst. An even greater crisis is forming ahead … the global aging crisis. According to the estimates of the IMF, government debt of the advanced member nations of the G20 is expected to more than triple relative to today's levels over the next four decades. The world will continue to face grave financial struggles even post GFC.

14

GLOBAL FINANCIAL APOCALYPSE PROPHESIED: THE WORST YET TO COME

"You ain't seen nothing yet." That was the sunny declaration of U.S. President Ronald Reagan at the end of his re-election speech in 1984. The popular Reagan declared: "America's best days lie ahead."[88] Indeed those were sunnier times for America. As we have already contemplated, America's outlook no longer appears so bright.

The GFC does not just concern a small set of countries or America alone. Significantly, we recognize that the GFC this time has the entire world in its grip. Any rational person can recognize that the world has an appointment with destiny...a coming judgment. In the previous chapters, we proved that such expectations are a logical deduction no matter what one's religious persuasions. Even the atheist cannot discount the notion of various types of world apocalypses occurring in the future.

Not only can conditions become much worse for America and other countries as a result of the current GFC, there still lies ahead the global financial apocalypse. In fact, the Bible makes one thing clear:

"We ain't seen nothing yet." In this chapter, we briefly review possible scenarios both for America and the world, as well as examine what Bible prophecy reveals about a final collapse.

TYPES OF APOCALYPSE

What does the word "apocalypse" actually mean? Its usage today is confused. We will not be able to properly discuss various future scenarios if we do not first clarify its definition. The origin of this word is found in Greek thousands of years ago. However, its meaning then was quite different from its various definitions today. Technically, the word originally meant an "unveiling" or "revelation" given to a person. That is why the book of Revelation in earlier times was referred to as the "Apocalypse of St. John"—the unveiling given to the apostle John. Since that time, the word "apocalypse" has come to have additional meanings, referring to anything having to do with the end times or the "end of the world," whether or not of Jewish and Christian origin. The word "Apocalypse" (capitalized), on the other hand, also is taken to mean the seven-year Tribulation period that is described in Revelation. Therefore, using the full breadth of common usage, it is possible that some apocalyptic trends may have nothing to do with the actual Apocalypse. They may be seen to be apocalyptic by secular commentators—namely, leading to an end or a catastrophe—however, are not prophetically identified in the Bible to happen during the Tribulation period itself. Of course, other trends evident today surely are the forerunners of processes and events prophesied to occur in the Tribulation period.

Now that we have this definition sorted out, we will be careful to distinguish between developments that are merely apocalyptic and those that either lead to or fulfill prophetic events inside the Apocalypse.

Things Could Have Been Worse

How much worse could the GFA or another future crisis yet become? It may be surprising to learn that the GFC to date could have been a lot worse than it was. As we briefly observed in Chapter 3, declines in U.S. housing prices and stock markets have not exceeded the historical precedents of similar crises in the last century. Also, consider that the major financial market declines only involved a relatively small amount of the world's capital actually being sold or bought. For example, in the case of the United States, only 3 percent of the $7 trillion in U.S. mutual fund assets were actually liquidated in the eighteen-month period between mid-2007 and the end of 2008. If stock market declines of 50 percent and more were associated with only 3 percent of investor assets exiting mutual funds, one wonders what would happen if 10 percent or 25 percent of all mutual fund holders wished to sell during a crisis period.

The same question applies to pension funds. In the case of the U.S. pension sector, they continued to be net buyers of bonds and stocks throughout 2007 and 2008. Again, we ask: What would have happened if this financial sector, the largest holder of securities assets in the world, had embarked upon massive capital flight? Stock exchanges would surely have been shut down around the world. In that case, equity and bond markets would have been nearly worthless. The world's financial system would have come to a sudden standstill. Similar declines in value would occur for many other assets. Even gold, the supposed sure harbor of safety, could prove utterly worthless at such a time.

OTHER COMPLICATIONS POSSIBLE

Other large powder kegs lurk within the world's financial systems that could some day explode with nuclear-like force. To this point, the world's colossal over-the-counter (OTC) derivatives markets have held together, though shaken. Valued at $516 trillion in notional terms before the GFC began (June 30, 2008, equivalent to some eight times the annual output of the entire world economy at that time), this market continued to grow even throughout the crisis. By mid-2008, already a year into the GFC, the outstanding value of these instruments had risen 32 percent further, to $684 trillion. Even outstanding credit default securities (CDS), a relatively new innovation that had boomed in size and value prior to the GFC, had not faced a fatal market disruption. Since that time, due to growing risk aversion and the deleveraging of the various financial institutions, the outstanding value of derivatives has begun to decline, though still remaining significantly higher than at the start of the crisis.

Despite enormous losses being borne by some participants in this market due to the high-profile bankruptcies of such firms such as Lehman Brothers, this market did not collapse. One reason is that the U.S. government underwrote some $170 billion of the losses in these instruments suffered by AIG. In so doing, the financial fortunes of other firms who were the counterparties to AIG on these contracts were saved. The point here is that had the world's derivatives markets collapsed—which would have been likely had the U.S. and other country governments not intervened—the entire financial world would have been virtually immobilized.

Another highly unstable condition that could yet upend the entire world economy is that other countries own a very large amount of U.S.-dollar securities. China's State Administration of Foreign Exchange (SAFE) and several other of this country's investment agencies alone may own in excess of $1 trillion in U.S. securities, mostly held as U.S. Treasury bonds. That is an enormous amount, equivalent to roughly 7 percent of the current size of the U.S. economy and nearly 25 percent that of China's.

What would happen if China were to sell these securities? Should China choose to do so, it would surely cause a collapse in the U.S. dollar. Such a situation could still threaten the U.S., and is similar to a situation that occurred between Britain and France in the early 1930s. Then, France was in the position of China today, and Britain in the equivalent position as the U.S. It ended quite disastrously. The UK pound (Britain's currency) eventually crashed and the French central bank, which was privately owned at the time, needed to be bailed out by the French government due to the catastrophic losses this bank sustained.

These few situations we have reviewed will give ample evidence as to how much worse the GFC could have been…or how much worse future crisis may yet become. With this realization, we can better imagine just how utterly catastrophic the collapses set to occur will be during the Great Tribulation.

How Much Worse for America?

It appears to be a logical deduction from Bible prophecy that America will decline in relative world influence, as we proposed in Chapter 11. However, this expectation still gives us no sure basis for any near-term predictions, nor does it provide the exact mechanism that will lead to this state.

Any seasoned global trend watcher will humbly admit that the future can indeed be surprisingly different than ever imagined. Even long-term trends—perhaps spanning twenty to fifty years and more—can be interrupted by abrupt and extended reversals before again resuming their longer-term direction. At these points of temporary reversal, it is easy to lose sight of the long-term trend.

Nevertheless, a number of different scenarios may lead to a global multipolar power structure…with or without the U.S. However, forecasting is a hazardous exercise, especially when it concerns financial markets and geopolitical shifts. We will therefore be careful not to make any unfounded predictions.

To forecast what may happen to America is one thing. But what effect such changes may have upon currencies, stock markets, or any other development must also encompass a perspective on what is happening in the rest of the world. Forecasting in this respect is a relative game.

For example, when forecasting the future developments of a single nation, this cannot be done without also anticipating the outlook for other nations. That is why, for example, so many forecasters are very wrong in their currency forecasts. This has certainly been the case with the U.S. dollar. It zigs when people think it will zag, and zags when it is predicted to zig. Why? Not only are currencies notoriously impacted by a wide range of factors, they are instruments that trade relative to each other. It is not enough to have a correct opinion about developments in America; one must also be able to assess these factors relative to the rest of the world. It is possible that America may be in a declining trend while a demise of Europe is unfolding even more rapidly. Therefore, to the consternation of uninformed observers, the U.S. dollar will rise even while conditions look rather black.

We must remember that the "love of money" remains a primeval force on earth. It drives the ways of the world. The very best and most devious minds are applied to the goal of accumulating money. As the saying goes, "It takes a thief to catch a thief." In like manner, to outwit the majority of people who are all panning the world for profits and gain requires a sharp intelligence and intrepid shrewdness. Having such characteristics is not necessarily unbiblical. Christ did say, "I am sending you out like sheep among wolves. Therefore be as shrewd as snakes and as innocent as doves" (Matthew 10:16). If we do not have these characteristics, we will have poor prospects of becoming relatively rich in the world's eyes. But would it be logical that Christians as a group will excel in such task? Likely not.

If learning anything from decades of moiling for portfolio gains in the world's financial markets, it is that economic and financial prediction requires either a great deal of humility…or naïveté. One will be wrong frequently. Unfortunately, too many organizations and ministries unnecessarily cause misdirection when they delve into financial prediction. They are hardly experts and thereby can unwittingly become part of the emotional swings that so often part people from their money.

With that clear disclaimer, can we make any predictions at all about America and the further outworkings if the GFC? Yes. Citing the famous quote of Friedrich von Schiller, the German philosopher and playwright,[89] "In today already walks tomorrow." We can surely discern how trends may continue, given the conditions of today.

Taking that perspective, we must conclude that there is the potential for a very grim future for America as well as other Western nations. The GFC, while it may be nearing the end of its first phase, will likely lead to even more challenging times ahead. We will consider some of the possible scenarios.

THE ROAD AHEAD WELL TRAVELED

In times past, when all else has failed, policy makers have always resorted to policies leading to inflation. Given the lawless and immoral character of the times, we consider it high odds that such an outcome is surely now underway. However, we must on guard for very deceptive manifestations of inflation that are likely to fool most people. The

Bible clearly outlines that a mark of the last days is deception, not only spiritually but also politically and economically. Such conditions play a chief role in fooling and entrapping many people during that prophesied period.

Already, many of the world's major central banks—the Bank of England, the U.S. Federal Reserve, the Swiss National Bank, the Bank of Japan—have begun to print money, and lots of it. The U.S. alone at one point announced plans to "create" $1.25 trillion. In a desperate attempt to "refloat" the world's economies, these central banks have thought it allowable and necessary to simply create money out of thin air. That this is a corrupt act, there is no doubt. Most people accumulate their savings through hard work and stewardship. For a central bank to simply create money through its wizardry effectively devalues the monetary savings already in people's possession.

These actions by central banks must be considered a bellwether event. There must be an inflationary repercussion of some kind if these policies are not soon reversed, because there is now rampant "monetary" inflation. This is the essence of inflation and all its outworkings. The only question remaining concerns the manner of its manifestation. Will inflation be reflected in consumer prices, financial asset prices, real assets, changes in the external accounts of countries, currency movements, or relative wealth transfers? One or more of these outcomes could occur. These are the questions that citizens of the world must now grapple with.

DECEPTIVE FALSE DAWNS AHEAD

The "reflationary efforts" by central banks should be expected to at least produce a perception of economic recovery. But here, it is important to distinguish between the real "living standard" conditions of people's lives and the trends of financial markets. Stock and bond markets can very well be brought back to a boil of new speculative highs in future years. As investors come to recognize that inflation stands to devalue their cash savings, they may run to any asset that will rise in value faster than their cash is depreciating. While financial markets and the prices of commodities such as foodstuffs and energy could soar in this type of environment, true economic conditions would continue to deteriorate—perhaps with unemployment remaining high and incomes and interest rates staying very low. It would be an environment similar in character to that suffered in Germany in the early 1920s (Weimar period of 1919 to 1923), various Latin American countries in ensuing years, and more recently in Zimbabwe. The only difference this time is that mildly similar conditions could be a global phenomenon.

All in all, the scenario considered could very well align with the prophecy found in Revelation 6:6: "I looked, and there before me was a black horse! Its rider was holding a pair of scales in his hand. Then I heard what sounded like a voice among the four living creatures, saying, 'A quart of wheat for a day's wages, and three quarts of barley for a day's wages, and do not damage the oil and the wine!'" (Revelation 6:6, NIV).

This verse speaks of a time when agricultural prices are drastically out of line with incomes. Effectively, a full day's labor will be required just to pay for a subsistence of food. While admittedly speculation, this prophecy nevertheless provides an indication of the severity of at least one of the stages of the coming global financial apocalypse of the future.

Nevertheless, we live in a world where almost all resources, minerals, and agricultural products have been "commoditized." That means that prices of such items are set on a worldwide basis—for the rich and poor countries alike. That's one of the effects of the last-day globalization that has swept the world. It is a condition that has really only come about in the last one hundred to one-hundred-fifty years. We can at least conclude that the prophecies of the Bible are in indeed aligned with the globalized, commoditized world already evident.

THE FUTURE OUTLOOK GUIDED BY PROPHECY

What lies ahead both near-term and long-term? We must remain open to the possibilities. After all, major global changes can happen rapidly today. Consider that during 1997 and 1998, the entire Asian continent seemed submerged in the financial crisis of that time. Who would have predicted that the next economic powerhouse and store of world surplus reserves would reside on this very same continent less than ten years later? In less than a decade, from conditions of deficits and economic depressions, countries such as China, Singapore, Taiwan, and others ended up as major creditors to the world. Most significantly, China ended up as the major lender to the largest economy in the world, namely the U.S. We can surely anticipate that the world will be even more remarkably different a decade from today.

Bible prophecy can help us probe into the future and evaluate scenarios. After all, "we have the word of the prophets made more certain, and you will do well to pay attention to it, as to a light shining in a dark place" (2 Peter 1:19). Then just what sure word does Bible prophecy tell us about the future that we can use to frame our range of expectations?

To begin, Scripture clearly states that a time of wrath will come when God says He will bring down the pride of mankind. Most understand that this will occur in the Tribulation period for the entirety of mankind. However, as part of this is unfolding, there are possibly as many as six different judgments involving collapses or wealth over-turns, all yet to occur.

Isaiah sheds light on some of the different manifestations of the "day of the Lord" (referring to the Tribulation period or possibly just the second half).

> The LORD Almighty has a day in store for all the proud and lofty, for all that is exalted (and they will be humbled), for all the cedars of Lebanon, tall and lofty, and all the oaks of Bashan, for all the towering mountains and all the high hills, for every lofty tower and every fortified wall, for every trading ship and every stately vessel. The arrogance of man will be brought low and the pride of men humbled; the LORD alone will be exalted in that day, and the idols will totally disappear. (Isaiah 2:12–18)

Here we see that economies will be brought low (trees), and trading systems (ships) as well as individual nation-states (mountains) will be humbled. Reading the above text, readers may wonder how we derived such a conclusion. If so, this may be due to unfamiliarity with the Bible's use of symbols and types. (For those interested in further examining the symbols found in this prophecy, a brief explanation is found in Appendix 2 at the end of this book.)

MORE THAN ONE TYPE OF COLLAPSE PROPHESIED

While it is prophetically factual that mankind's systems will come to a total collapse in the Tribulation period, this does not occur as one event but rather as many. What Isaiah calls the "day of the Lord" has a number of meanings. It can refer to the long or the short day (i.e., the seven-year period in entirety or the last half of the Tribulation, respectively), allowing for a number of collapses to take place. Here, in no particular order, are some major judgment categories that are ahead as part of our premillennial view, with brief explanations.

1. Wrath upon Israel/Jerusalem. Jerusalem is overcome while the remnant escapes into the wilderness. While Israel may be a rather tranquil area of the world (relatively) in the first half of the Tribulation following a covenant with the Antichrist, anyone hoping to remain unscathed and safe from loss in the second half will be disappointed.

2. Wrath upon All Mankind. This category includes judgments on individual nations as well as globalism itself. Ultimately, this is completed at Armageddon and in a short period thereafter. In this category we would include such judgments as upon Edom and Moab. Not only does God "consume the whole earth" (Zephaniah 3:8), but Israel also plays a role in exacting judgment upon the nations and peoples that have persecuted her (Micah 4:13, Jeremiah 30:11).

3. Wrath upon the Great Whore. Revelation 17 reveals that Mystery Babylon, the Mother of Prostitutes, will be burned by fire. Whatever wealth this religious entity represents, as part of the grand ecumenical movement of religion and money, she will come to naught. "They [the ten kings] will bring her to ruin and leave her naked; they will eat her flesh and burn her with fire" (Revelation 17:16).

4. Wrath and Judgment upon Mammon/Commercialism. It is not generally well understood that the judgments upon commercialism and the manmade pride that derives from these "Babel-like" systems take more than one form. Actually, they appear to occur on three separate levels. A remarkably large amount of prophecy focuses on these related judgments, which would require a separate book were we to attempt to present this entire thesis here. However, suffice to say that the Bible's heavy prophetic emphasis on this general topic—only second in volume to the prophetic material referring to future Israel and her peoples—alerts us to the importance of God's plan of judgment in this area.

Consider briefly that there are three stages in the collapse of Babylon the Great, at least one of these aligning with prophesied judgment of a modern-day re-emergence of ancient Tyre—a global, trade-based system—that Ezekiel and Daniel foresaw.

They are clearly different aspects of the judgment upon Mammon/commercialism. For example, in the case of Babylon the Great, its wealth is "...never to be found again" (Revelation 18:21); while that of revived Tyre is only never to be hoarded again, but is to "go to those who live before the LORD" (Isaiah 23:18). These are different results, and therefore must refer to more than one judgment.

Also, events befalling Babylon the Great must be separated into at least three judgments. We must note that "death, mourning and famine" will overtake her in one day (Revelation 18:8), while the sudden collapses and destruction of wealth are said to occur in "one hour"—three separate times involving three different groups of people (Revelation 18:10, 17, 19). The facts that some judgments occur in one hour and that the entire fall of Babylon the Great occurs over "one day" suggest that the downfall cannot be reconciled in one event, but rather involve multiple events.

Finally, at the end of all these collapses and wealth overturns, one more great and final overturn occurs at the start of the Millennium period. It is the great wealth transfer to Israel. Much of the world's riches that are not destroyed in the Tribulation period flow to Zion. Even here, there are at least two types of flows; that which apparently is seized as part of the "threshing" of the nations that rise against Israel is treated differently. These are "ill-gotten gains" of the nations (Micah 4:13, translated as "illicit" profits) that go before the Lord.

Other flows are more in tribute or as a result of Israel's dealings with the rest of the world. For example, "Then you will look and be radiant, your heart will throb and swell with joy; the wealth on the seas will be brought to you, to you the riches of the nations will come" (Isaiah 60:5; also see Isaiah 60:11, 61:6, 66:12; and Zechariah 14:14).

THE ROAD TRAVELED TO THE FUTURE COLLAPSE

Now that we have a better understanding of some of the financial aspects of the future Tribulation—what we are calling the global financial apocalypse—we may well want to ask how the world will get to that future time from here. What might be the intervening steps…the various scenarios? Let's begin to tackle this question from the perspective of secular advisors who are fighting the GFC tooth and nail.

These scholars are peering into the past to guide their way forward. Importantly, they are intensely analyzing the 1930s Great Depression and other significant economic busts, such as the slow-motion version that occurred in Japan between 1989 and today. Why? They are hoping to avoid repeating the mistakes of policy makers of the 1930s or of Japan. Great confidence is put in the fact that the current governor of the Federal Reserve Board, Dr. Ben Bernanke, is an accomplished historian of the infamous dust-bowl 1930s. Just what were these alleged mistakes made by old-time policy makers that are to be avoided in today's GFC?

Believe, it or not, there is little agreement on the answer to this question. Actually, the entire focus of debate is somewhat backward. A key point is that the questions here only focus on the aftermath, the financial and economic crises themselves once they have already occurred. Therefore, this discussion is largely only between economists who either didn't foresee a crisis or had little idea as to how prevent the conditions that led to such instabilities in the first place.

Wouldn't it have been better to avoid a crisis in the first place? As in healthcare, preventative behavior is much cheaper and less painful than medical treatment—possibly, invasive surgery or cardiac intervention. In this sense, it is the mistakes and bad habits before the crisis that are the real cause.

Where, then, are the big policy mistakes to be found? Actually, they occurred a long, long time ago. The conditions of speculation and rampant inflation that eventually led to instabilities and vulnerability to collapse were uncritically allowed to fester and build for a long time. To no surprise, the 250 or so economists with doctorates who work at the Federal Reserve protest that it is not possible to identify such developments ahead of time. These policy makers and many other economists collectively like to maintain that it is not possible to recognize a bubble until after the damage has been done. Really? This is one of the greatest absurdities, as the symptoms of unstable bubbles and busts are well known and quite simple.

Classical economists have always had a ready definition…a reliable diagnostic test with which to identify a bubble. The booms that led to bubbles, graft, and greed of the elites all had the same basic ingredients, though with some variation. Here is a diagnostic list of the major factors:

- A large expansion in debt, either driving an overconsumption or overinvestment binge. Credit and debt therefore grow faster than overall savings.
- A heavy reliance on capital gains for income and reported profits. People turn to the pursuit of easy gains rather steady income and profits.
- A sharply higher participation level in the stock market or some type of marketable asset that can be readily

borrowed against, either directly or indirectly. Real estate served this function in recent years.

- Crucially, a misreading of underlying credit and inflation trends. Policy makers allow themselves to believe that their monetary inflation is not harmful and holds no future consequences.

- A "great new world" impulse or theme convincing everyone of a new sustained era of prosperity, usually represented by a technological shift of some kind. For example, the telephone and the automobile were impulses contributing to past booms.

- Chronic external deficits—for example, a current accounts deficit—requiring a country to rely upon international borrowing to sustain its spending.

- Shifts on the household's balance sheet that led to a plunge in personal savings rates. Households may be accumulating nonproductive assets (consumer goods, for example) and overpriced houses in relation to their income and ability to support debt payments.

- Widening income and wealth skews in the general population. The rich get richer and the poor more so—to unsustainable extremes.

- Gross distortions in the input/output structure of an economy. This is a technical concept best explained with this example: When U.S. retail store space doubled from nineteen to thirty-eight square feet per capita between 1990 and 2005, this was definitely a distortion of the input/output structure of the American economy. By comparison, most European countries have less than ten square feet per capita.

All of these conditions occurred simultaneously as never before in recent years. A crucial point is that these imbalances have not yet been fully unwound to this point in the GFC. Then how much more pain of adjustment is still to be expected?

CAUSE AND CONSEQUENCE ARE RELATED

There is a sound principle observed by the Austrian School of economists. It is the idea that mistakes and excesses have consequences that cannot be avoided. Simply put, the damage suffered is equal to the damage done. Quoting Gottfried Haberler, the well-known Austrian School economist, "The length and severity of depressions depend partly on the magnitude of the 'real' maladjustments which developed during the preceding boom and partly on aggravating monetary and credit facts—the scramble for liquidity, destruction of bank money, and similar events on the international level."[90]

His view was simply that the severity of the following consequences—whether financial or economic, and in whatever other form—were related to the excesses and distortions that preceded them. Therefore, to find out how deep an economic downturn will be, first observe the extent of the imbalances and damage that occurred before.

This is not such a radical idea. In fact, the Bible teaches a similar principle. The consequences of mistakes cannot be avoided and must be atoned for: "A man reaps what he sows" (Galatians 6:7). Sins must be atoned (Romans 3:25). However, this is not a popular concept, certainly not among policy makers and politicians. Society is more likely to vote for what it wants to hear, as opposed to what is realistic. Not surprisingly, mankind has wanted to escape this connection to consequences from the dawn of time.

Efforts to avoid the repercussions of past excesses have long been evident in policy responses, most certainly in the U.S. economic realm. In fact, if anything, policy makers are doing their best to slow down correction and are hoping to restart the previous manias. Unfortunately, in doing so, the causes of the underlying disease have not been dealt with. Why? Societies want effortless prosperity and consumption in excess of their earnings; and politicians want to be seen delivering on such unrealistic expectations.

Therefore, problems are being covered up or papered over rather than cleaned up. Excesses have accumulated and prior bubbles have simply been converted into other types of unsustainable bubbles. A sure sign of this continuing deferral is rising total debt and skewing wealth and income distribution. For example, the enormous U.S. stock market bubble of the late 1990s, then capped off by the technology share mania, was later converted into a real estate mania as the policy responses of the central bank in trying to ameliorate the damage of the prior excesses allowed speculation and inflation to vent into a new direction.

Ultra-low interest rates, it is now well known, soon encouraged people to refinance their mortgages and cash out equity from their homes. This in turn led to overinflated real estate prices. During this entire period, debt growth continued to rise relative to income levels, far outrunning savings. We live today with consequences of this last and unfortunate craze

WHERE NEXT? FUTURE CHOICES

What will happen next? Will there be another bubble? Can there be a sustainable economic recovery? The correct answers here are related to two other questions we must first ask. They will confirm the likely prognosis.

First, will policy makers choose to continue to try to outrun consequences of past mistakes, or will they face up to them? The answer is eminently clear by now. Governments and central banks around the world have chosen to try to escape the results of past folly. In so doing, they are setting up the conditions for much greater future economic collapses in the future. However, this need not necessarily happen in the very near future. A major recovery period may occur—at least in some parts of the world—before this eventuality again looms.

To date, many countries are aggressively raising national debt levels by boosting government spending and bailing out various industries, above all companies in the financial sector. For example, Britain, itself home to the second largest financial center in the world, has now breached government debt levels greater than 100 percent of GDP (annual gross domestic product of the economy), and is risking a downgrading of its credit rating. Incredibly, this former world empire has finally come to this shameful point. It is now recklessly pursuing inflationary monetary policies.

The U.S. government at the time of this writing had already committed to more than $12 trillion in expenditures, bailouts, and contingent guarantees in its effort to forestall further financial collapse. This is an almost unfathomably large amount, equating to almost forty thousand dollars for every man, woman, and child in America. According to estimates, this is ten times the intervention of any other postwar recession. Such policy responses surely cannot lead to sustainable prosperity. They lead to even higher debt—ever-higher burdens for future generations.

Without a doubt, policy makers—both in America and around the world—are choosing to outrun their problems with monetary manipulation. That must lead us to conclude that any economic and financial recoveries must be considered temporary and will certainly not be sustainable. The options chosen are monetary manipulation, deception, and cronyism. It will lead to even greater impoverishment for America and certain other nations relative to the rest of the world.

It is a desperate situation. Some see it as the last chance for the vindication of humanist monetary theories. Again, quoting the influential Martin Wolf of the *Financial Times*:

> This is no small matter. Over almost three decades, policy makers and academics became ever more confident that they had found, in inflation targeting, the holy grail of fiat (or man-made) money. It had been a long journey from the gold standard of the nineteenth century, via the restored gold-exchange standard of the 1920s, the monetary chaos of the 1930s, the Bretton Woods system of adjustable exchange rates of the 1950s and 1960s, the termination of dollar convertibility into gold in 1971, and the monetary targeting of the 1970s and 1980s.... Most of us—I was one—thought we had at last found the holy grail. Now we know it was mirage. This may be the last chance for fiat money. If it is not made to work better than it has done, who knows what our children might decide? Perhaps, in despair, they will even embrace what I still consider to be the absurdity of gold.[91]

His sentiments are eerily correct, though he himself sees no other hope. While gold surely isn't the answer in the long term, though it may very well be a convenient store of value as an investment over the near term, he can smell despair. Here again he is correct. There indeed will come a time when the entire world will be in despair as humanist philosophies prove bankrupt. The world then will not choose gold or any other kind of idol. In fact, people will throw them into the streets (Ezekiel 7:19). They will choose a false messiah.

NATURE OF PEOPLE: AN IMPORTANT FACTOR

The second question we must ask in our diagnosis is this: Attitudinally, what type of people does society today comprise? Can they bear hardship...will they persevere through troubles? Or, will they feel entitled to rebel and fall into anarchy? We already commented on the role Prosperity Theology has played in polluting the expectations of Americans, no matter the denomination of Christianity. The same nonsensical expectations have been promoted on a secular level. To this point, most people are still somewhat hopeful that government actions might bail them out of their troubles.

But what would happen if these expectations were disappointed? Just what would be the response of the majority of people whose personal net worth has been devastated; whose house values have fallen below the value of their mortgages; who have discovered that a very small group of rich people have become even richer? Any range of answers will include some frightening scenarios.

To gauge the potential severity of any future outcome, it is useful to get a sense of the wealth devastation the average American household has experienced. While it is true that people must be held accountable for the consequences of their own stewardship decisions, the fact remains that the impact of the GFC has been of a shocking scale.

DEEP DESTRUCTION AND DESPERATION

A study by the Center for Economic Policy Research surveyed the wealth effect of the GFC for older American households.[92] It included the effects of the declines in real estate values as well as financial markets to the end of 2008. The results are chilling; they reveal the potential for severe desperation.

Many people between the ages of forty-five and sixty-four still have not paid off their houses. In fact, the situation is even much worse. Though perhaps owning their residences for more than two decades, a large number of households do not have positive net equity in their homes. Imagine! "Nearly thirty percent of the households headed by someone between the ages of forty-five and fifty-four will need to bring money to their closing (to cover their mortgage and transactions costs) if they were to sell their home. Technically, they have negative equity in their home. For people between the ages of fifty-five and sixty-four the percentage is 15 percent." The authors of this report state that the median household between the ages of fifty-five and sixty-four has experienced a drop in wealth of 50 percent since 2004.

Consider that these estimates do not include the effects of further price declines in real estate and financial assets, which continued to fall in the early months of 2009. Quoting further from the study, "The baby boom generation for the most part has insufficient time remaining before retirement to accumulate substantial savings. Therefore, they will be largely dependent on social insurance programs to support them in retirement."[93]

The most worrisome aspect of the massive declines in household net worth is that it has impacted the middle class disproportionately, and comes at a time when many baby boomers are approaching retirement years. The disaster that has befallen American households couldn't have come at a worse moment.

A DEMOGRAPHIC BOMB ON TOP

Viewing the high debt levels in America and other nations, some people may ask: Debt levels have been high before in America's history, and yet in these instances the nation has recovered to even higher levels of prosperity. Can't this happen again?

No, it's not likely this time. High debt levels indeed occurred in the early 1930s and then again in the late 1940s. However, the prognosis in these cases was entirely different, as the causality was not the same. The 1940s debt obligations were the result of a world war. Because of World War II, government debt soared (to over 100 percent of GDP), in turn driving real spending in the production economy. This was followed by a post-War population boom, helping to boost economic growth. In a very short period, government debt levels fell as new households saved, raised families, paid off their houses, and invested. Household debt throughout this entire period remained relatively low.

In the early 1930s, high debt-to-GDP levels also occurred. However, at the start, the main cause of this rise was not government debt, but debt in the private sector (businesses and households). Then as the economy collapsed in the 1930s, government debt soared. Here the denominator shrunk (the economy) as debt continued to rise after the onset of economic crisis. To think that today's debt levels in the U.S. are far higher than at any other time—even the 1930s—even before an economic depression has begun—is sobering.

There can be no doubt: The legacy of the current GFC will be radically higher government debt levels. As mentioned, non-financial debt-to-GDP was already at an all-time high before the crisis period began. Indeed, this itself was an important enabler and catalyst to the crisis in the first place. But as the choice has been to outrun problems, the U.S. government is plunging into even more debt.

Quoting Frederich Hayek, another well-known Austrian School economist, "...to combat the depression by a forced credit expansion is to attempt to cure the evil by the very means which brought it about; because we are suffering from a misdirection of production, we want to create further misdirection—a procedure which can only lead to a much more severe crisis as soon as the credit expansion comes to an end."[94]

Effectively, a blood-letting has been prescribed following an application of leeches. In a desperate attempt to restart the previous asset price manias, to again inflate stock markets and real estate to forestall the devastation of the net worth suffered by the average middle-class family, the solution is more debt. It is a response similar to that of a drug addict. An addict requires an ever-increasing dose to maintain a similar level of euphoria, until finally the veins collapse.

Yet, even these dynamics are not the worst developments of this desperate time. This honor goes to a different factor—demographics. The most sobering realization of all today is that an aging crisis is underway. Therefore, it will not be so easily possible to outgrow cripplingly high debt levels as it was in the 1940s–1950s. It would not be an outrageous forecast that U.S. government debt will triple relative to GDP over the next seven to ten years.

GFC OUTLOOK

I surely wish I could present a single scenario with 100 percent probability! However, it simply is not possible. There are just too many complexities that could unfold over the next several years. However, we can at be sure of at least a few facts. We know with certainty, as presented previously in this book, that there will be at least one more time of global prosperity. This must be so, or the world trading conditions depicted for Babylon the Great in Revelation 18 could not occur. However, this period of apparent prosperity needs be nothing more than one more temporary inflated bubble. In fact, this scenario could be a false dawn that emanates from the current GFC.

We also know that a relatively balanced power coalition of ten nations will emerge. That means that, in some fashion, the United States and possibly some other countries will decline in influence. This development must involve an economic decline, though not exclusively. All other outcomes or scenarios that precede or are outside of these two certainties are a subject of speculation.

REMAINING QUESTIONS

What world events drive the earth into the waiting arms of the final ten kings? We have already noted how global crises in the past have accelerated globalism. The pivotal question is this: Have there been sufficient crises and global power rebalancing to create the necessary conditions for the ten kings to align in the near future?

Two observations will guide any speculation. Firstly, the GFC to this point has not yet produced sufficient impetus for a global coalition of ten nations to emerge. Neither the major changes required to support the powers of any global organization nor any major global policy changes have yet occurred. At least one other round of global crisis is required. Why? Already, global policy makers are congratulating themselves for successfully averting a world financial meltdown.

In May of 2009, U.S. Treasury Secretary Timothy Geithner was prattling: "...major policy intervention (including Emergency Economy Stabilization Act—EESA) was, in the end, successful in achieving the vital but narrow objective of preventing a systemic financial meltdown."[95]

"We continue to expect economic activity to bottom out, then to turn up later this year;" opined Ben Bernanke of the Federal Reserve.[96]

He is forecasting that the worst is behind. Internationally, the same sentiment has prevailed. "We are, as far as growth is concerned, around the inflection point in the cycle," said Jean-Claude Trichet, president of the European Central Bank.[97]

If the heat of the crisis is over—or so policy makers may think—we can be sure that momentum will be lost with respect to any of the high-minded policy prescriptions and pronouncements of the elite G20 (Group of 20) meetings, the various transnational organizations, and the current political administrations. Already, some policy analysts are bemoaning that a "good crisis has gone to waste." It will take at least one more big crisis, if not many more, to bring about the prophesied globally coordinated condition of ten kings. In fact, it is not unreasonable to think that an even greater crisis than the GFC must occur. It need not be a new crisis. It could simply be the second stage of the GFC that is shortly ahead. Therefore, please note that the probabilities are very high that a much bigger crisis could still occur before the Tribulation period begins.

A plausible scenario that falls out of our speculations is that the GFC or one or more future crisis finally drives the entire world into the ten-nation ruling structure. By that time, America and a number of major European nations would already be severely decimated economically. The ten-king coalition then plays a role in coordinating global conditions that would create at least one more period of apparent prosperity leading into the Tribulation period. Following that point, the final global financial apocalypse finally occurs. Ultimately, an enormous, world-crippling deflationary bust is inevitable.

Whatever our speculations, readers must conclude that the outlook for America is not promising, though conditions may indeed look better for an interim period. However, policy makers and people with much wealth who can benefit from insightful and timely advice realize this, too. That implies that desperate and selfish actions must be expected. In fact, as already reviewed, such actions on the part of the government have already been underway. Many unprecedented measures and initiatives have already been pursued in response to the GFC.

TIMES OF BRINKMANSHIP AND DESPERATION

Turning our attention to the very near-term and focusing in upon North America, is a deflationary depression to be expected? Could an inflationary spiral emerge? Or, could velocity-type inflation occur with a mix of different types of inflation and deflation?

For a number of reasons, the answers are not yet crystal clear. Policy makers are desperately trying to inflate the economy, financial markets, and real estate values. Will they be successful? Trillions of dollars of investment capital must game questions such as these. Given the enormous buildup of financial capital, its concentrated ownership, and the centralized management by professional money managers—for example, large pension fund or hedge funds—as soon as the outcome is clearer, the responses will be both sudden and enormous. Billions and trillions of money will be on the move in an attempt to preserve its relative wealth or make new profits.

Very likely, prices of all types of assets could soar in this environment. While this sounds hopeful, it is not. It may present a profit-making opportunity to investors for a time, but it also is a disaster scenario leading to further economic imbalances and skewing of wealth. The underlying destruction of America would certainly continue in earnest.

Thoughts to Ponder

We cannot know the exact course of future events. Of one fact we can be certain: The final financial apocalypse for the entire world is very likely in the near future. The Day of the Lord, meaning the Tribulation, will involve far greater trials than the world has ever seen. It will be a global judgment, as made clear by the utterances of several Old Testament prophets besides Isaiah. Prophesied Obadiah: "The day of the Lord is near for all nations" (Obadiah 1:15). Zephaniah also repeatedly emphasized the global scope of the coming judgments: "On the day of the Lord's sacrifice I will punish the princes and the king's sons and all those clad in foreign clothes" (Zephaniah 1:8). "Neither their silver nor their gold will be able to save them on the day of the Lord's wrath. In the fire of his jealousy the whole world will be consumed, for he will make a sudden end of all who live in the earth" (Zephaniah 1:18). Assuredly, the financial collapses of the Great Tribulation are among the lesser trials of that time. Famines, plagues, wars, and the loss of a large number of human lives will take place.

Reviewing global trends currently underway, there is little doubt that the world is rushing toward that day when the final global financial apocalypse will occur. If anything, judging from the responses of global policy makers, regulators, and central banks to date, the GFC of recent times will prove yet another catalyst that accelerates the world to the that prophesied outcome. However, a few twists and turns will occur first. Some possible scenarios are discussed in the next chapter.

But must America, Canada, and other countries today participate as willing members of this prophetic progression? Are all outcomes inevitable right away? Could the actions of America delay its ultimate demise?

Yes. In the end, America's own choices will determine its future course. Indeed, what is prophesied in the Bible must indeed someday happen because it is the foreknowledge of God. But that does require that this present generation of Americans has the opportunity to choose to repent or to change its ways.

Is a change of course likely? We pray this will be the case. Yet, the predispositions and spiritual state of American citizenry cause heartfelt concern. Our conclusion to this point is that satanically deceived gospels, camouflaged under the cloak of Christian godliness, and a highly advanced state of paganism have deeply corrupted and dissipated America. We can only hope and pray for a change of heart and character.

However, if there is no change of direction, much worse conditions and hardships are ahead for the United States. That conclusion also applies to such countries as Great Britain, Canada, and others facing similar diseases. Plenty can still go wrong or deteriorate further, whether in the near- or long-term future for these countries. In any case, some of the policies pursued by the governments of these countries virtually guarantee even greater crises ahead.

While false dawns are likely to allure every so often (if at all), the economic, spiritual, and ethical conditions of these nations only point to further rebelliousness and deep-seated deceptions. The spirits of consumerism and lust do not easily give up their penchants for easy comforts and pleasures. Despite the clear and painful consequences of past excesses and sins, people will still pine for the days of revelry that landed them in trouble in the first place.

But of what consequence to Christians are such hoary prophecies, particularly if there is a possibility that these outcomes may be far in the future? If so, why worry so soon…so unnecessarily? Many evangelical Christians who believe there will be a Rapture expect to be snatched away before proverbial "hell" breaks loose upon the earth. In this view, why should one then care about dire predictions? Indeed, many evangelical Christians do reflect such an attitude, thinking they will remain secure and protected no matter the times. Somehow, they believe, God will harbor their coveted prosperity during any storm.

Whether or not one believes in an imminent Rapture, such an attitude couldn't be more foolhardy and dangerous. God will not insulate anyone from his or her idolatries. We reap what we sow, and ultimately all our idols will fall down.

While the global financial apocalypse surely lies ahead for the world, conditions for Christians during the current pagan times are already lethal. It is an apocalyptic time for Christians, who in many countries are being slaughtered by the millions. In fact, this is happening even in America even now. Do you recognize it?

It is a type of faith-killing apocalypse that is even much more dangerous than the coming global financial apocalypse, as we will show in the next chapter.

CHRISTIANS KEEPING THE FAITH

Figure #16

World Income By Major Religion
Per person GDP, Annual, Current US dollars, 2007

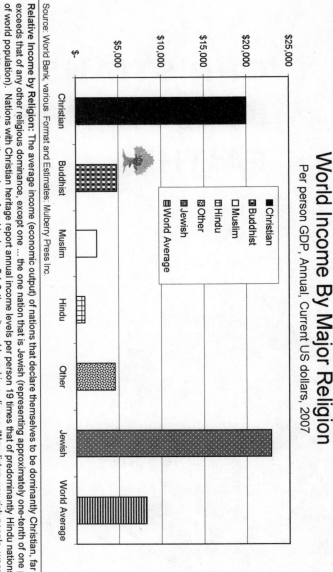

Legend:
- ■ Christian
- ▨ Buddhist
- ☐ Muslim
- ⊞ Hindu
- ⊠ Other
- ▩ Jewish
- ▤ World Average

Y-axis values: $25,000 / $20,000 / $15,000 / $10,000 / $5,000 / $-

X-axis categories: Christian / Buddhist / Muslim / Hindu / Other / Jewish / World Average

Source: World Bank, various. Format and Estimates: Mulberry Press Inc.

Relative Income by Religion: The average income (economic output) of nations that declare themselves to be dominantly Christian, far exceeds that of any other religious dominance, except one ... the one nation that is Jewish (representing approximately one-tenth of one percent of world population). Nations with Christian heritage report annual income levels per person 19 times that of predominantly Hindu nations and 8 times that of Muslim countries. In the prophecy found in James 5:1-6, the writer address his audience, "Now listen, you rich people, weep and wail because of the misery that is coming upon you." Could James have been referring to this world condition today?

15

APOCALYPSE NOW
FOR BELIEVERS

To this point, I have presented the dangers of our times and have alerted any who would listen to its grave prospects. The final scenes before the time of the Lord's wrath—the Great Tribulation—are unfolding in full view. But while that time of Apocalypse is the culmination of the wrath of God upon an unrepentant world, we can recognize that present times are also terrible. But, who are the intended victims of this current time of moral and societal upheaval, a time of anguished cares for the things of this world? Both Jews and Christians are in its crosshairs, I contend. I have already pleaded concern for our brother, the Jew, and have warned against participating in the tide of rising anti-Semitism, unwittingly or otherwise.

But what of the threat to Christians? It is part of an end-time conspiracy to entrap and persecute Christians. Christians today are in a relentless and brutal process of being slaughtered by the thousands. A virtual spiritual genocide is underway.

Truly terrible and perilous times have come upon believers. Most don't even realize this. Let's try to understand why this is so. We'll begin with a question: Just what is the core, existential purpose of society today? Without a doubt, it is the humanist goal of attaining the earthy "good life." Who wouldn't agree that this is the ultimate capstone of human existence? This is the gilded life marketed to consumers today: so within grasp, and always paraded before our eyes. Our entire commercial culture is tilted towards the imagined cares of this good life.

The result is that we are witnessing a hyped, last-days stage of what was already a glimmer in New Testament times: "To what, then, can I compare the people of this generation? What are they like? They are like children sitting in the marketplace and calling out to each other: 'We played the flute for you, and you did not dance; we sang a dirge, and you did not cry'" (Matthew 11:16–17). The whole world has increasingly accepted a materialist perspective of life. As the world sees it, we have only lived if we had a chance at greatness, consumed luxury items, are living in ease, and have excess wealth. Anything less means that we have not attained the ultimate hope of human existence. In some circles, we might even be considered a failed Christian were we not blessed with such a lofty existence. Of course, this represents blindness to eternal, "true riches" at its most complete.

Today, this humanist view of the world—unfortunately, one many Christians also endorse—is the successful standard bearer of life. The Humanist Manifesto 1 even expressly states that "the quest for the good life is still the central task for mankind.... And that he alone is responsible for the realization of the world of his dreams."[98]

Given that so many Christians have capitulated to this belief system, we must conclude that an end-time money trap is already far advanced upon the world. True to the script, it reveals an over-commercialized culture, itself a significant end-time sign. We must turn our attention to the key target of this strategy to flood the world with such humanist, materialistic values—the true church of the last days.

A MOST FALSE MESSAGE

Sadly, many movements identified as Christian are peddling the same visions and techniques as the marketing wizards of Madison Avenue. They are "…like children sitting in the marketplace calling out to each other" (Luke 7:32) with the latest marketing sciences that have been adopted to deliver attendance and revenue results. The message that slyly underpins many of today's church "marketing" programs is that the Christian life is the same as the "good life" the world wishes to attain. We can have worldly ease, comforts, the "good life," and all our trials solved. This is supposedly the promise and manifestations of the Christian life.

All of the trends apparent in the secular world of commerce and pop psychology are evident in the "church business." Just as a Wal-Mart and other "big-box" retailers squeeze out the smaller stores with their massive buying power and become ever bigger, so the mega-churches are draining attendance at the "drab and boring" churches, wherever they are. After all, it requires "bigness" and "success" to afford Jumbotrons and to attract Hollywood entertainment stars to perform during worship services. Church-growth consulting services are even operated as "profit centers." The net result is that "big-box" church-goers are being taught that to be Christian is to be materially blessed, expertly entertained, culturally relevant, and perhaps even to be lauded and recognized by the world.

There is only one problem. While it is possible that some Christians may have fewer trials than others, nowhere is the "good life" presented as the identifying mark of the Christian in the New Testament. Actually, if anything, the inverse holds true, according to many Bible verses: "In this world you will have trouble" (John 16:33); and "If they persecuted me, they will persecute you also," said the Savior

(John 15:20). These are factual statements. Far, far more warnings about persecutions appear in the New Testament than possible indications of attaining the worldly "good life." In fact, of the latter statements, there are none. Rather, persecution and trials are held up as being good and commendable. They are the hallmark of the faithful, resolute Christian who is not a friend to the world: "Rejoice and be glad, because great is your reward in heaven, for in the same way they persecuted the prophets who were before you" (Matthew 5:12); and, "For it is commendable if a man bears up under the pain of unjust suffering because he is conscious of God" (1 Peter 2:19).

TROUBLE AT AN INOPPORTUNE TIME

In direct contrast to the sugary message of popular Christianity today, the Bible tells us that in the last days there will be terrible times for Christians, so awful in fact, that the "love of many will grow cold" (Matthew 24:12).

The timing couldn't be more tragic or better planned for what we see in Western Christendom today. At the most inopportune and dangerous of times, a coddled Christianity is looking for the reward of the "good life" in the here and now. As such, these people are made captives of the "deceitfulness of wealth" (Matthew 13:12), the "worries of life" (Mark 4:19), and "desires for other things" (Mark 4:19), and are no match for the type of brutal environment the Bible prophesies will typify the last days before Christ's return. The recent GFC provides sufficient evidence that many "prosperous" Christians were found highly overindebted. They allowed themselves to fall prey to hollow promises and hopes.

There are many indications that those terrible times are already here and intensifying. Sadly, many Christians in North America and other high-income countries are therefore falling away for other gospels. Their shepherds have led them astray.

WHAT KIND OF GOOD LIFE?

As Christ said, "There is only One who is good" (Matthew 19:16). Just what should life be like for the people who have the "Good One" living within them during the "last days"?

Remarking on this time, the apostle Paul provided a key warning to the church about the conditions it will face in the last days, saying, "But mark this: There will be terrible times in the last days" (2 Timothy 3:1). Paul is speaking to the church—believers, in other words—and not just the world overall.

Just why will the "love of many grow cold" at that time (Matthew 24:12)? The Bible says, "Because of the increase of wickedness" (Matthew 24:12). The original Greek word used for "love" in the above text is *agape*, meaning the type of perfect love that is godly and selfless. We see here that the faith of many Christians will wither and die.

Apparently, the prophesied boom in wickedness will test Christians like never before. Of course, persecution of some form has characterized the life of the faithful from the beginning. But as the parable of the sower anticipates, not only physical persecution can make one's faith grow cold. "When trouble or persecution comes because of the Word, they quickly fall away. Still others, like seed sown among thorns, hear the word; but the worries of this life, the deceitfulness of wealth and the desires for other things come in and choke the word, making it unfruitful" (Mark 4:17–19).

Everyone who takes a literal interpretation of Bible prophecy will agree that horrible events will certainly occur in the end times. The events and conditions predicted for the Great Tribulation are of course apocalyptic. A third of the earth's population will die and various other difficulties, including a complete economic and financial collapse, are described in graphic terms by numerous prophets throughout Scripture. These are all certainly terrible events, but they occur inside that seven-year period that is also called the "time of Jacob's trouble" (Jeremiah 30:7). This Tribulation period is the time of wrath that comes upon all those, both Jew and Gentile, who have not yet recognized the Messiah. Therefore, the "terrible times in the last days" mentioned by Paul specifically speaks to another group—those who have already recognized and "bowed their knees" to the Messiah. In at least one sense, this period being addressed can be seen as even more terrible than the Great Tribulation—just how terrible?

TERMINALLY TERRIBLE

Let's take a moment to confirm what Paul meant by the word "terrible." Actually, this word is not an ideal interpretation of what is originally expressed in the Greek. Of all the main Bible translations, the King James in this case probably uses the best-fitting word: "perilous." The original Greek word is *chalepos*, having among its meanings "troublesome," "dangerous," "harsh," "fierce," and "savage." Not once is this word found in the book of Revelation. The only other time *chalepos* is used in the New Testament is in Matthew 8:28, where we find Jesus encountering two demon-possessed men living in caves, who were "exceeding fierce, so that no man might pass by that way" (KJV). Here we can postulate demonic connection to these "perilous times."

We do know that the period just before the Great Tribulation will be a time of complacency, when "people will be eating and drinking as in the times of Noah" (Matthew 24:37–40). It is a perilous time, spiritually treacherous. Much of the church will have been neutralized and deceived. We see the characteristics of that time with great intensity already today.

It will be different during the Great Tribulation. Yes, the world will see the height of Christian purging—genocide—during that period. All those who become Christians then will be persecuted and killed. But will that time actually be "perilous" for Christians living then? No, not likely. After all, Scripture says, "Do not be afraid of those who kill the body but cannot kill the soul" (Matthew 10:28). In that sense—in the spiritual—the answer is "no." In the end, their souls will be safe...for an eternity, no less. They may be slaughtered, but there will be little jeopardy with respect to them winning the race, and rejecting the grace that was theirs through Jesus Christ. We see this group under the altar in heaven as the "...souls of those who had been slain because of the word of God and the testimony they had maintained" occurring at the time of the fifth seal (Revelation 6:9).

These post-Rapture Christians will be forced to make a clear-cut decision when it comes to the point of accepting the "sign of the beast." Any person who is or becomes a believer during that time and refuses to the take the sign of the beast is certain to die physically (Revelation 14:11). True believers will know that their decision will lead to one type of death, most likely two—certain spiritual death should they take the "sign of the beast," with physical death still possible over the remaining Tribulation period. With such facts, what sane person who recognizes Christ as eternal Savior would take the sign?

The "perilous times" Paul mentions occur well before the Great Tribulation. Paul is saying that for Christians who are living in the last days—before the Great Tribulation and before Christ's return—conditions will become fierce and harshly dangerous to faith. The faith of many will turn cold. Though true Christians do not lose their salvation, they can fall out of circulation spiritually—becoming ineffective, ignoring the truth, refusing to run the race, remaining totally dormant, or worse. On the other hand, it takes much more courage to remain the "salt of the earth" during a time when wickedness is increasing and most churches have become purveyors of sugar and saccharine highs.

If we are already witnessing the very last of the last days, then shouldn't Christians be experiencing (or at least observing) fierce, harsh conditions now? Would we be overstating the case to say that we should be observing a firestorm of activity, a veritable flood of terrible and demonic things... today? The Bible provides us with an answer.

SIGNS OF THE PERILOUS TIMES

Scripture tells us exactly what conditions and consequences to antici-pate during these "perilous" times. These indicators may not be rec-ognized for what they are. Above all, they evidence a time of great deception. In fact, we are even given the specific signs of the "perilous times" occurrence. Eighteen alone are mentioned in 2 Timothy 3:2: "People will be lovers of themselves, lovers of money, boastful, proud, abusive, disobedient to their parents, ungrateful, unholy, without love, unforgiving, slanderous, without self-control, brutal, not lovers of the good, treacherous, rash, conceited, lovers of pleasure rather than lov-ers of God—having a form of godliness but denying its power. Have nothing to do with them."

Shockingly, these behavioral characteristics even take place under the license of institutionalized religion. Interestingly, the number eigh-teen could be seen to represent the final or highest form of mankind's rebelliousness that the world will see against God. This figure is the product of three times six, the numbers of completeness and of man, respectively. All of these conditions are observable today.

We have no trouble documenting the emergence of each of these characteristics as accepted norms in today's societies, many in so-called Christian countries. They are whitewashed by theologians and religious organizations. For example, starting at the beginning of the Paul's list, consider these observations:

1. "Lovers of themselves": Myriad surveys cite the increase of narcissism, selfishness, etc. The best indirect evidence of this is the high incidence of depression. The World Health Organization has produced studies on this trend in recent years, calling it an epidemic. While this phenomenon has different causes, it is also promoted by the empty values society incessantly promotes. Self-love is deceitful. It tricks people into believing they can imagine something better for themselves than what God has in mind for them.

2. "Lovers of money": The love of money is today worshipped as a central doctrine of economic growth and the chief measure of national and personal achievement. In recent decades, policy makers of many countries have advanced the deceitfulness of wealth by tantalizing citizens with effigies of effortless (but false) wealth. We reviewed some of these concepts in Chapter 3.

3. "Boastful": Once upon a time, people were encouraged to be discreet, humble, and understated. The Bible counsels us to give God all the glory, and whatever we do, to do it for Him. One telling statistic aptly documenting today's acceptance of "boastfulness" is the incidence of lies and overstatements on résumés submitted for job positions. A survey of this issue found that more than 95 percent of U.S. college students were willing to make at least one false statement on a résumé to get a job.[99] And of course, today, it is legitimized to have "bragging rights."

I could provide statistics that document the widespread emergence of the other fifteen characteristics listed in 2 Timothy 3:2–5. I only wish to make the point that all of these occur under the guise and structure of godliness and apparent piety, and "...denying the power of Godliness. Have nothing to do with them" (2 Timothy 3:5).

True believers, those who will be faithful to the end and whose love hasn't turned cold, will not succumb to these conditions and can expect persecution of many types. Christ, when outlining the signs of the last days in Matthew 24, told the disciples this: "Then you will be handed over to be persecuted and put to death, and you will be hated by all nations because of me. At that time many will turn away from the faith and will betray and hate each other, and many false prophets will appear and deceive many people. Because of the increase of wickedness, the love of most will grow cold, but he who stands firm to the end will be saved" (Matthew 24:12–14).

These are among the last conditions Christ points to before His return. Only one other condition follows: the preaching of the gospel to all the earth, which occurs during the Tribulation. If so, then where is the persecution today? We hear of Christians being slain for their faith in Muslim countries, in China, and in various third-world countries, but not in North America or Europe. However, Christ mentions two types of persecutions during this perilous period—discrimination or maltreatment and being put to death. Persecution can take forms that are much worse than a quick death. In fact, we argue that Christians are being persecuted in a much more dangerous and cunning fashion in countries such as America, Canada, and others. These Christians have fallen for the false "good life." Their form of godliness denies the power of God, which is what? Paul tells us in Romans 1:6: "I am not ashamed of the gospel, because it is the power of God for the salvation of everyone who believes: first for the Jew, then for the Gentile." Grievously, many Christians are today "ashamed" of the gospel.

As "wickedness increases" and more and more of society and church take on the characteristics we already examined—under the structural appearance of godliness, no less—it takes much courage to go against the flow.

Consider these situations and how they may compromise the Christian life:

- If you have a retail business, it is virtually impossible to close one day a week and stay profitable. What to do—sell the business, go bankrupt, or stay open on Sundays?
- Society is given over to massive speculation and indebtedness. Why not "plunge with them into the same flood of dissipation" (1 Peter 4:4)? Doing so, it's even possible to rub shoulders with other successful Christian businesspeople who seem perfectly suited to the corrupt business morality of the day. After all, it is not uncommon to see the wiliest businesspeople honored at the gatherings of Christian business associations.
- You forthrightly uphold God's Word, literally interpreting the Bible. But now, even your Christian friends think you are a narrow-minded nut and consider you an intolerant pariah.
- You work in a large, multinational corporation that enforces a highly incentivized performance structure, and you discover that honesty and attempts at maintaining a balanced family life render you unfit. Do you quit and give up the "good life"?
- Your children may be subject to deep insecurity and depression. They don't possess the latest designer jeans and can't see themselves matching up to the ideal image our culture demands. Counteracting the thousands of media messages your children hear every day is a thankless, never-ending task.

- A "man-on-the-street" TV interviewer asks you whether you think homosexuality is a sin. Even though you don't condemn the sinner—after all, we are all sinners—you evade the question because your comment could be considered a hate crime. Simply stating that the Bible considers homosexuality sin may even cause repercussion for your business or place of employment.

- An apparent Christian inexplicably takes you to court. He was a trusted business partner at one time, maybe even a member of your "Christian" investment club. Undeservedly, you lose your house as a result. Your life is in ruins.

- You find yourself out of a job. Sending out résumés with inflated qualifications would be doing what is simply the norm. Why not? The cares of this life are pressing. You need to get your daughter into the right school to ensure her chances for an elite job. And, everybody in your circle is buying a summer lodge.

Legions of other possible of pressures and invitations to compromise could be cited. We have not even considered that specific demonic activity may also be directed against "front-line" Christians. As we can see from these scenarios, the time of persecution is already here. The bottom line is that being a Christian today has a price, and it involves a sacrifice. But how could that be? Haven't we been taught for years that being a good Christian brings rich blessings?

Many therefore will choose to give up hope and active faith due to the disappointments brought about by persecution and wickedness. Instead of seeing it as a privilege to share in the sufferings of Christ, they have been conditioned by apostate teachers to expect the "good life" in the here and now. They repudiate their faith as a result of hardship and forced sacrifice. After all, God didn't come through with His side of the deal, as the pastor promised. Better to go through the motions of godliness while endorsing the tactics and mindsets that will not forfeit the chance for the "good life." "Country Club Christianity" has become an elite religion with the ultimate appeal.

UP, UP, AND AWAY?

A major difference between various Christian sects concerns the topic of the Rapture. Some interpret Scripture to reveal that there will be a "snatching away" (1 Thessalonians 4:17) of the faithful at some point before Christ's feet again physically touch the Mount of Olives. Others are equally adamant that there is only one event. Though I am persuaded of the pretribulation view, I choose not to make this a point of debate in this book. I only make one observation: Of the two views—Rapture or no Rapture—it is the latter that should be seen as the easier, less "perilous" outcome.

This is in direct contrast to the popular caricature of evangelical Christians who are considered "escapists" waiting for a divine rescue from the tough times of the Tribulation period. While this is of course is not an argument disproving the Rapture, it unfortunately represents a correct and embarrassing view of the state of most Christians. Some are so idolatrous about the "good life" they want to enjoy, they are relieved to believe that their comforts will not be take away from them before they go to heaven. They have it backwards. They love the world more than they fear God. Reflecting this earth-dweller view, we remember the comment of one high-profile Christian who expressed relief at the thought that his investment portfolio would be secure until the time of the devastations that are likely to occur during the Great Tribulation. He was comforted that he wouldn't suffer any major losses before the Rapture.

As we have reviewed, the really "terrible times" for Christians are today. Today is the dangerous period when the "love of many" becomes cold. In contrast, there will not be spiritually perilous times during the Great Tribulation. Those with eyes to see and ears to hear during that time will clearly recognize the times. How could they not?

THOUGHTS TO PONDER

Francis Ford Coppola's 1979 movie, *Apocalypse Now*, tells the fictional story of U.S. Army Captain Benjamin Willard, who is sent on a mission into a treacherous region of Cambodia during the Vietnam War to find Col. Walter E. Kurtz.[100] This colonel reportedly had become insane, enforcing a brutal rule in the region. He took no prisoners and resorted to strategies of intimidation and horror. His willingness to employ cruel atrocities was far outside the comfort of Western sensibilities and accepted war-time conduct. Yet, his program of terror was effective in intimidating the enemy.

Christians today indeed are experiencing a spiritual form of "apocalypse now." A ruthless enemy, the deceiver, is attempting to kill the faith of Christians. He is using brutal strategies of intimidation and fear, specifically targeting those who have allowed humanist and materialistic values to infiltrate their beliefs. Christians who aren't rooted in the true reality of eternity are extremely vulnerable.

Today is the dangerous time of deception, apostasy, and complacency. If that is the case, dedicated Christians who truly strive to serve God and walk with Jesus Christ should be facing perilous times right now, or at least expect such conditions. All the strategies of the

Mammon world and the "prince of the air" will be engaged, a "rise of wickedness" with the express objective of annihilating the church and true believers. True Christians who really want to be in the presence of the Lord will not be inclined to sell out their precious faith for the cheap and temporal promise of the earthly "good life." They expect to look into the Savior's eyes some day, at the bema seat, repenting of their faithlessness and lack of eternal perspective.

On a personal level, just how terrible are things for you today? What forms of persecution are the enemy directing at you? And what price are you willing to pay in order to follow Christ? Many can't bear to pay the price of forsaking the "good life," so they retreat, shutting down their witness.

Of course, the most effective way of competing to attain the "good life" as the world and some churches would define it, is to pursue the eighteen characteristics listed by the apostle Paul. Given the present, hyper-competitive and deceitful financial environment of the world today, these characteristics are most likely to be rewarded in the here and now. It is no coincidence that the apostle Peter presents nearly the same list as the description of the false prophets in 2 Peter 2.

Given the "feel-good," pop psychology being preached by many teachers and "smiling" preachers these days, Christ's statements that we should expect to share in His sufferings will surely seem incongruous and surprising to most Christians on the wayside and main path. It shouldn't be. Peter warned exactly otherwise: "Dear friends, do not be surprised at the painful trial you are suffering, as though something strange were happening to you. But rejoice that you participate in the sufferings of Christ, so that you may be overjoyed when his glory is revealed" (1 Peter 4:12–13).

Christians may have the opportunity in these last days to prove their faith genuine: Grief is being suffered in "all kinds of trials...so that your faith...may be proved genuine" (1 Peter 1:6). With Christ, it is possible to stand firm to the end (Matthew 24:13). Paul provides hope, saying: "For I am convinced that neither death nor life, neither angels nor demons, neither the present nor the future, nor any powers, neither height nor depth, nor anything else in all creation, will be able to separate us from the love of God that is in Christ Jesus our Lord" (Romans 8:38–39).

For Christians, the terrible times are worsening now…before any prospect of the "up, up, and away."

Figure #17

Widening World Wealth Skew:
Comparison of percentiles, Population versus Wealth

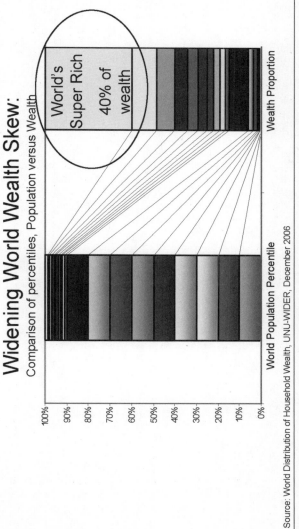

World's Super Rich

40% of wealth

World Population Percentile

Wealth Proportion

100% 90% 80% 70% 60% 50% 40% 30% 20% 10% 0%

Source: World Distribution of Household Wealth, UNU-WIDER, December 2006

Rich Become Richer: According to *The Worldwide Distribution of Household Wealth*, issued in December 2006 (the first global wealth survey in history), the top 2% and 1% of the world's population is estimated to own 51% and 40% of world household wealth, respectively. Very likely, the world today has a much more imbalanced wealth skew — the rich being richer, and the non-rich relatively poorer — than ever before in history. How extreme might this condition yet become in the future? James 5.3 says, "You have hoarded wealth in the last days."

16

SEARCHING FOR AND FINDING
TRULY GREAT RICHES

Now listen, you rich people, weep and wail because of the
misery that is coming upon you. Your wealth has rotted, and
moths have eaten your clothes. Your gold and silver are corroded. Their corrosion will testify against you and eat your
flesh like fire. You have hoarded wealth in the last days. Look!
(James 5:1–3)

The entire prophecy found in James 5:1–6 lists at least six financial or economic signs of the last days. In studying the Bible, I
have counted almost fifty such general signs. This passage in James
is the most concentrated assembly of such indicators. They include
hoarding, accumulation of wealth, wage inequities, different classes of
workers, luxuries, and indulgence—consumerism at its peak!—conditions of economic brutality, and perhaps even widespread obesity.
Most significantly, the edifice of wealth is then turned into a curse as
it corrodes and is proven illusory. Not only does this prophecy presage
the Tribulation period, it also speaks to the idolatries evident among
end-time Christians.

James' pronouncement here indeed is a prophecy. He clearly refers to "the last days" (verse 3). Though it is true that the last days already had already begun during his time in the first century, it remains that the last days—the very last days—are in force today.

The prophecy that rich people will "have hoarded wealth in the last days" is clearly in view. Specifically, in this chapter, we wish to focus on the prophecy concerning wealth.

FIRST WORLDWIDE SURVEY OF WEALTH PROVIDES CONFIRMATION

In December 2006, a ground-breaking report entitled "The Worldwide Distribution of Household Wealth"[101] was released. It was the first global wealth survey in history. The results were much worse than had been previously indicated by other studies that surveyed income. Wealth and income, though related, are quite different. Income is generally defined as the annual flow of earnings, while wealth is the accumulation of income and hoarded assets.

According to the report, the top 10 percent of adults in the world owned 85 percent of global household wealth (2005). The average member of this wealthy group therefore has 8.5 times the holdings of the global average. Furthermore, the top 2 percent and 1 percent of the world's population were estimated to own 51 percent and 40 percent of world household wealth, respectively. This is a more extreme distribution than had been estimated by surveying global incomes in previous studies.

Very likely, the world today has a much more imbalanced wealth skew—the rich being richer, and the non-rich relatively poorer—than ever before. How extreme might this condition become in the future?

It is hard to say. However, there comes a point when a further distortion becomes highly toxic for the world's economic healthfulness. No doubt, this condition already contributed to the severity of the economic impact of the global financial crisis.

While we discern that prophecies about the distribution of earthly wealth have come into fulfillment, there are additional prophecies about the treatment of another kind of wealth. In the last days, just before the time Christ returns, there will be a low valuation of heavenly wealth.

WRONG TEACHING AND FALSE PROPHECY

Prophetically, Christ asked, "when the Son of Man comes, will he find faith on the earth?" (Luke 18:8). This is probably the most important prophecy for the Church Age. Yet, in the New Testament, it seems almost hidden. It is only half a verse long, found in only one of the four Gospels, and seems entirely disjointed from the text before and after. Jesus is clearly saying that very little faith will be found on earth when He returns.

We can better understand why by using an inverse equation. The Bible substantiates an inverse relationship between wealth and faith. For example, "Blessed are you the poor, for yours is the kingdom of God. But woe to you who are rich, for you have already received your comfort" (Luke 6:20, 24, the "Sermon on the Plain").

James emphasizes this perspective a different way, saying: "Has not God chosen those who are poor in the eyes of the world to be rich in faith and to inherit the kingdom he promised to those who love him?" (James 2:5).

Most assuredly, there are many exceptions to this general equation of faith versus riches. We are dealing here with a general correlation and not any specific persons or households. There clearly is an inverse relationship with faith and wealth and comfort.

Again returning to Christ's prophecy, and now reversing faith for wealth, when He reappears, will He find wealth on earth? As we established at the outset of this chapter, according to James, the answer is yes. When Jesus uttered His question, He knew the faith of His flock would face a great onslaught from worldly wealth and comforts in the last days, also revealing that "the love of most will grow cold" (Matthew 24:12). While this statement was probably spoken directly to the Jews, it only follows that it also applies to Christians.

Without a doubt that cold day has arrived—certainly for Western Christianity and Jews alike. Without pretension, faith in Europe is largely dead. In North America, there are indeed many who profess a Christian faith, but it is of the type that is without power. Many use faith as nothing more than a contractual indemnity policy with God, or as a device to "get wealth" or warm comforts.

This state of mind is easy to fall into...no premeditated plan is necessary to do so. Once one attitudinally becomes totally reliant upon the bank account, technology, and the pride and accomplishments of mankind, the power of God diminishes—at least as is utilized in daily life. No longer does our faith rest in the notions that God will care for us, has a purpose and a destiny for us, and wants to lead us not by sight, but by faith.

SEARCHING FOR EARTHLY SOLUTIONS

Witnessing the late, great stage in which we find the world, we are persuaded that perilous times are now. Then how are we to grapple with the pressing challenges and anxieties that assault our lives at this very moment? Times of economic and financial trouble do cause human hardship and stress in this present, three-dimensional realm. This cannot be denied. Families may be living under the constant barrage of creditors, perhaps wondering when the fateful eviction or foreclosure notice may arrive on the doorstep. Some people are experiencing hunger and homelessness. Frankly, when financial survival is the immediate objective, who will find comfort in the eternal? Why be so heavenly minded that solutions are of no earthly good?

Yes, eternal perspectives are all so noble and "spiritual" sounding. We may imagine our hopes being lifted upon the diaphanous wings of fairies into the opened heavens to the background music provided by cherubim. We may convince ourselves to believe that everything will be fine, seen over the eternal timeframe. But just how do such beliefs fill our stomachs now?

This indeed may be the attitude and questioning of people, certainly also of many Christians. Then, what steps should one take to deal with the trials of the present times—the economic oppression, the traps, the confusing and volatile developments and trends of our world?

ETERNAL PERSPECTIVES FIRST NECESSARY

Actually, we cannot find any reliable answers for this world unless we first center our eternal perspectives and reaffirm our belief in heavenly reward. It is here that we must find our foundation. Only if we truly believe we will attain the heavenly riches of eternal life will we bring the needed perspective to deal with earthly conditions. There are several reasons this must be the case.

In the first place, the very reason the faith of so many Christians is being annihilated today is precisely because eternal perspectives are no longer believed. If one places little value in eternal riches, then one is vulnerable to becoming entrapped in the cares of this world. Many Christians have clearly staked their hopes upon earthly prosperity. They have been captured by a culture of pagan beliefs, wanton consumption, and the enticing images of effortless wealth. Swimming in this surfeit of materialism, they have adopted an aberrant Christianity—laced with the deadly and false gospel of Prosperity Theology—that validates their lusts. A new culture of "Christian values" has emerged that conveniently serves to whitewash the man-made idols of prosperity. Of wants there is no end. Therefore, "There was not end to his toil, yet his eyes were not content with his wealth" (Ecclesiastes 4:8).

Mankind overlooks the fact that God, who is the Creator, could not possibly have brought a creation into existence in which lesser idols could supersede Him. He is a jealous God, tolerating no other gods besides Him (Deuteronomy 5:9, Exodus 34:14). As presented in Chapter 4, idols, by definition, must topple. It is a physical aspect of the natural law of this world. Notably, it is a condition most evident in the realm of money and Mammon, whether attributable to the laws of economics or mathematics.

For example, as soon as the majority of mankind settles upon a belief or expectation that is apart from an infinite God (by definition this then being an idol), it can no longer hold true and therefore becomes invalid. If everyone came to the idolatrous belief that buying tulip bulbs is the sure way to security and comfort here on earth, we know that ultimately this cannot prove true. While this is an overly simplistic example (although it did happen in Holland between 1634 and 1637), we can understand that some people will end up making quite a bit of money as tulip bulb prices soar in response to a mass rush of buyers. However, in the end, most people will end up losers. Once everyone has enough tulips, no one will be left to buy more. Ultimately, expectations will be disappointed and the tulip idol toppled. As it is, not all people can be rich. Wealth remains a relative concept and therefore its attainment is a never-ending competition.

We see a more complex type of idolatry taking place today in the form of idolizing retirement schemes. While, of course, it is reasonable to plan for retirement, our indulgence-seeking societies fail to recognize that if everyone collectively has fewer children, the value of retirement funds in the future will not be sufficient. In the created order, it is impossible for people to retire if there are not enough workers to perform services or underpin the income requirements of the retirees. An idolatry has developed that mankind's financial systems can bestow promises independent of the limitations of the created order.

STEWARDSHIP AND FAITHFULNESS LINKED

Only one belief can be held by the totality of mankind that will remain true and stable. It is this: "…without faith it is impossible to please God, because anyone who comes to him must believe that he exists and that he rewards those who earnestly seek him" (Hebrews 11:6). Placing faith in anything else is putting hope in a god that doesn't exist, with no reward.

If we do not truly believe that our riches are hidden and preserved in a place other than "where moth and rust destroy, and where thieves break in and steal" (Matthew 6:19), but rather are stored up as "treasures in heaven, where moth and rust do not destroy, and where thieves do not break in and steal" (Matthew 6:20), we will not have the required anchor to deal with the current trials.

Christ clearly linked our stewardship and faithfulness on earth with the ability to appreciate real eternal riches. "He that is faithful in that which is least is faithful also in much; and he that is unjust in the least is unjust also in much. If therefore ye have not been faithful in the unrighteous mammon, who will commit to your trust the real riches? And if ye have not been faithful in that which is another man's, who shall give you that which is your own?" (Luke 16:10–12, KJV).

Consider the significance of that verse. If we cannot even be faithful with temporal things—our earthly lives and bodies in the service of Lord Jesus Christ—then how could even eternal promises and riches be appreciated by such mortals? It is a humbling question that confirms our eternal perspectives must be put right first. Only then can we deal with our own temporal circumstances, no matter what they may be, how they came about, or whether they are our fault or that of others.

WHY THE TRIALS OF THE PHYSICAL LIFE

If eternal values are so important, then why did God create us to sojourn in the physical realm of earth, booby-trapped with concepts of money and Mammon, and replete with bodies and souls that have natural spiritual and genetic proclivities to want to serve Mammon and love money?

Why is there opposition between faith and money, the kingdom of God and Mammon? In the pleasure of God's creation, it is a condition of the world. Jesus said: "You cannot serve both God and mammon" (Matthew 6:24). This statement struck right to the heart of the cosmology of opposites—good and evil, sin and righteousness, the kingdom of light versus the forces of darkness. Were it any different, it would not be possible for us to choose to bring a meaningful sacrifice of faith and love to our Lord. Otherwise, to do so would simply be an automatic, programmed response of no value.

Christ made this comment to His disciples right after He told the rich young ruler to "sell his possession and give to the poor" (Matthew 6:21). It threw the disciples into an immediate debate. They were daunted by the challenges of property and the requirements of the kingdom of God. While on the one hand, to be wealthy was to be considered a blessing of the godly (after all, Abraham was wealthy); on the other hand, Christ admonished that "...it is easier for a camel to go through the eye of a needle than for a rich man to enter the kingdom of God" (Matthew 19:24). "Who can then be saved?" the disciples asked (Matthew 19:25). Christ replied, "With man this is impossible, but with God all things are possible" (Matthew 19:26).

Here we see two systems that contradict each other: the kingdom of God versus the domain of Mammon. These two realms have completely different wealth systems. They have two singular currencies, respectively: faith and money. A constant tension between these polarities continues.

As with the constant force of gravity, we never fall upward. Rather, we can only fall downward. Similar to gravity, Mammon to human flesh is a force that we can never fully rest against, as it is always pulling down. As Paul said, we are to continue to "work out your salvation" (Philippians 2:12) and bringing praise must be a sacrifice (Hebrew 13:15). Therefore, the acts of choosing to serve God and being vigilant against the entreaties and seductions of Mammon require initiative, active thought, and constant awareness.

Therefore, there is never a resting point in the endeavor to choose to serve God. It is a condition of this dispensation, this present stewardship under God's kingdom. Just as Gideon required a trait of constant vigilance for his chosen three hundred warriors, it is also required for the Christian today. The final army selected by Gideon included those who drank cupping their hands, eyes looking forward, not down.

Though we are ever so thankful that it is by the grace of God that we are saved, whether we are beset by the deceitfulness of riches or not, the sad reality is that most people in high-income countries are seriously blinded to the true nature and wealth potential of faith.

AN INCREDIBLE DEAL

We have enormous opportunities to lay up riches while we are still here on earth. Consider this statement of Christ: "I tell you, use worldly wealth to gain friends for yourselves, so that when it is gone, you will be welcomed into eternal dwellings" (Luke 16:9). This is a puzzling statement, as it seems to endorse the rather devious actions of the wicked servant (see Luke 19).

This parable confirms that we can use worldly wealth—whether monetary capital, assets, skills, or other possessions—and turn it into eternal riches. What an incredible offer: We can turn temporal materials that we cannot keep into eternal riches that we cannot lose! This being the case, it is such a travesty to try to turn eternal riches into temporal payoffs in the here and now. This may sound ludicrous. Yet, so many popular teachings (Prosperity Theology, most prominently, as we have reviewed) are based on that very idea.

Again, there are incredible opportunities to store up wealth in heaven. That is especially true during troubled and difficult times such as now. Whether the sun may shine or storms rage, whether health or sickness, fortunes or mishaps, economic recoveries or financial busts, God's love for us endures. Our salvation remains secure; our eternal hopes are not lost; our riches in heaven are safe; and our faith leads to heavenly treasures. God remains on the throne and the order that He has set upon earth endures.

Where should we look for wealth and power? "Worthy is the

Lamb, who was slain, to receive power and wealth and wisdom and strength and honor and glory and praise!" (Revelation 5:12).

THE MOST PRECIOUS COMMODITY IN THE WORLD

As we observe, the contrast between earthly riches and true riches—wealth, prosperity, material satisfaction, or worldly confidence—is a theme repeatedly presented throughout the entire Bible. True faith itself is considered the most valuable and real of all possessions. Scripture repeatedly portrays our faith and salvation as real riches and asserts that the price of their procurement in the first place is inestimable.

"For you know that it was not with perishable things such as silver or gold that you were redeemed from the empty way of life handed down to you from your forefathers" (1 Peter 1:18).

"For you know the grace of our Lord Jesus Christ, that though he was rich, yet for your sakes he became poor, so that you through his poverty might become rich" (2 Corinthians 8:9).

The apostle Peter reflects these evaluations of faith in this passage:

> In this you greatly rejoice, though now for a little while you may have had to suffer grief in all kinds of trials. These have come so that your faith—of greater worth than gold, which perishes even though refined by fire—may be proved genuine and may result in praise, glory and honor when Jesus Christ is revealed. Though you have not seen him, you love him; and even though you do not see him now, you believe in him and are filled with an inexpressible and glorious joy, for you are receiving the goal of your faith, the salvation of your souls. (1 Peter 1:6–9)

Without a question, according to Scripture, real faith is much more valuable than property and worldly wealth. Peter assesses it as more valuable than gold. Why? Because without it we cannot please God...nor can we receive the "goal of our faith," the salvation of our souls and eternal life.

While the world strains for the attainment of material wealth, the most precious acquisition of all—faith—today lies cold in many countries, especially wealthy countries of Christian heritage. Yet, there is nothing absolutely more worthy than faith.

LOOKING AHEAD TO THE SECURITIES OF GOD

We can only speculate as to the exact turn of events ahead...world events, the challenges of unpredictable financial markets, the soon-coming, world-power coalition of ten kings, and so on. Though we may use our minds to work out the best ways to husband our savings and resources as good stewards here on earth (the next chapter will present a suggested guideline for doing that), our ultimate hope is much greater. Provided we live as obedient stewards, we have a portfolio full of securities—the promises of Jesus Christ—we can rely upon. Just look at these valuable securities and instructions we find in the Bible:

Jesus Christ will never forsake us: "Keep your lives free from the love of money and be content with what you have, because God has said, 'Never will I leave you; never will I forsake you.' So we say with confidence, 'The Lord is my helper; I will not be afraid. What can man do to me?'" (Hebrews 13:5–6).

Relying upon our money and seeking our security in the infinity of financial gains is fruitless. When God's disciplining—or judgment, in the case of those who will live in times of great tribulation—finally comes, our worldly investments will provide neither refuge nor eternal reward.

Do not worry about things that are beyond our control: "Therefore do not worry about tomorrow, for tomorrow will worry about itself. Each day has enough trouble of its own" (Matthew 6:34).

We are not to preoccupy ourselves with the future. Spending our time and energy to overcome the boundaries of risk and the unknown will prove unsuccessful. God alone knows what is unknowable to us. He alone sees the future perfectly. If we live in total service to Him, then we have absolutely nothing to worry about.

"Rejoice in the Lord always. I will say it again: Rejoice! Let your gentleness be evident to all. The Lord is near. Do not be anxious about anything, but in everything, by prayer and petition, with thanksgiving, present your requests to God. And the peace of God, which transcends all understanding, will guard your hearts and your minds in Christ Jesus" (Philippians 4:4–7). Also, a similar security is found here: "The LORD is the strength of his people, a fortress of salvation for his anointed one. Save your people and bless your inheritance; be their shepherd and carry them forever" (Psalms 28:8–9).

Ignore the wicked who may become wealthy: The labors of the rich whom the world idolizes will all go to waste with no eternal reward. Their payoff is only for a very short season. And even for this brief time, riches provide no peace. Seeking earthly wealth, they suffer much anguish and deceit. According to Bible prophecy, there is little doubt what is in store for the wicked and their wealth: "The arrogance of man will be brought low and the pride of men humbled; the LORD alone will be exalted in that day, and the idols will totally disappear" (Isaiah 2:18).

Are we just getting by in this world, with little in our bank accounts? If we are serving the Lord faithfully, it doesn't have any impact upon our eternal prospects. "Better the little that the righteous have than the wealth of many wicked; for the power of the wicked will be broken, but the LORD upholds the righteous" (Psalms 37:16).

Be gentle with others, seeking to save them from the consequences of complicity in an end-time money snare during the perilous times: "Be merciful to those who doubt; snatch others from the fire and save them; to others show mercy, mixed with fear—hating even the clothing stained by corrupted flesh" (Jude 22–23).

Occupy and look up, for the Lord's return draws near: "But you, dear friends, build yourselves up in your most holy faith and pray in the Holy Spirit. Keep yourselves in God's love as you wait for the mercy of our Lord Jesus Christ to bring you to eternal life" (Jude 20–21).

Do not bow down to the "image of gold"—God will save us: We can glean hope from the experience of Daniel's companions, Shadrach, Meshach, and Abednego. They refused to give into the idolatry forced upon them by King Nebuchadnezzar, no matter the price. If they had to die in the fire or live on the fringes of society as outcasts in order to stay faithful to their God, then so be it: "If we are thrown into the blazing furnace, the God we serve is able to save us from it, and he will rescue us from your hand, O king. But even if he does not, we want you to know, O king, that we will not serve your gods or worship the image of gold you have set up" (Daniel 3:17–18). Though the great financial/commercial colossus of our end-time world may entice us to worship it, even attempting to entrap us, it is better to accept an existence on the fringes of society as outcasts than have complicity in its sins.

Expect Persecution: "…without being frightened in any way by those who oppose you. This is a sign to them that they will be destroyed, but that you will be saved, and that by God. For it has been granted to you on behalf of Christ not only to believe on him, but also to suffer for him, since you are going through the same struggle you saw I had, and now hear that I still have" (Philippians 1:28–39).

Here we are told that Christian persecution, whether subtle or direct, is to be expected. In fact, it is a sign that we are on the right path and are indeed living out our faith. If you are walking down the wide road of ease or surfing on the leading edge of society's values or world trends, you will not experience any persecution (whether spiritual or physical). Chances are that your understanding of true stewardship is also worldly. If so, you will find yourself caught deep in the net of Satan's end-time money snare.

A FINAL PERSPECTIVE OF THE LAST DAYS

Have you ever wondered what that "great cloud of witnesses" (Hebrews 12:1) would think of our world today? Viewing the world from above, they would be observing mankind's crowning capstone of humanism and materialism rapidly taking form—the globalization of mankind, the "666" system coming into view. They would be dismayed that mankind yet again is intoxicated by the vision of another Tower of Babel, saying "let us make a name" (Genesis 11:4) and determine our own destiny. Most of all, wouldn't that cloud of witnesses be most grieved to see how many supposed Christians have been thoroughly blinded by false but alluring promises and cares of our present age?

Seen from the broad specter of long-term world trends, evident is a human timeline the Bible has long prophesied. We have suggested that the systemic aspects of the "Beast," also symbolized by the number 666, are already operative in our day, right under our very noses. Some day, likely soon, this world system will be headed by the Antichrist and used to oppress the entire world. To the believing and pure Church, this advent will be of no concern. The church—the Philadelphian church—will be kept from this period. Christ said to the Philadelphians, "I will also keep you from the hour of trial that is going to come upon the whole world to test those who live on the earth" (Revelation 3:10).

Though this literal reading of Scripture may provide a comforting interpretation, it does not refer to the present era but rather to the future Tribulation.

On the other hand, world conditions today are absolutely treacherous to the Christ-indwelled person. This is a key characteristic of end-time conditions. The Bible mentions many victims and casualties of that time. We recall Christ prophesied that not much faith would be left on earth when He returns (Luke 18:8). Why? Some people will be drawn away from their faith because of lust for riches and the deceptions of wealth; others will become victims through entrapment and economic oppression (Matthew 24:12; Luke 21:34; 2 Timothy 3:1–7). Either fate can be the result of our own actions or those of others. In whatever situation we may find ourselves, we will be hard-pressed to maintain a contented and peaceful attitude.

But, every challenge also offers an opportunity. We can again remember what Peter tells us, which we read earlier. We have reasons to rejoice, for our struggle is only for a little while and there awaits the eternal reward of real riches: "In this you greatly rejoice, though now for a little while you may have had to suffer grief in all kinds of trials...for you are receiving the goal of your faith, the salvation of your souls" (1 Peter 1:6–9).

STEWARDSHIP TODAY

Figure #18

Changing Values of Thrift and Work

National Savings Rate, 1990 to 2008, Forecast 2009-2010, Quarterly

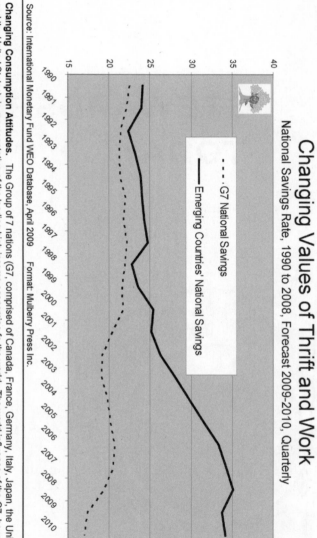

Legend:
- - - - G7 National Savings
——— Emerging Countries' National Savings

Y-axis: 15, 20, 25, 30, 35, 40

X-axis: 1990, 1991, 1992, 1993, 1994, 1995, 1996, 1997, 1998, 1999, 2000, 2001, 2002, 2003, 2004, 2005, 2006, 2007, 2008, 2009, 2010

Source: International Monetary Fund WEO Database, April 2009   Format: Mulberry Press Inc.

Changing Consumption Attitudes. The Group of 7 nations (G7, comprised of Canada, France, Germany, Italy, Japan, the United Kingdom and the United States), is representative of the leading high-income economies to the world. The world influence of the G7, however, is gradually waning. In recent years, the G20 group of nations, including such other countries as China, India, Russia, and Brazil, is emerging as a more influential, policy-making group as world economic and financial power is shifting away from the G7. Generally, the latter group has suffered from declining savings and investment as there has been a cultural shift towards consumption and lower savings.

APPENDIX 1

PRACTICAL STEWARDSHIP GUIDELINES: HOW CHRISTIANS SHOULD STEWARD THEIR POSSESSIONS

Just how should Christians steward their savings? It is a more challenging question than ever, given our conclusions in the previous chapters. In these troubled times of hyper-charged financial markets, desperate "cares of this world," and volatile economic swings, just how is it possible to steward anything? Wouldn't some certainty about the future be useful aid in this task? Instead, looking ahead, we face widely disparate scenarios.

In these times of great financial uncertainty, volatility, and intense temptations to join the world in the mad rush to build a heaven of material prosperity on earth, just how should we manage our savings and investments? After all, we live in this world—as corrupt and deceitful as it may be—and still carry a duty of practical, day-to-day stewardship for our families and possessions. The checks we write must clear our bank accounts.

Therefore, stewardship is a real, "rubber-on-the-road" issue many godly Christians want to resolve. For a start, it will be encouraging to know that one doesn't need the benefit of accurate economic forecasts to be a good Christian steward.

At the same time, the task of stewardship has its own complications. Successful stewardship requires personal involvement and unique individual application. Any prescription will vary for each person, as it involves both subjective and absolute issues. Uppermost, the question concerns itself with the condition of the heart. As such, no investment advisor or financial planner can truly provide a comprehensive answer for you. You must be involved.

Despite the complexity of the economic and financial conditions in the world, as well as the uniqueness of individual situations, I believe that it is possible to present a guideline that can be helpful to Christians in this most important matter. This chapter offers a brief primer on Christian stewardship.

NOT THE BIBLE ON INVESTMENT

Just what is the objective of faithful stewardship in the first place? Before answering, we need to clear away some misconceptions and impediments. We observe that the Bible's perspective on the topic of stewardship leans against popular teaching today. Why? The current vogue in Christian circles is to consider the Bible as the "best investment guide in the world."

Hear the invitations that call out to us these days, many times from the pulpits. In spirit, they are as these: "Let us consult the Bible so that we may prosper." Or, "Let's find what we may in Scripture that will bless and support our desires." It would not be surprising to hear an advertisement on Christian radio: "Invest with this Christian financial advisor and you will enjoy excellent investment returns from world stock markets." These pitches will surely bait people "who want to be rich" (1 Timothy 6:9a). Unfortunately, these entreaties miss the essence of stewardship entirely, not to mention open the door "...to fall into temptation and a trap and into many foolish and harmful desires that plunge men into ruin and destruction" (1 Timothy 6:9b).

Teachers, preachers, and financial planners who promote these impressions of stewardship may be well meaning; however, they are misguided. Most certainly, the Bible provides clear guidelines on stewardship. After all, matters related to money and possessions are dealt with more than any other topic in the Bible. In addition, stewardship also includes the responsibility of managing our gifts, time, and talents. We will mostly limit our discussion here to the stewardship of possessions.

IMPEDIMENTS OF POVERTY AND RICHES

Two other impediments exist—the extremes of riches and poverty. Neither is helpful in the task of stewardship if only for the reason that it brings attitudinal biases to the task. The Proverbs writer wrote, "Keep falsehood and lies far from me; give me neither poverty nor riches, but give me only my daily bread" (Proverbs 30:8). In fact, it is only "our daily bread" that we are to pray for, according to the Lord's Prayer (Matthew 6:11).

God does not wish poverty for the world. If only humanity would live selflessly according to godly precepts, there would be no such thing as poverty. The fact that a large part of the world is plagued with poverty and is destined to remain this way is mostly a result of sin and idolatry. Just as sin is a part of the world condition, so are the poor. Christ, recognizing that sin would be part of the world, said, "The poor you will always have with you" (Matthew 26:12). This was not so much a prophecy as it was a statement of fact.

Even as Scripture sets out principles that can technically help humanity avoid the suffering of abject poverty, at the same time, the Bible was not inspired to be a "get-rich-quick" book. The very reason so much of the Bible deals with the topic of money is to counter a basic weakness of mankind, namely the "love of money." Money provides the greatest leverage point for Satan and his cosmic agenda. Therefore, the Holy Spirit seeded the Bible with lots of advice and admonishments about the many sorrows and deceptions of Mammon.

Without question, the "love of money" is the most powerful force for evil on earth. Coming against this powerful demonic force in our day will not be easy. The love of money shouts out to us from every quarter to consort with it, to run after it, to possess it. After all, the Bible says that a deep, perverted love of money will be a condition of the end times: "But mark this: There will be terrible times in the last days. People will be lovers of themselves, lovers of money, boastful, proud..." (2 Timothy 3:1–2).

To call the Bible an "investment guide" is perverse. This is directly opposite to its true intent. Rather it is a "disinvestment" guide, teaching us to be godly stewards while not becoming attached to the things of this world or being ensnared by money and materialism. The Bible invites us to place our hope in the promises that are eternal, escaping the claims of a temporal world that will pass away.

In this sense, the Bible clearly lays out the proper principles of stewardship. Follow them and you will be blessed. You will be content. However, you may not be rich. In fact, for some—and perhaps most—to be rich would be the worst curse. A taste of wealth would quickly hinder their relationship with God. Competing idolatries set in. Satan knows this, too. Therefore, financial abundance is not always a blessing from God. Indeed, a global boom in wealth would do more for Satan's cause than Christ's. After all, a worldwide boom in wealth is one of the prophesied conditions of the end times (James 5:1–6).

BIBLICAL STEWARDSHIP PRINCIPLES

Let's begin grappling with the question: How should Christians invest their savings? We will need to tackle this question in two parts: the conceptual and the practical. The conceptual principle will apply to everyone. However, the practical application will differ depending on individual situations and callings. This is the approach professional portfolio managers employ in applying investment policy to different clients. They separate the strategy—the investment policy, as it is more formally known—from the portfolio implementation. In the case of the investment policy—for example, perhaps including the view that the U.S. dollar is expected to rise or fall, or that general stock market levels are too expensive—will apply to everyone in the same way. To illustrate this point in another way: The U.S. dollar will not rise for some investors and fall for others at the same time. This is not possible. Therefore, there is one investment policy.

However, what will be different for individuals is in the application of any investment view to their own financial affairs. Some people are wealthy; others are on a tight budget and require ready access to their savings; and yet others are retirees. There are different needs, planning objectives, risk tolerances, and comfort levels. In the same way, some people have a God-given calling to earn much money in order to give generously, while others feel inclined to take vows of poverty as their means of honoring God. Each will find a different application of the investment policy appropriate. Therefore, there are no real absolute guidelines in this question of investment implementation.

But, isn't this an unbiblical concept? No, not really. The apostle

Paul embraces the concept of individualistic application, saying: "One man's faith allows him to eat everything, but another man, whose faith is weak, eats only vegetables.... One man considers one day more sacred than another; another man considers every day alike. Each one should be fully convinced in his own mind" (Romans 14:2, 5).

This variability in implementing an investment view surely complicates the answers we are seeking. It is the same contrast as between these two questions: What is God's plan of salvation and what is God's will and particular calling for my life? The answer to the first applies to everyone; the second will be diverse. We all come to salvation through Jesus Christ, yet we are given different gifts, talents, and callings. Each fulfills a different part in the body of Christ. "As it is, there are many parts, but one body" (1 Corinthians 12:20). Given this variability of application to each situation, we therefore cannot give advice that will apply to everyone specifically.

However, what can be done is to provide general principles that will help everyone in making decisions with respect to personal stewardship matters.

MOTIVES MANAGEMENT

Christian stewardship is 90 percent motives management and 10 percent practical investing. In fact, being a good steward may not require you to be an investor at all. Of course, the message of the financial industry is otherwise. They like to promote the view that being a successful investor is the evidence of good stewardship. It is otherwise. All the successes and blessings of knowledgeable stewardship will be lost for eternity if the motives and the condition of the heart are not right to begin with.

Therefore, let us set the correct foundation for our examination and first look at our own hearts. To begin, just what role do we allow the desire for gain to play in our lives? Greed is the main doorway leading to participation with and entrapment in the world and an end-time regime—the end-time money trap. The Bible commands that we "…seek first his kingdom and his righteousness, and all these things will be given to you as well" (Luke 12:33). Inverting this verse will help us better understand the consequences of not doing so. The verse would then read as follows: "Seek first money and earthly wealth, and his kingdom and righteousness will *not* be given to you." In contrast, impurities and sins will be given to us. The apostle Paul certainly held this view, saying: "Some people, eager for money, have wandered from the faith and pierced themselves with many griefs" (1 Timothy 6:10). Immorality and greed are interconnected.

To be blunt, greed is idolatry. It places money and gain ahead of God. A greedy person worships at the altars of Mammon, breaking the very first of the Ten Commandments, "Thou shalt have no other gods before me" (Exodus 20:3); and "Do not worship any other god, for the LORD, whose name is Jealous, is a jealous God" (Exodus 34:13).

Therefore, the Bible is uncompromising in its judgment of greed. "No immoral, impure or greedy person—such a man is an idolater—has any inheritance in the kingdom of Christ and of God" (Ephesians 5:6). Greed seeks its inheritance upon earth. To the contrary, true stewardship sets its hope upon godly obedience and eternal riches and reward.

AN ETERNAL PLANNING PROGRAM

A plan of attack for a proper stewardship focus is laid out in 2 Peter 1:4–7. Peter says, "For this very reason, make every effort to add to your faith goodness; and to goodness, knowledge; and to knowledge, self-control; and to self-control, perseverance; and to perseverance, godliness; and to godliness, brotherly kindness; and to brotherly kindness, love." Most readers will be surprised to learn that this verse has anything to do with stewardship. Yet, it has much to do with this topic. All of the characteristics Peter outlines are an essential foundation for insulating ourselves against the spiritual lures of an end-time, materialistic world. Without such a disposition, it would be impossible to be good and faithful stewards.

Peter's ordering of the mentioned characteristics is not accidental. He begins with faith. Without it, salvation would not be possible. We cannot be saved if we do not first have faith. And, if we have not first been saved, then no good can be found in us in any case, and godly stewardship would have no basis or purpose. God alone imparts His goodness to us through the atoning sacrifice of the crucifixion of Jesus Christ. Without this foundational characteristic, there would be little point in striving to be knowledgeable or self-controlled. Were we to meet all the remaining requirements of Peter's list except this first one of faith, we still wouldn't be saved. There would be no eternal riches to inherit and no promise of eternal reward.

The rest of Peter's outline is dealt with next, point by point.

Knowledge. First and foremost, we need information and insight. Through a study of the Bible, we can know the season of the times we live in, the wiles of Satan, and everything else we need to spiritually navigate our lives. We must not be unaware of his schemes. We should strive to stay informed about the factors and powers at play these days in world affairs and economies. Fewer and fewer North Americans have any notion of the times and trends affecting the whole world. This also applies to Christians. They have no knowledge and are lacking in wisdom. They therefore are "…like a wave of the sea, blown and tossed by the wind" (James 1:6). They will be herded and driven like frightened sheep through global crises and the whims of crowds.

Self-Control. We are called to guard our hearts and not fix our affections on earthly possessions. Everything we own or seek upon earth must be under the ownership of our Lord Jesus Christ. Everything—small or large—must ultimately be in His service. Christ Himself implores us to guard against all kinds of greed: "Watch out! Be on your guard against all kinds of greed; a man's life does not consist in the abundance of…possessions" (Luke 12:15). We can use money and technology, and enjoy God's global creation. However, we do not need to be in their service, worship them, or allow those things to set up a kingdom in our hearts in opposition to God.

Why are we saving or investing? Is a humble and balanced ethic of stewardship governing these activities? Or, is it purely the allurement of high financial returns, the temptation to engage the world in its competitive clamor to hoard wealth and comforts, to boastfully elevate ourselves over others? No eternal reward will accrue to our account in heaven if these impulses drive our lives. Disappointments could impact our lives upon earth if we chase such early objectives.

Perseverance. The most difficult part of stewardship these days is perseverance. This is the case for a number of reasons. Though we can conduct our lives to honor God, the wicked will continue to prosper. While God tarries with His judgment, wishing that none might go lost, we will watch many godless and evil people amass fortunes and kingdoms on earth. They flaunt it in our faces, exulting in their ease and comfort. The world venerates them, giving them high profile in magazines and other media, chronicling their lives as if they were gods on top of Mount Olympus. All this while we live quietly and humbly, with our eyes set up eternal promises and rewards.

If that weren't enough, we must contend with our close friends and Christian brothers and sisters. We meet them for coffee and they tell us of their conquests. Perhaps they boast about how much they have made staking their money in a risky, fast-growing mutual fund or a real property investment. We nod in affirmation, possibly even congratulating them in an attempt to conceal our pangs of jealousy. Over dinner in our homes, or during conversation at church socials, we hear of the material indulgences and financial exploits of our fellow Christians. Even in this supposedly safe harbor of our churches, we sometime venerate rich people, treating affluence as the sure blessing of godly living and as evidence of wisdom. After experiences like these, the passions for the world and its temporal towers of wealth can be inflamed. It can require hours of being alone with God to again quiet these fires of lust for material gain.

Practicing biblical stewardship today in full truth and spirit will win few accolades and publicity. If you think the challenge of perseverance sounds tough to this point, it surely stands to becomes worse. As it is now, few are able to endure the temptations of either consorting with the idols of hoarded financial wealth or to compromise their values in their bleak attempts to survive the troubled economic times. How many are walking away from mortgages and other unpaid debts or plunging into a pagan, survival mode at any cost? If Christians ever needed perseverance, the time is now.

Godliness. Just how can we remain godly in a financial world given over to greed and materialism? As mentioned, stewardship and investing are not necessarily one and the same. They are entirely separate activities. Stewards may never be required to be investors. On the other hand, investors must always be good stewards. This view runs contrary to the message of many of today's Christian financial counselors: To be a good steward you must heavily invest—for example, buy mutual funds. If you do not, they claim you are not stepping out in faith.

Naturally, it's not that simple. True stewardship is not born out of the question, "How far can I run with the bulls of the world without getting gored?"; "How can I grab onto the tail of an end-time money boom or trade the manic market swings and still preserve my soul?"; or "Why not carouse and frolic in the worldly financial markets—even though it is part of a complex system that seeks to ensnare the world of the last days —grab my share, and bail out by repenting just before Jesus returns or our possible sudden death?" According to the advice of many Christian financial planners, it is a greater sin to miss an uptrend in stock markets than to participate in a diabolically deceptive financial system. These attitudes do not reveal the spirit of a true steward who is fully serving Christ.

The apostle Paul makes some suggestions as to how we might live godly lives in an adulterous world. "Make it your ambition to lead a quiet life, to mind your own business and to work with your hands, just as we told you, so that your daily life may win the respect of outsiders and so that you will not be dependent on anybody" (1 Thessalonians 1:11). He recommended that the believers in Thessalonica work in low-profile professions and work with their hands. What did he mean by this?

Paul was suggesting that believers take jobs that do not lead them into complicity with a corrupt world. He chose to do so himself. He was a learned scholar, yet worked with his hands making tents. Supposedly, he could have been a consultant, a knowledge worker of some kind. Instead, he chose to work with his hands.

Paul's suggestions are good recommendations, though not commandments. For example, Paul recommended to Timothy that it would also be better not to marry. His view was that if one wanted to wholly serve the Lord without any diversions and unnecessary obligations, then it is better to remain single. Similarly, better not to have a lofty, elite job that will constantly throw you on the horns of compromise. But this isn't to say one should not be a knowledge worker, a lawyer, or a financier. God puts His people in all kinds of professions. Paul also said that "…each man, as responsible to God, should remain in the situation God called him to" (1 Corinthians 7:24).

However, Paul does make a point that is worth considering. Many professions require that you become an accomplice, or at least harbor knowing complacency in the corruption of the world or to enlist in an end-time conspiracy that sets itself up against God. Such people may find themselves subjected to unnecessary temptation or forced to endorse corruption. Should you leave such a job? Only God can provide personal direction on this difficult question.

PRACTICAL INVESTMENT OUTLINES

Investing in today's financial markets is a high-stakes game that has little to do with sound stewardship. Too often, it is all about brinkmanship and gambling, playing the world's frenzied and unprincipled game of wealth maximization. The fruits of this game are obvious: anxiousness, greed, fear, and lack of peace. In the meantime, it is luring many investors into the belief that wealth can be created from magic. The bust of the GFC will have disabused most people of this notion. However, if history is any guide, such lessons will be quickly forgotten.

For those of us who do have money invested in longer-term financial assets such as stocks and bonds, how should we manage them? Actually, it is a question that applies to almost everyone, as most will be exposed to financial market trends in one way or another. Even though we may not directly invest in stock and bond markets, our insurance policies and future pension claims are backed by such investments. Government pension systems also depend upon financial and economic conditions. The fact is this: Whether we are direct investors or not, our lives are inextricably tied up with the world's financial system. Even though we may have overcome the ensnarement of a materialistic world system within our hearts, the global financial/commercial colossus has become so pervasive and invasive that we must still take account of its dangers to our physical livelihoods.

Here are some approaches to consider when stewarding savings, beginning with the basics:

Always examine motives: We cannot overemphasize this matter, so again it is mentioned on the top of this list. Is a humble and balanced stewardship ethic governing your financial savings activities? Or, is it purely the appeal of high financial returns—yours, or those others are bragging about—and the intoxication of past gains that is driving your ambition? If so, disappointments lie ahead eventually, perhaps sooner than you may think. Those are precisely the emotions that conspire to pull you into the maws of a money snare. We are reminded: "For where your treasure is, there your heart will be also" (Matthew 6:21). Those who are rich are commanded "not to be arrogant nor to put their hope in wealth, which is so uncertain, but to put their hope in God, who richly provides us with everything for our enjoyment" (1 Timothy 6:17). Most importantly, the warnings of 1 Timothy 6:9 bear repeating, as they speak of a sure outcome when we have the wrong motivations: "People who want to get rich fall into temptation and a trap and into many foolish and harmful desires that plunge men into ruin and destruction."

Be a steward, not a hoarder: God's economy is mainly composed of flows, not overstuffed storehouses of idle money. Just as God is love in motion—love lived—so it should be with money. Of course, we need to save for our anticipated needs and to fund the activities of our businesses and livelihoods. However, there comes a point where the act of saving becomes hoarding. In this sense, for the saints, all savings must be done in a spirit of stewardship. In contrast, the world promotes the spirit of hoarding; the pursuit of earthly wealth as a measure of success; a bulwark of security; to satisfy boasts. Be a flow-person, not a hoarder. Most all of God's gifts to us, whether the gifts of the Spirit or material resources, are meant for sharing and blessing others through our giving.

Trust God and live humbly: Let the world go by in its frenzied hunt for wealth and prosperity. These days, investing in stock and bond markets requires discipline and informed knowledge. These markets are either the objects of a crazed lust for wealth or the horrible fear of loss. When at all possible, it is better to store savings in investments that are not subject to the extreme swings of fear and greed. In normal times, such investments would include short-term Treasury bonds and Treasury bills as well as investments in solid, private businesses. Yet in the chaotic maelstrom of the GFC, even these securities suffered substantial swings.

Gain control of your savings: Gain as much control of your savings as possible so that you can determine how they are invested. Though the investment recommendations of professionals such as pension fund consultants, actuaries, and mutual fund managers, etc., may be well-meaning, their recommendations can still be harmful. Many are simply unknowledgeable and deceived—a case of the blind leading the blind—who, like all of us, need to put bread on the table. Sadly, others who do know better may consciously recommend hollow solutions in the pursuit of their own narrow self-interests. Of course, it remains that no advisers, no matter how sincere and trustworthy, can reliably predict the future. As a rule, wherever you can, seek control of your own investments. Wherever you can't do so, such as may be the case in a company defined-benefit pension plan or an endowment insurance policy, or in the case of a complex investment that requires professional help (a real estate partnership or a special-ized mutual fund), scrutinize, scrutinize, and again, scrutinize. In the end, how your savings are invested is still your responsibility.

Follow common sense: If an investment or financial deal sounds too good to be true, it probably is. High returns usually require a higher level of risk or speculation. Whenever a promised interest rate for a given time frame is substantially higher than a competing investment, beware. There must be a reason. The financial institution offering this interest rate must earn enough on the money you invest in order to pay you the promised return. Given the competitive financial systems we have today, the only way a financial institution can offer a substantially higher interest-rate return is to take on more risk. Determine why one financial institution is able to offer substantially higher returns than another.

Understand risk and its popular perception: Risk is not always a bad thing. Why? It is virtually impossible to escape all risk. Nothing on earth is 100 percent secure or predictable. Therefore, it is important to assess the risk of any investment and determine whether it is personally tolerable and reasonable in price. Risk must always be equated with potential return. However, it takes strong discipline to be able to discern the price of risk. Most people will find themselves too influenced by popular opinion and mood. For example, when most people fear that financial market declines are in the future, risk is unusually cheap. This does not mean one should take a standard perspective of contrarianism. However, the notion that the madness of crowds is usually wrong has a biblical parallel: "For wide is the gate and broad the road that leads to destruction" (Matthew 7:13).

Research extensively: When researching an investment option, seek information from sources other than the firm or person offering the opportunity. The promoter of an investment is likely to have a one-sided perspective. Even better, seek financial knowledge from alternative sources with no obvious biased interests...in other words, an incentive in having you buy the investment from them. Sources for such information are newsletters or financial counseling services that do not derive any support or income from the sale of investments.

Don't make exceptions because of religious affiliations: If you are approached by a self-proclaimed Christian financial advisor, hold him or her accountable to the same standards you would apply to anyone from whom you would seek investment advice. There is no evidence that suggests people with religious connections are more successful investors than others. Why should Christians be more adept at beating the odds in godless investment markets than the wicked? All too often, Christian investors are fleeced by con artists. They like to prey on the faithful because they are quick to drop their guard the moment a religious association is implied.

Save more: Even though it will be difficult to find a good storehouse for your retirement nest egg—one that will remain secure for a long period of time until you pass on—you must continue to save. In fact, you must save more than other people if you wish to claim a higher-than-average income when you retire.

Get an ultimate claim upon income: Ultimately—especially in a world of declining population growth—all financial values must rest on basic income (labor). That's an aspect of the human economy that will always remain true, no matter how sizzling and futuristic the world may seem. Pay less attention to capital appreciation alone. Whenever opportunities avail, invest your savings in securities or ventures that have a strong prospect of continuing to deliver income—whether markets rise or collapse. To the extent possible, make absolutely sure that you have a claim on investment earnings—quality interest and dividend income. Along with liquidity, it's these things that are expensive and scarce during difficult times.

Try to avoid assets that can be manipulated: Choose investments that are least subject to manipulation. Admittedly, during this late stage of the age of global capital, a very large part total financial wealth is in the form of marketable securities. Securities markets are notoriously easy to manipulate by monetary authorities and owners or managers of large pools of financial wealth. For the long haul, minimize the type of investments with values that can fluctuate suddenly and wildly with supply and demand. As much as practicable, avoid securities markets and diversify savings into non-listed type of assets.

Seek other types of savings and income: Invest savings in stores of value other than in financial securities markets. Direct ownership of businesses and real property with good income prospects and/or real estate would be recommended ways of diversifying future income potential. In the first instance, solid and secure employment income is most important. Count yourself blessed if you have a secure job. To the extent possible, seek a job in a field that produces a service or a product that is not subject to foreign competition or imports. These days, a trade (such as being a plumber) has more than its usual attraction, as it is not likely to face competition from an overseas worker.

Diversification and more diversification: This is a discipline that cannot be emphasized enough. As the saying goes, "Never put all your eggs in one basket." Why? If the basket should ever fall, you can be sure that all the eggs will be broken. Given the volatile times and the near impossibility for the average person to anticipate future trends and to successfully navigate these waves (indeed, this also being true for professional investment managers), it is best to diversify one's investments across different asset types as well as securities. If some investments prove unrewarding in a certain environment, the hope is that others will not. While some baskets may fall, at least the eggs in other safer baskets will survive.

Invest in your extended family: Remember, in times past, retirement lifestyle depended on the amount of children and the size of the future extended family one had. It was the income potential of this group that could be relied upon to support you during retirement years. It's no different today, though mainly in a socialized form in developed countries. Here finances intersect families. Both are about developing future income potential and are directly related. So what to do? At the very least, it makes good sense to invest in relationships with children. You never know. You may need to live with them someday, as do more than two-thirds of the world's elderly. Encourage them to be productive future citizens and hope it will translate into superior income power for your extended family.

We have come to the end of the list. The approaches summarized may be subject to ridicule from a worldly perspective. Remember how Jeremiah whined to God, "I have never lent nor borrowed, yet everyone curses me" (Jeremiah 15:10). He was not participating in a financial system that operated to oppress the poor and transfer wealth to the "experts in greed" by way of a loose credit culture. And apparently because he wasn't, people thought Jeremiah was just being judgmental. He was. He didn't want to have any part in the corruption and vain pursuits of the society of his day.

The above points, though not intended to be a comprehensive stewardship guide, if followed along with the plan laid out in 2 Peter 1:4–7, should indeed produce at least two benefits: true wealth of eternal values and success in attaining a blessed life of contentedness upon earth, one that the idol-worshipping world cannot find: "Godliness with contentedness is great gain" (1 Timothy 6:6), for "godliness has value for all things, holding promise for both the present life and the life to come" (1 Timothy 4:8).

Figure #18

Changing Values of Thrift and Work
National Savings Rate, 1990 to 2008, Forecast 2009-2010, Quarterly

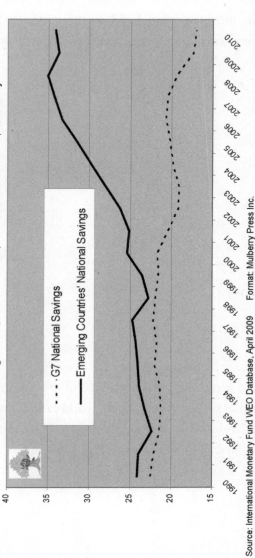

Source: International Monetary Fund WEO Database, April 2009   Format: Mulberry Press Inc.

Changing Consumption Attitudes. The Group of 7 nations (G7, comprised of Canada, France, Germany, Italy, Japan, the United Kingdom and the United States), is representative of the leading high-income economies fo the world. The world influence of the G7, however, is gradually waning. In recent years, the G20 group of nations, including such other countries as China, India, Russia, and Brazil, is emerging as a more influential, policy-making group as world economic and financial power is shifting away from the G7. Generally, the latter group has suffered from declining savings and investment as there has been a culural shift towards consumption and lower savings.

APPENDIX 2

SYMBOLS IN
ISAIAH CHAPTER 2

While we should always seek to interpret all Scripture literally, many aspects of "the things to come" explained or foreshadowed in both the Old and New Testaments are portrayed in symbolic language. The meaning remains literal, but through symbol.

Reviewing prophetic Scripture, we repeatedly see elements and events portrayed in the form of the same symbols—for example, in this case, mountains, hills, seas, trees and vines, to name some. To illustrate, it is broadly agreed that mountains refer to kingdoms and powers, and the seas to all humanity of the world. When mountains are "threshed" (Isaiah 41:15) or "laid low" (Isaiah 40:4), it is nations that are being dethroned from power.

Trees play a particularly strong role in this type of imagery, portraying at least three main meanings throughout the entirety of Scripture. Genesis 2:9 provides a key for three categories of meanings: "And the LORD God made all kinds of trees grow out of the ground—trees that were pleasing to the eye and good for food. In the middle of the garden were the tree of life and the tree of the knowledge of good and evil" (Genesis 2:9).

Here we see three completely different realms portrayed by trees:
1. the natural tree, those "that were pleasing to the eye for and good
for food"; 2. the "tree of life", and; 3. the "tree of knowledge." The
first speaks of the physical or material dimension; the second of God's
spiritual plan of eternal life and redemption—the kingdom of heaven;
and the third of the absolutes of the eternal existence of the "I Am."
All of these types appear repeatedly throughout the entire Bible. For
example, the Tree of Life is mentioned repeatedly from the book of
Genesis through to the Revelation. The phrase "tree of life" appears in
the last few verses of the Bible, Revelation 23:14 and 19. However, for
our purpose of discovering the Bible's message of end-time judgments,
we want to focus on the symbolism of the natural, earthly trees. There
are both general and specific meanings.

The tree is often depicted in the Bible as portraying the commercial power of nations and humankind. In modern terms, we would
define call this economic might. We see the tree spoken of in this way
many times throughout the Bible. For example, Nebuchadnezzar's
Babylon is depicted this way in Daniel 4. Assyria, at the apex of its
might, is also likened to a tree.

> Who can be compared with you in majesty? Consider Assyria,
> once a cedar in Lebanon, with beautiful branches overshadow-
> ing the forest; it towered on high, its top above the thick foli-
> age. The waters nourished it, deep springs made it grow tall;
> deep springs made it grow tall; their streams flowed all around
> its base and sent their channels to all the trees of the field.
> So it towered higher than all the trees of the field; its boughs
> increased and its branches grew long, spreading because of
> abundant waters. All the birds of the air nested in its boughs,
> all the beasts of the field gave birth under its branches; all the
> great nations lived in its shade. (Ezekiel 31:2–6)

Lebanon is also typified as a tree. "See, the Lord, the LORD Almighty, will lop off the boughs with great power. The lofty trees will be felled, the tall ones will be brought low. He will cut down the forest thickets with an ax; Lebanon will fall before the Mighty One" (Isaiah 10:33–34). Egypt is chopped down like a forest of trees (Jeremiah 46:23) and its Pharaoh is likened to the description of Assyria in Ezekiel 31, "'This is Pharaoh and all his hordes,' declares the Sovereign LORD" (verse 18). The earthly economies of Lebanon (Isaiah 14:8), Egypt, Assyria, and Babylon are all described metaphorically as big trees. Each was an economic powerhouse at one point—perhaps like Japan in the 1980s, or the United States today. At one time or another, all were prosperous, economic giants—big, tall trees. Each of the specific prophecies relating to these nations spoke of these big trees being cut or fallen down.

Even today, trees are associated with a prospering and fruitful land. If a country denudes its forests without replacing them, we recognize that this nation is being impoverished. When we hear of the rain forests of South America being decimated, that some countries in Africa are rapidly becoming treeless, we perceive a declining economic vitality. Any country razed of its trees is considered an economic wasteland.

Now with this understanding of the symbolism of trees, some of the opaque prophetic Scriptures will begin to open up. Isaiah is clearly prophesying a global collapse in the future and its devastating completeness indicates that this prophecy aligns with the events to occur in the mid-to-late stages of the coming Great Tribulation.

The author publishes the free on-line newsletter:

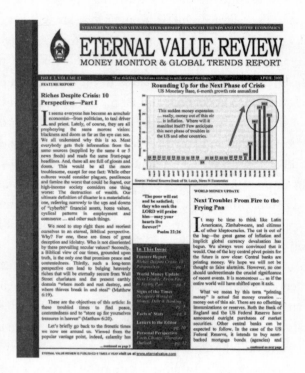

Readers wishing to receive regular updates on global perspectives and financial trends are invited to subscribe. Please visit the website www.eternalvalue.com and sign up for a free email distribution, or for further information, please write: staff@eternalvalue.com.

For a hard-copy subscription, contact Mulberry Press Inc. for subscription rates at admin@eternalvalue.com.

Mulberry Press Inc.

P.O. Box 2609, Station R

Kelowna, BC

V1X 6A7

ABOUT THE AUTHOR

Wilfred Hahn brings a unique skill set to the topic of worldwide money developments. He is both a seasoned practitioner in global economics and financial markets and an avid student of Scripture.

Wilfred has worked on the front lines of global money for almost three decades. He has overseen billions of dollars of global capital as chief investment officer for Canada's largest bank and global investment operation, and has also served as director of research for a major Wall Street firm as well as chairman of a major offshore mutual fund company. Because he is a respected senior financial executive, secular media often seeks him out for his credible and reasoned views regarding current global developments. His views are particularly relevant to Christians living in the end times, an era of great deception, wealth distortions, and economic oppression.

Hahn has written hundreds of articles and produced some forty books and booklets, including *The Endtime Money Snare: How to Live Free* (2002). For six years, he was also the associate editor of Dr. Kurt Richebächer's *Currency & Credit Markets*, an influential international report.

He and his wife, Joyce, founded The Mulberry Ministry in 1995. Its main communication tool is the *Eternal Value Review,* a periodical for *"thinking Christians seeking to understand the times."*

NOTES

Introduction

1. Martin Wolf, Op Ed, *Financial Times*, March 17, 2009.
2. Wilfred Hahn, "A Warning That Hits Home," *Midnight Call Magazine*, May 2004.
3. Ibid.

Chapter 1

4. Sean Cole, "American Public Media: Is There a Divine Hand in the Dow? Marketplace, October 13, 2008 (http://marketplace.publicradio. org/display/web/2008/10/13/armageddon/).
5. Daniel Taub, "Almost One-Quarter of U.S. Homeowners Underwater as Values Sink," *Bloomberg*, May 6, 2009 (www.bloomberg.com).
6. Thomas Ice, "The Earth Dwellers of Revelation," *Pre-Trib Perspectives*. February 2008.

Chapter 2

7. Dave Hunt, *Y2K: A Reasoned Response to Mass Hysteria* (Eugene, OR: Harvest House, 1999).
8. John Kenneth Galbraith, *The Great Crash: 1929* (New York: Houghton-Mifflin, 1955) 27.
9. "Walter Russell Mead," Wikipedia (http://en.wikipedia. org/wiki/Walter_Russell_Mead).
10. Walter Russell Mead, "The New Israel and the Old: Why Gentile Americans Back the Jewish State," *Foreign Affairs*, Vol. 87, No. 4, July/August 2008.

Chapter 3

11. "Big Three Will Run World's Media, says Murdoch," *The Australian* February 13, 2004.

12. Luc Laeven and Fabian Valencia, "IMF Working Paper: Systemic Banking Crises: A New Database," September 2008.
13. Carmen M. Reinhart & Kenneth S. Rogoff, "This Time is Different: A Panoramic View of Eight Centuries of Financial Crises," April 16, 2008.
14. Ibid., "The Aftermath of Financial Crises," December 19, 2008.
15. George Friedman, *Overture: An Introduction to the American Age* (John Mauldin, Outside the Box Special Edition).
16. David Colander, Hans Föllmer, Armin Haas, Michael Goldberg, Katarina Juselius, Alan Kirman, and Thomas Lux , "The Financial Crisis and the Systemic Failure of Academic Economics" (University of Kiel, Department of Economics).
17. John C. Edmunds, "Securities: The New World Wealth Machine," *Foreign Policy,* Fall 1996.

Chapter 4

18. Merriam-Webster Online Dictionary (www.merriam-webster.com).
19. Global Economic Crisis: Implications for Trade and Development (UNCTAD, May 7, 2009) 8.
20. "Economic Axioms," San Francisco School of Economics (www.sfschoolofeconomics.com).

Chapter 5

21. Clotaire Rapaille, "Marketing to the Reptilian Brain," *Forbes Magazine*, July 3, 2006, 44.
22. Paul B. Farrell, "Just Surrender to Wall Street's Weapons of Mass Manipulation," FoxNews.com, January 30, 2007. (http://www.foxnews.com/printer_friendly_story/0,3566,248590,00.html).
23. Daniel Kahneman, "Neurofinance: Cure or Malarkey?" quoted in Bloomberg News, February 2, 2006.
24. Adam Levy, "Money Drives Us Crazy: It's Official," *The Australian*, February 9, 2006.
25. James McNeal, "Trillion Dollar Kids," quoted in *The Economist*, December 2, 2006, 66.
26. Maurice Saatchi, "The Strange Death of Modern Advertising," *Financial Times* Op-Ed, June 22, 2006.
27. David Nicholls, quoted in *Financial Times* "Special Report on Innovation": "The Need to Get under the Skin of the Consumer."

Chapter 6

28. B.H. Newton, "Thoughts on the Apocalypse, 1843," *The Coming Day*, Vol. 2, The Babylonian System Revelation 17 & 18. (http://www. searchlight-missions.org/Periodicals/ComingDayIssues.cfm.).
29. Ibid.
30. Advertising slogan of Telus Inc., a communications company.
31. John Wesley, quoted in Max Weber, *The Protestant Ethic and the Spirit of Capitalism* (New York: HarperCollins Academic, 1992) 175.

Chapter 7

32. Lawrence E. Harrison, *The Central Liberal Truth: How Politics Can Change a Culture and Save it From Itself* (Oxford University Press, 2006).

Chapter 8

33. Joseph Thayer, *The Greek-English Lexicon of the New Testament.*
34. John J. Davies & John C. Whitcomb, *Israel From Conquest to Exile*, (Indiana: BHM Books, 1989) 337.
35. Guilo M. Gallorotti, *The Anatomy of an International Monetary Regime* (Oxford University Press, 1995).
36. Antal E. Fekete, "The Dollar: An Agonizing Reappraisal," Gold Standard University, May 30, 2007.
37. Nathanael West, *The Thousand Year Reign of Christ*, (Grand Rapids, MI: Kregal, 1993 [Originally published 1899]). Note that West references 1 Kings 10:14; 2 Chronicles 9:13; Isaiah 9:17,10,12; and Haggai 2:7.

Chapter 9

38. Max Weber, *The Protestant Work Ethic and the Spirit of Capitalism* (1905).
39. R. H. Tawney, *Religion and the Rise of Capitalism* (New Jersey: Transaction, 1998 [originally published by New York: Harcourt, Brace & Co, 1926]).
40. Calculated from Federal Reserve Board Z1 Report, June 11, 2009, reporting March 31, 2009 conditions.
41. "Prosperity theology," Wikipedia (http://en.wikipedia. org/wiki/Prosperity_theology).
42. Table: Income Levels of Major Religious Traditions, "U.S. Religious Landscape Survey, The Pew Forum on Religion & Public Life," February 2008, 60.

43. Ibid., "Income Level by Protestant Denominations," 80.

44. C. Peter Wagner, Personal invitation to this author to participate in an ad hoc, "invitation-only" Apostolic Roundtable on Kingdom Wealth, in Colorado, October 2004. On file with The Mulberry Ministry.

45. C. Peter Wagner, "Releasing Wealth in Apostolic Times," (http://www.globalharvest.org/index.asp?action=wealth).

46. Gerald Celente, World Trend Institute, www.trendsresearch.com.

47. Michael Medved, "Why the World Hates the Jews," (http://www.townhall.com/columnists/MichaelMedved/2006/08/09/why_the_world_hates_the_jews) August 9, 2006.

48. "Pew Forum on Religion & Public Life, U.S. Religious Landscape Survey," February 2008.

49. Robert Anderson, *The Coming Prince.* (Grand Rapids, MI: Kregel, 1957) 83.

50. Royal Decree, Expulsion from England, 1290.

51. Serigo Della Pergola, "Jewish Out-Marriage: A Global Perspective," International Roundtable on Intermarriage (Brandeis University, December 18, 2003) Table 1.

52. The North American Jewish Databank, National Jewish Population Survey, 2000–2001.

53. Aron Heller, "Think Tank: Jewish Numbers in Decline," reporting on The Conference on the Future of the Jewish People, July 12, 2007, *The Columbian.* (http://www.wwrn.org/article.php?idd=25655&sec=35&con=4http://www.wwrn.org/article.php?idd=25655&sec=35&con=4).

54. Serigo Della Pergola, Jewish Out-Marriage: A Global Perspective, International Roundtable on Intermarriage, Brandeis University, December 18, 2003 Table 1.

Chapter 11

55. Walter Russell Mead, *God and Gold: Britain, America, and the Making of the Modern World* (Alfred A. Knopf: New York, 2007).

56. Joseph Stiglitz, "Reversal of Fortune," www.vanityfair.com.

57. www.telegraph.co.uk, October 9, 2008.

58. Satyajit Das, "Only Global Action Will End This," *Business Spectator*, October 7, 2008.

59. *Asia Times*, October 9, 2008.

60. Nadim Kawach, *Emirates Business 24-7*, December 18, 2008.

61. Thomas Friedman, *New York Times* Op Ed, December 24, 2008.

62. Leslie H. Gelb, "Necessity, Choice, and Common Sense," *Foreign Affairs*, May/June 2009.

63. Roger C. Altman, "The Great Crash of 2008: A Geopolitical Setback for the West," *Foreign Affairs*, January/February 2009.

64. Yoichi Funabashi, *YaleGlobal*, March 23, 2009.

Chapter 12

65. The Globe and Mail/Worldwide Independent Network of Market Research Survey. This is made up of an international group of pollsters who have created the WIN Crisis Index to monitor citizens' perceptions in their country, which surveyed 14,555 people in seventeen countries during the fall of 2008.

66. Gerald Seib, "In Crisis, Opportunity for Obama," *Wall Street Journal*, November 21, 2008 (http://online.wsj.com/article/SB122721278056345271.html).

67. Kemal Dervi (United Nations Development Program) and Juan Somavia (International Labor Organization), "One Crisis, One World" (http://www.koreatimes.co.kr/www/news/include/print.asp?newsIdx=38298).

68. Dr. Robert A. Pastor, December 15, 2006 (http://www.worldnetdaily.com/news/article.asp?ARTICLE_ID=53378).

69. Klaus Schwab, "Foreword to Global Risks Report 2009," World Economic Forum.

70. Henry Kissinger, "The Chance for a New World Order," *Herald Tribune*, January 12, 2009 (http://www.iht.com/bin/printfriendly.php?id=19281915).

71. Paul Volcker, "We Have the Tools to Manage the Crisis," *Wall Street Journal*, October 10, 2008.

72. George W. Bush, September 15, 2005 (http://www.cnn.com).

73. Barack Obama, February 24, 2009, Associated Press.

74. Global Economic Research, "Economic Cycles," October 31, 2008, Societe General.

75. Philip Stephens, "Globalisation and the New Nationalism Collide," *Financial Times*, October 24, 2008.

Chapter 13

76. Sir Robert Anderson, *The Coming Prince*, 271.

77. "Globalization and Inequality," *World Economic Outlook*, September 2007 (Chapter 4).

78. World Institute for Development Economics Research, UN University (UNU-Wider).

79. The passage originally appeared in the "Dialogue Held With A

Certain Persian, the Worthy Mouterizes, in Anakara of Galatia"[3], written in 1391 as an expression of the views of the Byzantine emperor Manuel II Paleologus, one of the last Christian rulers before the Fall of Constantinople to the Muslim Ottoman Empire, on such issues as forced conversion, holy war, and the relationship between faith and reason.

80. Speech by Libyan leader Mu'ammar Al-Qadhafi, which aired on Al-Jazeera TV on April 10, 2006.

81. World Bank, World Development Indicators Database, 2006 statistics.

82. http://www.infoplease.com/ipa/A0005140.html.

83. Ricki Lewis, Ph.D., "The Rise of Antibiotic-Resistant Infections," U.S. Food and Drug Administration (http://www.fda.gov/fdac/features/795_antibio.html).

84. The group of the ten richest Christian nations, accounting for 10.7 percent of the world population and 60 percent of world annual income, comprises Australia, Belgium, Canada, France, Germany, Italy, Netherlands, Spain, United Kingdom and the United States.

85. References to the killing of Jews are found in a number of Hadiths. For example, one such saying, which is attributed to an account by Sahih Al-Bukhari, follows: "Allah's Apostle said, 'The Hour will not be established until you fight with the Jews, and the stone behind which a Jew will be hiding will say. "O Muslim! There is a Jew hiding behind me, so kill him."'" Volume 4, Book 52, Number 177: Narrated Abu Huraira: (Translated versions sourced from U.S.C-MSA Compendium of Muslim Texts.)

86. International Monetary Fund, "The State of Public Finances: Outlook and Medium-Term Policies After the 2008 Crisis" March 6, 2009.

87. Buckminster Fuller, *Twilight of the World's Power Structures*, St. Martin's Press, 1981.

Chapter 14

88. *The Guardian,* November 8, 1984.

89. Johann Christoph Friedrich von Schiller, November 1759–May 9, 1805.

90. Gottfried Haberler, *Prosperity and Depression*, (London: George Allen and Unwin Ltd., 1937) 470.

91. Martin Wolf, "Central Banks Must Target More than Just Inflation," Financial Times, May 6, 2009 (http://www.ft.com/cms/s/0/cace1a34-39d6-11de-b82d-00144feabdc0.html).

92. David Rosnick and Dean Baker, "The Wealth of the Baby Boom Cohorts after the Collapse of the Housing Bubble," Center of Economic and Policy Research (CEPR), February 2009.